# Chaos as Usual:

## Conversations about

## Rainer Werner
# Fassbinder

Rainer Werner Fassbinder
(1981)

# Chaos as Usual:

## Conversations about

# Rainer Werner Fassbinder

edited by Juliane Lorenz

with Marion Schmid and Herbert Gehr

translated by
Christa Armstrong and Maria Pelikan

APPLAUSE
NEW YORK • LONDON

**An Applause Original**
**Chaos as Usual: Conversations About Rainer Werner Fassbinder**

Copyright © Henschel Verlag GmbH Berlin 1995, 1997

*Library of Congress Cataloging-In-Publication Data*
Ganz normale Chaos. English
      Chaos as Usual: conversations about Rainer Werner Fassbinder / edited by
  Juliane Lorenz ; translated by Christa Armstrong & Maria Pelikan
        p.   cm.
        Filmography: p.
        Includes index.
        ISBN 1-55783-262-5 (cloth)
        1. Fassbinder, Rainer Werner, 1946- . I. Lorenz, Juliane.
  II. Title.
  PN1998.3.F37G3613 1996
  791.43'0233'092--dc21                             96-37914
  [B]                                              CIP

*British Library Cataloging-in-Publication Data*
A catalogue record of this book is available from the British Library.

APPLAUSE BOOKS

211 West 71st Street
New York, NY 10023
Phone (212) 496-7511
Fax: (212) 721-2856

A&C BLACK

Howard Road, Eaton Socon
Huntington, Cambs PE19 3EZ
Phone 0171-242 0946
Fax 0171-831 8478

First Applause Printing, 1997

Distributed in the U.K. and European Union by A&C Black

# Table of Contents

*in memory of liselotte eder*

# PREFACE

This book is an attempt to trace and illuminate, through interviews with colleagues, friends, and contemporaries, different perspectives about Rainer Werner Fassbinder. You may find, in the final analysis, that these interviews focus not on Fassbinder, the person, but on what he awakened and invoked in others.

In the first interviews, I found myself defending Rainer against critical observations about his working methods and lifestyle. However, I soon learned to smile at my personal "protectivism." I let go in order to take stock and assemble a clear picture of the man and his work. Ten years after his death, I found myself asking "What was it that made us swarm and buzz around this "sorcerer"? What was it that frightened some and repelled others, but fascinated all of us? What distinguished him from other artists and what remains of the things he achieved when no one else could? Is he a "myth" or did he just dare what none of us had the courage to attempt? Did he use people, or was he being used more than a man of his caliber could tolerate? A highly sensitive person who always approached life with enormous curiosity, did he finally give too much of himself?

In the course of my investigation, I became haunted by intensely personal memories, experienced by someone who had been confronted, at a very young age, with the death of a companion. These are feelings which even a lifetime cannot suppress. Much as I try, I will never overcome the memory of that early morning in June, 1982, when I found Rainer dead in our apartment. That day something ended, and not only for the history of German cinema. A driving force, a host of fantasies, skills, and talents, was no longer accessible, no longer open to attacks and exploitation. Nothing was the way it had been.

Rainer Werner Fassbinder left behind him a literary and cinematic oeuvre which will take a unique place in the history of European film and in the culture of the twentieth century. It is an oeuvre which evolved as the expression of an era, between 1966 and 1982, in a country which was then another Germany and which no longer exists.

I would like to thank all those who participated in these interviews for their willingness to reflect on their memories of Rainer. I thank the editor, Marion Schmid, for her critical detachment in working on the texts. I thank Tatjana and Andreas Peterson for their help with the transcripts. Above all, I thank the publishers in Germany and the United States, especially Glenn Young, who received this large volume of interviews with great curiosity and encouragement. My special thanks also to my agent, Maria Pelikan.

—*J. L.*
*New York/Berlin*

# A Fassbinder Photo Gallery

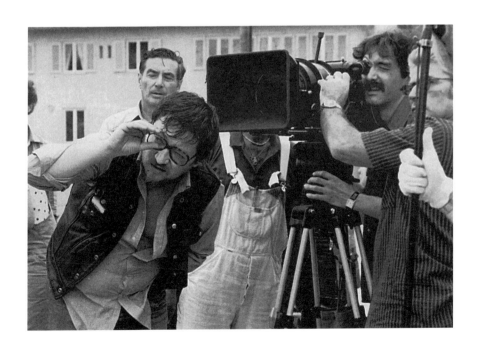

Rainer Werner Fassbinder      Dietrich Lohmann
*Rio das Mortes* (1970)

Ursula Strätz (1969)

Irm Hermann          Fassbinder          Margit Carstensen
Berlin Film Festival (1972)

Gunther Kaufmann     Hanna Schygulla     Harry Baer

Harry Baer     Peer Raben     Kurt Raab     Margit Carstensen

*Coffeehouse* (1970)

Margit Carstensen        Fassbinder
Berlin Film Festival (1972)

Fassbinder            Margit Carstensen        Karlheinz Böhm
*Martha* (1973)

Irm Hermann
*The Bitter Tears of Petra von Kant* (1972)

Brigitte Mira            Fassbinder
German Film Prize [Bundesfilmpreis] for *Ali:Fear Eats the Soul* (1973)

Michael Ballhaus
*Martha* (1973)

Ingrid Caven                    Daniel Schmid
Cannes Film Festival (1975)

Fassbinder
Gottfried John                    Brigitte Mira                    Michael Ballhaus
*Mother Küsters Goes to Heaven* (1975)

Fassbinder                    Peter Märthesheimer
*I Only Want You to Love Me* (1976)

Hanna Schygulla                    Fassbinder
*The Marriage of Maria Braun* (1977)

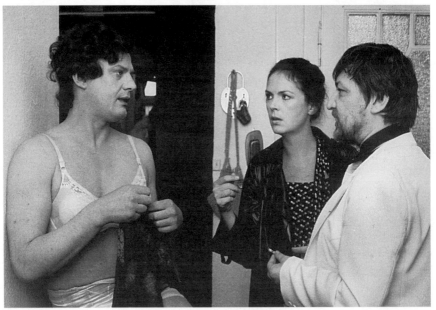

Volker Spengler          Elisabeth Trissenaar          Fassbinder
*In a Year with 13 Moons* (1978)

Hanna Schygulla as Maria Braun
(1978)

Juliane Lorenz        Fassbinder

(1978)

Dieter Minx      Fassbinder      Xaver Schwarzenberger

*Berlin Alexanderplatz* (1979)

Fassbinder                    Rosel Zech

*Veronika Voss* (1981)

Günter Lamprecht                          Fassbinder
*Berlin Alexanderplatz* (1979)

Armin Müller-Stahl                         Mario Adorf
*Lola* (1981)

Fassbinder                                        Hanna Schygulla
Venice Film Festival (1980)

Fassbinder                                        Barbara Sukowa
*Lola* (1981)

Fassbinder                                    Rolf Zehetbauer

*Veronika Voss* (1981)

Fassbinder                                    Barbara Baum

*Lola* (1981)

Theo Hinz       Juliane Lorenz           Horst Wendlandt       Fassbinder
Berlin Film Festival (1982)

Joan Fontaine   Xaver Schwarzenberger   Fassbinder   Rosel Zech   James Stewart
Berlin Film Festival (1982)

Liselotte Eder                    Juliane Lorenz
Fassbinder Exhibition, Berlin (1992)

Egmont Fassbinder                    Juliane Lorenz
Benefit Concert: *Fassbinder on the Road to USA* (1996)

# DANIEL SCHMID

B*orn in Switzerland in 1941, Mr. Schmid now lives in Paris and in Switzerland. Since 1970, he made a name for himself as director of numerous movies, among them* La Paloma, Shadows of the Angels, The Kiss of Tosca, *and* Between Seasons. *In Geneva and Zürich, he conducted such opera productions as Alban Berg's* Lulu. *His book,* The Invention of Paradise — A Spectacle in Five Acts, *portrays Switzerland as a stage set with the emotional background of the nineteenth century. The interview was conducted in Flims/Waldhaus.*

## SOMETHING DISTANT,
## SOMETHING MONGOLIAN

*You met Rainer in 1966 during the entrance exams for the newly founded Berlin Film Academy [Deutsche Film Und Fernsehakademie Berlin]. As soon as the names starting with "F" had been read, he knew, of course, that he had flunked. According to Rainer, he cried when he found out. Strangely enough, he told me that Werner Schroeter had also flunked and that day sat under a table, crying. Later I learned from Schroeter that he hadn't even taken part in that exam. I don't know whether I misunderstood Rainer or whether he was simply spinning out one of his melodramatic stories.*

Werner Schroeter definitely was not present. I was accepted and Rainer did cry. He was a total wreck. Although . . . you could never tell with him for sure. He had so many faces, it was crazy. Rainer could be totally perplexed, totally vulnerable, and quite sentimental as well as detached and present, all at the same time. So it's true, he cried, which is a kind of catharsis, but did he cry for a whole week? Hardly.

Even then, I think I understood what made Rainer tick. He reminded me of that line by Hasenclever: "Change and change again, and yet to ourselves stay the same." When he first visited me in the digs I shared my girlfriend, I felt as though someone had switched on the electricity.

*What form did this current take?*

His incredible awareness, his acute alertness, his rare lack of prejudice, his openness…you felt you could walk right through him, as though he were reflecting you. You instantly felt you would not be betrayed by this man.

His most striking characteristic was his childlike quality. I remember one very touching story. In 1974, we were both attending the New York Film Festival—he came with *Fox and his Friends* and I came with *La Paloma*. And there, during the screening of his movie, I saw Rainer with tears streaming down his face. The rest of us—Ingrid Caven, Werner Schroeter, and I—thought the movie was very German, dripping with self-pity. And he was bawling as he watched himself on the screen. I found it silly but undeniably touching. I thought, "Amazing, how he can pull that off." Then the lights came on, and right away Rainer was there with some smart-aleck cynical remark. You know what I mean? This rapid succession of emotions on different levels…

*I remember it well.*

One always runs the risk of simplifying or leaving out essentials about Rainer. There was an enigmatic quality about him. You know the line in *Shadows of the Angels*, "Myself is somebody else." He once asked me to read his play *The Garbage, the City and Death*. I asked him why he didn't want to direct the movie. "I can't do that," he said. "I don't even know what it's about." He didn't want to adapt it because it had simply poured out of him.

*The Film Academy exams were held in the villa on Wannsee where the Literary Colloquium is located today.*

I arrived late. Everybody had been seated, and many were in jackets and ties. Holger Meins was one of them. I stood in the auditorium, looking for a seat. There was only one left, way in the back, next to a young man to whom I felt attracted in a mysterious sort of way. He was looking at me as I headed in his direction. He seemed very curious, very demanding, very alert, and very transparent, yet quite distant. He also was shy, a quality I would sense in him all through his life.

*But you never spoke to each other?*

No, we did our thing and handed in the papers. Then we began talking. He came home with me because he had no place to stay. And somehow he entered my life. From then on he simply hung around. What can I say? Just imagine two young men meeting during exams and somehow staying together all those years. In retrospect, it seems logical enough to me. We told each other what we were planning to do in the future, the kind of films we wanted to make, the world we wanted to create.

*You are a few years older than Rainer?*

Yes, but I was a country bumpkin. I had come to Germany from Switzerland, to this ruined city in this ruined country, looking for a world which no longer existed because that world had been exiled or gassed. I had been raised in anti-Fascist ways. I brought an outsider's view to everything that came my way. At that time, my very first week in Berlin, I also met Andreas Baader. I keep asking myself, "Why did I meet them?"

*But after Rainer failed to get into the Film Academy, you went separate ways. He went back to Munich, continued with his writing, made a second short and, in 1967, applied again for the entrance exams. That time, he wasn't even allowed to take the test!*

Needless to say, the Film Academy didn't teach you to make movies the way Rainer or I would make movies all our lives. A "revolution" was going on. The children of the middle-class were frolicking in foreign gardens of Maoist provenance. It was a jolly life. Utopian. Munich was out of the question. That was yuppie-chic. Berlin, with its carefree arrogance, seemed like the center of the world. It was a heady atmosphere, quite ecstatic. At any rate, being a first year student at the Film Academy, I was pretty close to the action. Holger Meins was there, too. He had produced a movie, called *Wie mache ich einen Molotow Cocktail? [How To Make a Molotov Cocktail]*. He hadn't done it just for fun either. The revolution also took hold of the movies, at least in theory. It was crazy. Nobody was aware that the global internetting by computers and media had already begun. Nobody took to the streets to demonstrate against pictures.

*When did you next meet Rainer?*

In June 1969 Rainer attended the Berlin Film Festival with his first feature film, *Love Is Colder Than Death*. I met him in an elevator at Europa-Center. He was surrounded by people who later came into my life. We talked about all those revolutionary ideas. I think we were pretty confused. That same year I also met Werner Schroeter. Earlier I had met Rosa von Praunheim.

I was open to absolutely everything. However, I felt more and more suffocated by the formal training I received at the Film Academy. I wanted out. And who should appear at this juncture with Ulli Lommel and the "group" in the elevator? Rainer, of course. He asked me how long I was planning to stay in Berlin and whether I was still at that stupid school. I saw his movie, which the Festival had panned. To be honest, I didn't think that was any way to make a movie either.

*So you were not a Fassbinder fan?*

I had met him as a friend, and whenever we met again, we met on that basis. I always considered Werner Schroeter's cinematographic work more exciting. Rainer knew that. Our mutual attraction derived from my inner resistance to some, though not all, of his movies.

*And did you go back to the Film Academy?*

I was preparing my movie for the finals but interrupted my work to go to Venice as assistant director to Peter Lilienthal on the television film *Die Sonne Angreifen [To Attack the Sun]*, based on a book by Witold Gombrowicz. Through Peter Lilienthal I met so many interesting people who lived in Munich that I decided to move there, too. I shared a large apartment on Friedrichstrasse with Werner, Ingrid Caven, Magdalena Montezuma, and Ila von Hasperg. Those encounters with the circle around Rainer and Werner Schroeter became a sort of trigger for me.

*What did you mainly talk about? Movies?*

Movies? No, we never talked about movies. We talked about life! Rainer was filming *The Merchant of Four Seasons*, in which I played a small part. Together we conceived the idea of Tango-Film, although Rainer actually put up the production money. At one point I expected that my own movie, *Heute Nacht oder nie [Tonight or Never]*, would be produced next. But Rainer had other ideas. He literally told me, "No way. On Monday I start shooting *my* next movie." I got mad, said good-bye, and stormed out of the apartment. Ingrid followed me four days later and acted in my production. In due course several other dissidents joined us, among them Harry Baer. I still remember Rainer telling me, "You'll never pull that off. You're much too spoiled."

*Had Salem come into Rainer's life by then?*

Rainer met Salem in Paris before he started filming *The Merchant of Four Seasons*. Rainer was about twenty-five at the time. Salem was ten years older, a Berber who had a wife and two children back home in Morocco. They split early in 1974, after Rainer announced he couldn't stand Salem's drinking habit any longer. Rainer couldn't deal with it. He simply fled. And in this state, Salem allegedly assaulted two people. He virtually had to be smuggled out of Germany. I'll never forget how Rainer cried in the car all the way from Berlin to Cologne.

*I often ask myself why Rainer's relationships with men always had to end in tragedy. It had been much the same earlier with Günther Kaufmann and later, towards the end of the relationship, with Armin. Why couldn't these relation-ships have been different?*

Perhaps I can explain by way of a personal observation. I grew up without a father, as did Rainer. My brother and I came from a classic ma-triarchy. We had these "uncles" who each believed he had to put on a show of authority to replace the missing father. It was similar in Rainer's case. We experienced male authority only in this form and thus never ac-tually felt it. A balanced partnership is much harder to achieve between men than it is between women. I, for one, could never abide Rainer's au-thoritarian attitude. I dealt with him only in a playful way.

*Now I am going to say something I wouldn't have said or even thought fifteen years ago. Why were his male partners always men who, in some way or other, became dependent on him, if only because of their initial social and financial in-feriority?*

Were they inferiorities? It's hard to tell. People approach each an-other. Is the one who offers more guilty than the one who accepts? In fact, there is no guilt. Take this example: Goethe married Christiane Vulpius, much to the chagrin of Frau von Stein. It was a blow to the in-telligentsia and to his numerous mistresses in Europe. He, the monument, marrying Christiane, the washerwoman, a girl from the lower orders. She must have offered him something — the cuisinière, as they called her in the salons of Europe. Was Goethe superior to her?

*It's a good example, though it doesn't shed much light on the psychological process.*

Rainer had one peculiar quality: extreme dependence on others depending on him.

*Did you find him gullible in any way?*

No, but he was so transparent that he was like no one else. Our own reflections in his face were more complex than anything we had ever learned about ourselves.

*Let's now turn to the project you worked on together in 1975, the movie* Shadows of the Angels. *After barely a year in office, Rainer had been forced to resign his job as co-director of Theater am Turm [TAT] in Frankfurt. The grants commission had rejected his movie project* Die Erde ist unbewohnbar wie der Mond [The Earth is Uninhabitable like the Moon], *based on a novel by Gerhard Zwerenz.*

Rainer wrote his play late in 1974 on a trip to Los Angeles, independent of Zwerenz' novel and screenplay. He was going to rehearse it after his return to TAT. But then things developed rather rapidly. The play hadn't yet been published. Later, when it was available in print, the famous paragraphs containing the lines spoken by Nazis were quoted as the author's opinion and used against him out of context. It was the beginning of a provincial German tragedy.

Both scripts, the play and the movie, present a brilliant picture of Herr and Frau Müller, a twentieth-century German couple. It is very accurate, yet quite crazy. This Fascist saying, "I was a technocrat, I had no concern for the individuals I killed." And his wife, the Marxist-Leninist, who is paralyzed and in a wheelchair, saying, "We refuse to let ourselves be devoured by circumstances we have not created." Upon which he wheels her home for coffee and cake.

*When the play was in rehearsal,* Frankfurter Rundschau *carried a small item, alleging that something "anti-Semitic" was being rehearsed at TAT. And that was the beginning of the end.*

After the TAT debacle, Rainer often came to Paris. He asked me to read the play and give him my opinion. My instinctive reaction was that it was a nasty fairy tale, a German fairy tale. Then he asked me whether I would like to do the movie. By then I had made several movies which had received certain recognition in France. I had just decided to live in Paris. So I said, "Why not?" The script, which we wrote together, originated during his frequent visits to Paris. The movie was shot in Vienna.

*How did you actually write the script together?*

We did it in a rather playful way. The play was there. So we simply converted it, scene by scene, into a script, which we wrote in longhand.

Some clueless individuals later claimed Rainer had known perfectly well that the play would come under heavy attack and had deliberately pushed me to the fore to take the brunt. That is total bullshit. Neither of us took those attacks seriously. In my experience, Rainer was one of those rare people, maybe the only one, who was entirely without prejudice.

*I agree with that.*

What shocked Rainer the most was that former Nazis were suddenly and sanctimoniously presenting *him* as an anti-Semite! What's more, this total calumny went undisputed in Germany. Only in foreign countries did people understand the parable of the German couple, Herr and Frau Müller: the Communist in the wheelchair and the Fascist with time on his hands, who only goes out at night, dressed in women's clothes, to perform as a transvestite.

Foreign audiences and critics also understood that we were at the end of the century in a nameless city, where the sky is visible only in the execution scene. The character who is called "the rich Jew," and Lily, who in the play is called "Roma B.," are riding in a car. He doesn't really want to kill her, because it would leave him with no one to talk to. So he says, "I could forgive you," and she replies, "I don't need your forgiveness." After a long pause, he says, "Do you realize, we never listened to music together?" Then Lily takes his hand and, gazing out of the moving car, says, "I know, music might have deceived us." To which he replies, "And who would want to be deceived?" And Lily says, "Everyone. We all need those songs that sing of love." Then he stops the car, they get out, and he strangles her as she had wished. The key phrase is "Music might have deceived us." It is like Marie's attitude in Büchner's *Woyzeck*.

*Did you make substantial changes with your directing?*

I changed a few things. Mainly the music track he had suggested, which I redid entirely. And I changed his stage directions.

*Did he keep out of your way?*

Completely. He saw the final cut prior to the mix. I had a minor problem with the rhythm in the first five minutes of the film. I told him, he looked at it, and he agreed.

*You might have thought he would have interfered.*

Well, he didn't. In fact, he had to adjust to our rhythm. By then, I was already working on a regular basis with Renato Berta, who is quite different from the cinematographers Rainer worked with — in those days, it was Ballhaus. We simply needed more time, which he fully accepted. As a principal direction, I told him that he was Marilyn* and that he was beautiful. This preempted potential arguments, and he performed like a trooper.

*In 1976, the movie was presented at the Cannes Film Festival. There was an outcry against the play which in the meantime — in March 1976 — had been published by Suhrkamp. The Israeli delegation departed in protest. Suhrkamp stopped distribution of the printed play.*

Yes, people just lapped up those rumors at Cannes. Nobody bothered about the contents of the play, let alone the movie. It was like a train that could not be stopped. Charges of anti-Semitism were all the rage. Yet the movie was never banned; it played all over the world.

*The movie was shown in your American retrospective in 1993. Nobody — not even the members of the Jewish community — voiced that criticism then or in 1988, when the play was produced in New York.*

The play was never properly performed, although it opened in Copenhagen in 1986. A proper performance is still due.

*Rainer Werner Fassbinder, the person and the friend. What remains?*

When a man is gone, as Rainer is, he easily becomes the subject of projection, of interpretation, of explanation. Who was he? Perhaps he

* "Marilyn" refers to the glamour that Marilyn Monroe came to represent.

himself never knew. Perhaps it is not all that important. I personally have very good memories. I'm not going to ask myself who he really was for the rest of my life. I was very young when I met him; we were both young. The day I stepped into that auditorium he caught my attention and I obviously caught his. Who knows why?

It all had something to do with those utopian years between 1967 and 1972, and with the people we met during those years. The time turned us on and, because of the opportunities it gave us, it has left us with an obligation. Rainer, with his brilliant awareness, inspired us, pushed us ahead.

If ever anyone gave testimony about Germany, it was Rainer. He made up for what the defunct German cinema — with the exception of Helmut Käutner and Wolfgang Staudte — failed to express in the fifties and sixties. Yet there was something distant, something Mongolian... Chinese about him. Something very remote. I often told him that. To which he would giggle and say, "Oh, stop it." I thought of him as an ancient Chinese, or an old Chinese woman, or a very young Chinese child. So many faces, father, son, mother, all in one.

*One more question on the subject of love, of give and take.*

Rainer had an enormous capacity for love, although, it was often combined with demands, like the example of the little finger: first it's just the little finger, then the whole hand. If you failed to set limits, you were lost. At least, I was. I needed to get away whenever things got beyond me. Yet to him that was the point when the relationship became interesting. He was greatly interested in disengagement and how to play with it.

There is such a thing as being damaged by happy days, childhood and youth, the paradise from which you cannot be expelled... were we in paradise? At least, the first years of his work were happy even for him. That was before he knew too much about the system and how it works, how dependence works, how people act out their fantasies.

*What, in your view, is a "damaged utopia"?*

To be alive in such an era and witness its passing. Those were the only free, utopian years. Perhaps the era stretched into the Brandt/ Heinemann years. But then everything happened at once, the end of utopia, of ideologies, of the familiar landscape. The change began in 1966, especially a change away from formality. People simply behaved toward each other in a more relaxed way. Until then life had still been somewhat Victorian. It was the end of an epoch. And perhaps we owe this epoch a duty — which is an anachronism in our day and age.

# HANNA SCHYGULLA

H*er somewhat accidental stint, in 1964, at the drama school in Munich, and particularly her encounter with Rainer Werner Fassbinder, ended Ms. Schygulla's academic career. Beginning in 1969, she acted in about half of Fassbinder's movies. At first she played working-class Marilyns, whom she described as "almost the exact opposite of myself." Living on the very edge of society, vainly dreaming of bourgeois happiness, they are chasing after illusions, from* Love Is Colder Than Death *to* The Bitter Tears of Petra von Kant. *She later played major female characters, "my tragic sisters," as she called them, who put off happiness until a tomorrow that never comes: Effi Briest, Maria Braun, and Lili Marleen, symbolic figures in German history. After Lili Marleen, her last Fassbinder movie, she played in foreign productions by avant-garde directors such as Ettore Scola, Jean-Luc Godard, Andrzej Wajda, and Kenneth Branagh. She has received numerous national and international awards. At present she lives in Paris. The interview was conducted in Munich.*

## LIKE BROTHER AND SISTER

*I realize now that something snapped after* Querelle. *In 1982, I did not see it. I always thought he was a healthy person.*

Which is not surprising. He himself thought he was stronger than everybody else.

*When I look at photographs of him today, I can see how tired and exhausted he was. He always exuded this incredible strength. But after* Querelle *he was*

*tired and even told me so. I said, "So sleep for a few days." But there was this*
*pressure about getting the movie to Cannes on time...It was the first time I*
*said, "I can't do it. I can't edit a Dolby-stereo film in ten days." He was des-*
*perate. His total exhaustion did not come from drugs but from work, from con-*
*stantly pushing himself to the limit.*

Rainer hardly ever slept. In the early days, he refused to touch drugs.
Drugs made him nervous. Maybe he knew that, once he started, he
wouldn't be able to stop. Of course, it was all related to the obsessive
character of his creativity, his calling, his conviction that he needed to
do everything fast. I remember his telling me even in drama school that
he wouldn't get old. He was then, I don't know, maybe nineteen or
twenty? Where did he get it, this premonition of dying young? Though
in the final analysis, he brought it upon himself.

*It contradicts his Buddha-like quality.*

There was something oriental about his features. He always looked
as though he had blown in from some faraway steppes, from the hordes
of Genghis Khan.

*How did you first meet?*

I went to Paris for a year when I was nineteen. Then I came back
and entered the university. That soon got on my nerves, and I decided
to drop out as fast as I could. And then there was this girl who told me,
"I'm going to drama school at night; it's really interesting, why don't you
come along?" So I went, and there was Rainer.

*Did you feel what he described as an instant understanding between you?*

Nope, I always thought Rainer didn't like me. That was my first impression. I can't say that I liked him much either, but I was fascinated by
him. That brooding quality of his...In the beginning, his acting had
something of Marlon Brando. Of all the students he was the most interesting to me. Whenever we were improvising—which I often found
embarrassing—I thought: "Oh my God, what is he thinking?" Somehow the look in his eyes mattered to me.

*Yet you never asked him?*

No. I can't even remember speaking to him all that much. All I remember is that he struck me as someone special with a special talent, an

outsider like myself, but that he didn't like me. One day we were rehearsing a scene from Goethe's *Elective Affinities*, where a sister loves her brother but doesn't want to let him know. She talks to him while she is stitching away at her embroidery, trying to hide her love. It seemed incredibly old-fashioned to me. Afterwards Rainer let me know through Christoph Roser that he had liked my performance very much. I was amazed. I couldn't imagine Rainer liking this kind of thing. In those days, I considered him a rebel, a guy in search of something new. Strange, how all the switches had already been set. It's possible that something like the heart of our relationship was already ticking in that scene, and that it had touched him. Because that's what we were: brother and sister. Our reactions toward each other always remained the same, although we rarely addressed each other directly. I also kept being surprised at the things he liked. Of course, he was surprising in general. The moment you thought he was like this or that, he turned out to be completely different. Then I left drama school.

I really believed acting was not for me. My performances went from bad to worse. I became more and more artificial, I became very tense . . . and then I left.

I don't remember Rainer and I ever acting together in anything. All I remember is meeting with a group at a coffee shop now and then. He once said he didn't like Capricorns. I am a Capricorn, so I took it as another proof that he didn't like me. I always felt this mixture of attraction and warning not to get too close lest I be burned. I felt I had to keep a certain distance. I thought he might become dangerous if I gave in to him body and soul.

*How do you mean "dangerous"?*

He would drive you into a corner and not let you go. He had this obsession with seeing how far he could go with a person. I knew I'd be lost once I was cornered. I can only function if someone believes in me. There is a deep-seated anxiety in me that nothing I expect of myself will ever come true. It's an inferiority complex I grew up with. Some people are born with a plus, others with a minus. I believe Rainer, too, was born with a minus. It was probably one of the subliminal connections between us that we were able to convert the minus into a plus.

A few days after my hasty departure from drama school, I found this note: "We are playing *Antigone*. The opening is in three days. Why don't you drop by? Rainer." Another person might have said, "No way. This needs to be rehearsed." But to me, being plunged into a situation with no time to question myself was a great chance. It was also typical of Rainer. He would fling himself into a project and things would just evolve. I knew he was remarkably sure of his talent. There was always something like a sound-proof area between us, where nothing upsetting could penetrate from the outside; a safety zone, where nothing could go wrong.

*Did you ever try to break out of this zone?*

In the beginning, I didn't want to break out. By the time I did, it was too late. After *Maria Braun*, I opened up to Rainer. I had come to realize that he was the person I had to commit myself to, the person who was my fate. I also realized that *The Marriage of Maria Braun* had something to do with our unconsummated relationship.

*Then why not break out of that safety zone?*

When Rainer entered the room, everyone stood at attention. People with masochistic tendencies became so hysterical that he could squeeze them dry. The rest kept their distance. Whenever Rainer appeared, I actually found it hard to be myself. I was tense, hoping he wouldn't hurt me, yet also wanting to please him. It made me unable to stand up to him.

But he was also afraid of me. Rainer never wanted to sit close to me. He built up a wall between us. Yet how quickly the wall disappeared whwn we happened to start talking to each other. The thing that always fascinated me about Rainer was that you could never see beyond the horizon into the inner sanctum. Whenever you thought you knew him, an area that you hadn't seen before would open up. Perhaps this ambivalent feeling about truth was precisely what bound us together. Rather than this *or* that, it's this *and* that. It's how Rainer made his movies. Things were like this, on the one hand, and like that, on the other. His movies are about things that don't fit together at all and don't follow any theory. That is why his movies are still valid. He was a product of his time, like the rest of us, and he believed in the slogans of his time. Yet he never failed to question them.

*To what extent were the women you played an aspect of yourself?*

The love story in *Lili Marleen* was our theme, so to speak, as it was in *Maria Braun*, which became our hit movie. Passing each other by, saving something for later until it is too late . . .

Those women I used to play, inarticulate, naive, working-class girls, glued to their men, were the complete opposite of myself. All I wanted was to be free, at all times and under any circumstances, like a bird of passage. It was always there deep inside me. And there was this urgent desire to escape from the intellect, from what I had become during that time at the university.

I had somehow stumbled into studying literature, because I had written good essays in school. I thought, "O.k., I'll do something related to language," because in fact I had no idea what to do. I thought about teaching school, because I liked children. Maybe I can trigger something in their minds. I was delighted that my encounter with Fassbinder brought my studies to an end, although for the longest time I thought that acting wasn't for me either.

*During the shooting of* Maria Braun, *Rainer said, "Now she finally realizes that this is right for her." It was important to him that you accept your talent.*

In the early days, I was thrilled to see myself on screen. It was new and what I saw was quite different from my real self. The parts I played were like photographic negatives.

*At the time, you said that the part of Effi Briest constricted you like a corset.*

Yes. I actually wanted to play it with more expression. I realize now that the movie is so good precisely because I was not allowed to express myself. At the time it was frustrating for me just to stand there and not be able to let anything out. I was not allowed to give in to any impulse. I had to be composed. But at that phase of my life, this composure was what I most wanted to shed.

*But wasn't that also a part of yourself?*

It was, but a part I wanted to shake. Of course, it all fits together, my development and this part I was playing. But I wasn't mature enough to see it that way and say, "Well, what do you know! How interesting, there is a parallel . . . " Apparently that's how life is, the moment you want to shake something, you have to go through it once again very intensely.

*Did you try to persuade Rainer to let you try something else?*

No. I was still very much under his spell. I could only break that spell by leaving his sphere of influence. I finally put that into words sooner than I planned, during a break on *Effi Briest*. He said, "When this is over, we are going to do *World on a Wire*, and then we'll do whatever...and then..." And I heard myself saying, "No way, then we'll do nothing at all for a while, I need a break." I remember his face. A look of shock and total distress. As though someone had hit him from behind. Which, of course, I had in the sense that I had never told him where I stood before, what I wanted, what I was dreaming of.

*Did you think it was over for good?*

Yes, I did. I watched what he was doing from a distance, and when I saw *Chinese Roulette* I thought, "Thank God I'm not in this movie!" Still, I never doubted we'd reunite some day. The bond was too strong.

*Let's go back to the early movies. Rainer told me that everybody in the group had jointly wanted to make the first ten movies. Later it was reported that he was the only one who wanted to make them. Of course, that hurt his feelings. What about it — were all of you behind him, or was there some dissension?*

Nothing like that. It was an adventure for us all. But, of course, it was he who wanted the movies. We were the pawns in his game. For us, it was exciting to be part of it, but he was the driving force. Willi [Peer Raben] also played an important part, mustering the courage to get those projects off the ground. Willi supported him all the way. He spread such ease. We were all amateurs, after all, and Rainer let us be.

That's another reason why I thought acting was not for me. I sometimes felt out of touch with myself. Rainer picked up on that and worked it into his vision of life, he portrayed it in his movies. Reality became something like a dream or, more frequently, a nightmare. The characters act as though they are moved by remote control, in keeping with the slogans of those days. We were convinced that society was to blame for everything, that we were the way we were because society had programmed us that way.

The characters in his early movies are not simply social creatures but intelligent sleepwalkers. That's why those early movies have this ethereal quality. In those days, the world was still relatively intact, even if disfigured by Man. But it was not yet a world likely to be annihilated. We were not aware of an ozone hole or of the fact that Man had fiddled around with nature to the extent that it might be beyond salvation. It was Man, the creature who had become estranged from himself by his work and by the social system. We believed in a utopia where life could be completely different. We had grown up in the soil of Nazi Germany, and we wanted to do everything differently. Those were the impulses that sent us into the street to stand up for ourselves, exposing evils and bringing them to light. Or, as Rainer would have said, showing where it stinks.

Rainer always worked with double-exposures in pictures. On the one hand, as in *Alexanderplatz*, there is Man at his animal worst, the arch-enemy. On the other side, there he is, an angel with broken wings. It was his vision of Man, and it still works: I am one and the other. He always chose lovers quite different from himself, who perhaps had been wounded to the same degree he had. He felt their pain but had no need to live it. He was an outsider by choice. He extracted and distilled that sense of alienation and shaped it into something powerful. He provoked it. He took pleasure in confusing, vexing, shocking, muddling up things. He grabbed the people he worked with by their talents and gave them the space they needed.

*And they put up with everything else.*

He was basically a giver. He was the cornucopia of their lives. Had they been honest, though, they would have admitted that they never felt very much at ease with him.

*There were phases which were truly awful. Yet the good times outweighed them.*

And that lay like a curse on his relationships, and probably made him suffer, too. Of course, there were blithely exuberant moments, when we had fun and things were refreshingly anarchistic. There were sudden moments when something wonderful would take shape and you were part of it. There was this tension in the room. There was always this fear of being exposed or learning more about yourself than you wanted to know. He had something of a cougar, that watchful tension of his eyes. Those eyes could be very soft and tender, yet you never knew if he was about to caress you or pounce on you with his claws.

# IRM HERMANN

Born in 1942, Ms. Hermann met Fassbinder in Munich in 1965, where she played a part in his first short, The City Tramp. She followed him to Action Theater and, after its demise, to the antiteater. Fassbinder wrote major female characters for her in nineteen of his movies. Completely different from the female clichés created by Hollywood, these characters have become an important part of German movie history. In 1972, she was awarded the Film Prize of the German Federal Republic for her performance in The Merchant of Four Seasons. Since 1975 she has acted in over fifty movies by such prominent directors as Percy Adlon, Hans W. Geissendörfer, Reinhard Hauff, and Werner Herzog. In 1980, after several years of separation from Fassbinder, she acted in Berlin Alexanderplatz and in Lili Marleen. At present she lives in Berlin, where the interview was conducted.

## TOUCHED A NERVE

*How did you meet Rainer?*

A friend of mine was at drama school while earning her living as a secretary. She sometimes invited me to her apartment on Kaulbachstrasse. There was a young man, a fellow student of hers at drama school, who occasionally read there in the evening from novels of young writers. That was Rainer.

*What did he read?*

Something unpublished by a friend of his. It was total kitsch, the kind of novel that is sold in supermarkets. He read all through the night, smoking one cigarette after another. Later, we all went to hear Christoph Roser read *Only a Slice of Bread* at a drama competition. After the reading, we all went to a pub across the street, where I met Liselotte Eder. I was fascinated by Rainer, but months went by before we met again. Then one day Christoph Roser called to ask me whether I wanted to act in a movie. I said obviously I couldn't, because I wasn't a trained actress. But that didn't seem to be a valid argument to him. So I went to Café Monopterus on Kaulbachstrasse near Englischer Garten, where Rainer was waiting. He was incredibly shy, very polite and reserved, which I found very attractive.

*Did they start shooting right away?*

They were shooting in Susanne's apartment, just around the corner. Everything had been prepared: lights, camera, sound...

*This was* The City Tramp.

That's right. Three months later, Rainer called and invited me to a screening of the finished movie at Arri Cinema. After that we met more frequently. Eventually he would just pick me up at the office every day. We walked through Englischer Garten and he talked about the movies he wanted to make.

*What fascinated you about him?*

He was the first person who took me seriously. He recognized something in me which I was not yet aware of myself. He liked things about me that no one else liked — my style and my manner of speaking. The fascination was mutual, though, a mutual flame. We saw each other every day. At some point he told me I should stop working as a secretary, and I agreed. He went to see my boss and told him I wanted to quit. That was my first step out of a bourgeois existence. Soon thereafter he moved into my apartment on Ainmillerstrasse. Love gave me wings. Suddenly I could do whatever I wanted. Every door was open to me, because I wanted them to be.

*In the summer of 1967, Rainer finished his second short.*

That's right. That summer we went to Oberhausen together in the hope that we could show the two shorts we hadn't been able to register in time. I managed to see Hilmar Hoffman, who was in charge of the festival. But the program was full, we were simply too late. Rainer insisted that there had to be a slot somewhere in the program where the work might be shown. We waited in the cinema café for a decision that never came. Then we hitchhiked back to Munich with all our frustrations on our backs.

*What did you do when nothing seemed to work in movies?*

Rainer had this idea that I should open an agency for actors, and I did. Later my clients included Hanna, Christoph Roser, Susanne Schimkus, and Rolf Bosse. For a while, I traveled all over Germany with the photos and resumés of my actors, visiting casting agencies and offering them my clients. At the same time, I tried to persuade the television editors to show Rainer's two shorts on television, without success. Rainer met the group on Müllerstrasse in the fall, which marked the end of our close relationship.

*Rainer said you were the only person he had actually forced to become an actress.*

It's true. He put me on stage in Ferdinand Bruckner's *Verbrecher [Criminals]*, his first Action Theater production. I was paralyzed with fear. Next I played a major role in *Krankheit der Jugend [The Sickness of Youth]* with Jean-Marie Straub, a frequent guest star at Action-Theater. The production later became part of his movie, *Der Bräutigam, der Komödiant und der Zuhälter [The Bridegroom, the Comedian and the Pimp]*.

I was curious about life, and I loved Rainer with all my heart. I despised all things middle-class: the stuffiness, the hypocrisy, and, above all, the ignorance. But my chief motive was a yearning for love. Working as an actress was an extension of my dreams which, in my early youth, only movies had fulfilled.

*Movies of a very different character…*

True. The fantasies Rainer turned into movies were quite different. Soon we were all wrapped up in his world of perception, his ideas of reality. His world also became my own.

*How did you feel about the roles Rainer created for you?*

As time went on, I felt constricted in the parts he wrote for me. But, you see, I had no choice. I had to accept them if I wanted to be with him. It was that simple. Whenever I had personal disagreements with him, I would simply be dropped from the next movie or stage play. There you are.

*But you were able to live with the image he projected through you?*

That image exists only in people's minds; it has nothing to do with my true personality. The real question is why later other directors wanted to simply lift this image as if it were an artificial decal and apply it to their own work. "She was so good in what she did for Fassbinder, so why can't she play it for me?" With Rainer, I acted much less self-consciously. I took on whatever Rainer saw in me—like a perfume. Of course, it also had something to do with the image I had of myself and what I wanted to be. I'll never forget the first time I saw myself on screen in *Love Is Colder Than Death*. I ran out of the cinema in tears, and Rainer ran after me. He understood what had happened. Because to me it wasn't a matter of whether I was plain or beautiful, but that this was truly me. And he instantly understood what was going on inside of me.

*Beware of a Holy Whore in 1970 signaled the end of the antiteater era. When you think back to that time and all the hurt feelings and estrangement, what are your conclusions?*

The years with Rainer are an essential part of my life. They shaped my character and my awareness. I am grateful for the experience and I don't regret anything. I am surprised today when people on the street still recognize me as a "Fassbinder actress." His movies must have had a profound impact on people...

*How is it that his movies can still stir up people's emotions today?*

He shoved a mirror into their faces, and not always a flattering one. He simply showed their flip side, mostly the middle-class side. Foreign audiences react more tolerantly, because they believe, incorrectly, that his movies don't address their own society. As long as it's about the Germans, it's fine with them. Rainer touched a nerve. He showed how people behave, pure and simple. It was bound to shake everybody up.

# URSULA STRÄTZ

Born in *Schweinfurt in 1940, Ms. Strätz began her stage career at Residenztheater in Munich. In 1966, she founded the Action Theater in Munich where, in due course, Rainer Werner Fassbinder also had his first stage experience. Except for a few small movie parts — in* Love Is Colder Than Death *and* Fontane Effi Briest *— her interest focused mainly on the theater. In 1974, she followed Fassbinder to TAT in Frankfurt. After the collapse of this experiment, she discovered her talent for painting. At present she lives in Munich, where the interview was conducted.*

## A THUNDERCLAP

*You met Rainer quite early on, when you were managing Action Theater in Munich in 1966.*

It was actually Action Cinema at the time.

*Action Cinema? What was that?*

A group who had studied at the same drama school in Munich decided to put on new, modern plays. I dreamed of a new, "different" theater. But not a theater on the outskirts. I wanted to be right in the center of Munich. We found Nationale Lichtspiele, an old movie house at 12 Müllerstrasse. Needless to say, we rented all the movies we wanted to see ourselves.

*How did Rainer join up with you?*

One day, it must have been in 1967, the door of the cinema opened and two guys who couldn't be more different from each other walked in. One of them was stylishly dressed. He made his entrance and then posed beside a movie poster we had put up at the entrance, saying nothing. That was Christoph Roser [actor and producer of Fassbinder's first two shorts]. The other was a lively, agitated fellow, who started talking non-stop about movies and the theater. When I told him about the theater I was planning to open, he said he was ready to enlist. That was Rainer Werner Fassbinder. He asked me about my favorite movies and I asked him about his. He mentioned *Der müde Tod [Tired Death]* by Fritz Lang. We talked about setups and movie pictures.

*Did Rainer come back?*

He did, though not immediately. I don't remember whether he attended our first theater performance.

He frequently dropped by after rehearsals for *Publikumsbeschimpfung [Offending the Audience]* by Peter Handke. Some members considered him an intruder, because he hadn't been with us at drama school. Healways wanted to participate and constantly interrupted our discussions. When he brought his play *Katzelmacher* for us to read, people were indignant and refused to have it performed. I told them, "Sorry, we are going to produce it." Willi [Peer Raben] and I had decided to try him out.

Anatol Gardener broke his arm during Willi's production of *Antigone* and Rainer stepped in, which turned out to be his first performance in our theater. For our next play, Büchner's *Leonce and Lena*, I thought we'd "try out" Rainer as assistant director as well as an actor. The women were to direct the men and the men to direct the women. In the end, Rainer ended up directing the entire production; those fabulous crowd scenes bore his distinctive mark even then. He had beautiful ideas.

*Such as?*

I would call them cinematic elements in the form of slapstick interludes. I am thinking of the scene where the subjects are lining up to welcome the royal couple. They are blowing their noses and topple down in formation. The entire row would topple whenever something silly was being said. There was the stage set which addressed political events of the day. The partitions were lined with pictures of the Shah, who happened to be on a visit to Germany. There was a lot of dancing throughout the production, and sometimes the partitions were knocked over, Shah and all.

We watched Rainer's shorts — *The City Tramp* and *The Little Chaos* —

both of which impressed me very much. After the screening I went for a walk with Rainer. We were alone for the first time and I told him that I loved him. He was still with Irm Hermann and had started a relationship with Willi while I was still living with Horst. So we decided this wasn't the most propitious moment. Things were complicated enough. Too much emotional confusion. Instead, Rainer showed up every morning with rolls fresh from the bakery, and we all had breakfast together.

Day by day our relationship became closer. In the end it was Rainer, Willi, and I who discussed the plays and decided with ones we were going to produce. Since I liked the two shorts so much, I offered to direct *Verbrecher [Criminals]*. It was obvious to me even then that Rainer wanted to make movies and that nothing would stop him.

But working in the theater gave him enormous pleasure. When Jean-Marie Straub told me that his adaptation of *Die Krankheit der Jugend [The Sickness of Youth]* would not run all that long, I suggested we perform *Katzelmacher* as a second play. Meanwhile, Willi and I moved in with Irm Hermann and Rainer, who then had a small apartment on Ainmillerstrasse. The two women were sleeping in the bed, by the way, with Rainer and Willi on the floor.

*Rainer told me it was a 250-square-foot apartment. Why did you move in with them?*

Horst had returned from the hospital and, needless to say, had caught on to my enthusiasm for Rainer. He was not terribly pleased by this development. In order to avoid foreseeable problems, I moved out.

*Then the next crucial event occurred, your accident.*

That accident affected the whole future of our theater. That morning Rainer and I had left the apartment together. I was going to walk with him through Englischer Garten. But at the last minute I changed my mind. The car I hitched a ride in was a mini. The driver was seriously injured; his wife, who sat with him up in front, ended up a paraplegic. I spent a long time in the hospital with a brain contusion. But I made sure that the show went on.

*What happened during your stay at the hospital?*

Horst took advantage of my absence to fire Willi and Rainer. The two subsequently joined the Büchner Theater and did *Zum Beispiel Ingolstadt*, Rainer's adaptation of Marieluise Fleisser's *Recruits in Ingolstadt*.

Rainer visited me faithfully every day in the hospital and reported on the *Ingolstadt* rehearsals.

*How long were you gone?*

Six weeks. By the time I came back, everything had collapsed. The theater was gone, as was the large apartment on Holzstrasse where Horst and I had lived. He had just stopped paying the rent.

*What did you do? Where did you go?*

I moved into the theater. I was determined to go on with my theater.

*And where was Horst?*

He disappeared. I learned from the newspapers that he had joined Andreas Baader and had taken part in setting fire to that department store in Frankfurt. It was horrible. Not only did I no longer have a theater or an apartment, I no longer had a husband. Besides, the brain injury seriously affected my equilibrium and my cognitive functions: every street seemed to end in a steep descent. Nothing was the same.

*What brought antiteater into being?*

That was entirely Rainer and Willi's work. I didn't want to see any of them; I was furious with them and with myself. The next thing I remember was *The Beggar's Opera*. They had found space for their antiteater in Witwe Bolte, a pub somewhere in back of the university.

*That was antiteater's fifth performance.*

By then, in 1969, I was back on the team. We now lived at Nördliche Auffahrtsallee near Schloss Nymphenburg. Again it was Irm, Rainer, Willi, and myself—a wonderfully creative time. Rainer was writing a new play, *Preparadise Sorry Now*, with Willi making contributions along the way. Then we moved from Nördliche Auffahrtsallee, which was becoming too cramped for us, to Stollbergstrasse in the center of town. For the first time we became a large commune. There were Rainer, Willi, Gottfried Hüngsberg, Ingrid Caven—who was living with Gottfried at the time—and myself. Irm did not move in with us. I honestly don't know why.

*And now you began making movies as well. Was it* Love Is Colder Than Death?

It was. Rainer wanted to make movies and naturally we all wanted to be part of this new development. He was writing non-stop. One production followed another in rapid succession. Needless to say, it was unequivocally a Fassbinder theater, no doubt about that.

*Meanwhile the name Fassbinder had become a household word.*

That had been true since *Leonce and Lena* in 1967. Rainer had made a lasting impression on the critics as an outstanding actor. The year 1969 was extremely productive and successful. *The Beggar's Opera* became a hit. Rainer wrote *Preparadise Sorry Now, Anarchy in Bavaria, Dedicated to Rosa von Praunheim*, and *The Coffee House*, based on Goldoni. He made his first feature film, *Love Is Colder Than Death*, which was shown at the Berlin Film Festival.

*Then there was a serious crisis. The Department of Taxation descended and suddenly confronted him with a debt of close to 200,000 marks. He was barely twenty-six. All the members of the commune vanished. Nobody felt responsible for the financial demands. The confusion caused a total collapse. Rainer set up his own company and shot* The Merchant of Four Seasons. *He continued to be creative and active, but antiteater ceased to exist. At that moment, many of those who had earlier disapproved of Rainer's dominating leadership could have continued with their "own" theater. Why didn't they?*

As far as I was concerned, the accident had somewhat stifled my enthusiasm for plunging into new ventures. Besides, I had my regular job. And I needed to pay back my own debts.

*When did you come back again?*

Late in 1974, Rainer became co-director at TAT in Frankfurt. He asked me if I wanted to be part of it. I think he accepted the co-directorship partly for the sake of the group. Perhaps that is why he appointed Kurt Raab as co-director which, I believe, was a real mistake. But Kurt needed the job, since Rainer was not always able to cast him.

*Why would Rainer take on the directorship for your sake?*

I once blamed him for the entire collapse. I hadn't meant it all that seriously but it apparently hit him very hard. In those days, he was blamed by a lot of people. In fact, the energy and the ideas had all come from Rainer and from Rainer alone. Perhaps he took those accusations too much to heart and tried to defuse them by accepting the director-ship. Yet in the final analysis, people were no longer interested. They preferred to act in his movies in order to become famous. They all wanted a share of the fame. It couldn't last.

*The whole thing lasted less than a year, and of course Rainer was responsible for the debacle. Then there was the scandal about his Frankfurt play.*

I couldn't stand the turmoil, those endless battles between us and the remaining TAT ensemble. It was a circus with collective management as the clown. That was when I started drinking, and drinking in earnest. Rainer begged me to go for treatment, and I did.

*And after that you began to paint.*

I did, much too late. But I made it.

# PEER RABEN

Born in 1940 at Viechtafell in Bavaria, Mr. Raben studied drama and musicology in Munich. His friendship with Fassbinder evolved while they worked together at Action Theater and later at antiteater in Munich. He worked mainly as a stage musician, dramaturg, conductor, and composer. He also acted as production manager in several productions of antiteater-X-Film. He wrote stage music for productions by Peter Zadek, Klaus-Michael Grüber, Luc Bondy, Hans Neuenfels, and Hansgünther Heyme, among others, as well as for Fassbinder. He was responsible for the music of almost all of Fassbinder's movies. His music is also heard in movies by Werner Schroeter, Daniel Schmid, Robert van Ackeren, Reinhard Hauff, Ulrike Ottinger, Luc Bondy, and Bernhard Sinkel. Apart from ballet music, he composed all the chansons for Ingrid Caven. In 1980, he received the Prize of the German Federal Republic for his music in Die Ortliebschen Frauen [Luc Bondy], and in 1983 the Prix Futura. Herbert Gehr conducted the interview with him in Munich.

## WORK WITHOUT END

*How long had Action Theater been around when Rainer appeared?*

Action Theater started operating early in 1966. I joined in the summer of 196, just before Fassbinder first appeared in the audience.

*In the audience?*

Yes. After the performance, the audience was invited for a discussion with the actors. One night Fassbinder was there, hanging out at the theater bar afterwards, telling everybody he was an actor and anxious to join the theater. You could tell right away that he was serious. His comments on the performance of *Antigone* were very much to the point and he knew how to assert himself. Everything he said added up to, "I've got to stay here and work here."

He had come to see my production of *Antigone* — not the classic text by Sophocles but Brecht's adaptation. Fassbinder liked the fact that several texts had been woven together. I wanted a separation of text and emotional presentation. If a line was emotionally very highly charged, I had the entire cast speak it in a very cold manner. If, for instance, the lines disclosed great suffering on the part of the character, I told them to completely separate themselves from that emotion by speaking the lines simply and clearly, even though the character herself might be on the verge of tears. Speak your lines, and then have a crying fit. That was something new in those days. In the States, the Living Theater had done a lot of it. We were influenced by them, as was Fassbinder.

*Was Fassbinder committed to the process of collective work on a play?*

Not committed; not interested. In fact, you could say he was against it. After *Antigone* we were planning to collectively direct Büchner's *Leonce and Lena*. Rainer promptly made himself unpopular. He said this made no sense at all. There could be only one director, leaving no doubt that he meant himself. This caused a violent argument among the cast. Most people resented his attitude, saying, "Where does this guy come from anyway? We don't even know him. Does he know what he is doing?" Then rehearsals began, and no one brought up those questions again.

*Yet, in his personal life, Fassbinder was not at all adverse to the idea of communal living.*

Communal living worked reasonably well most of the time. Of course, it is easier than handling the text of a poet, where it's hard to make a collective decision about where the focus should be.

*If he favored a traditional hierarchical division of labor, he must have already assumed a very strong position.*

As we worked on the play, it rapidly became evident that Fassbinder's ideas were sound. His leading position was accepted because of his obvious artistic talent, not because we wanted to submit to the spirit of collectivism. In the late sixties, drama school students used to say, "For Heaven's sake, why do we study all that junk? We don't want to do what the state theaters are doing. We want to do our own thing." We established our own theater, because we wanted to do a new kind of theater. When Fassbinder staged scenes from *Leonce and Lena*, people immediately said, "Yes, that's what we are looking for." He simply understood. His ideas were new. They represented a change from the traditional theater and they showed Action Theater the way.

*To what extent did those ideas concur with the slogans of 1968? Was the production affected by current politics?*

The production had a lot to do with the current political scene. *Leonce and Lena* is packed with strong political situations. And certain members of the group wanted to emphasize them even more.

*At what point did you decide not to return to your engagement in Wuppertal?*

The prospect of working with Fassbinder at Action Theater confirmed my decision. I had played in Wuppertal for quite a while. I had been on stage night after night, repeating the same things over and over again. I realized this was not what I wanted to continue doing.

*Fassbinder has been credited with turning many of his collaborators into professionals, people who, initially, had not been experts in their fields.*

No, he did not turn them into professionals. It was his genius that he knew how to use them the way they were. It would have been all wrong if they had turned into professionals. That was part of the novelty we created: he did not try to direct dialogue in the traditional sense of the word. The actor was to remain on stage the person he was in actual life. He was to adapt the ideas of the character he played to his own personality.

*Did that also apply to your compositions? Did Fassbinder say: this is Peer Raben, the person, his music has more to do with him than with the purpose of the specific project?*

Music was inserted as part of a performance. In the performance of *Leonce and Lena*, for instance, we used songs by the Beatles. The music remains an element in itself and does not dissolve into the play.

*Was it a logical step from your work in the theater to the movies?*

Fassbinder's visual conception of the stage was essentially derived from the movies. He was the first to introduce cinematographic elements into stage productions. *Katzelmacher* was the first major movie adaptation of a play in which actors from Action Theater performed. It was practically an adaptation of the play we had done on stage, with the same cast.

*Did you have a new concept for the screen version?*

It naturally had to be thought through again. *Katzelmacher* has a style of its own. As a movie it represented something entirely new for the screen. We were shooting scenes where the characters don't move at all but appear before the camera as though they are sitting on a stage.

*How do you visualize the collaboration between the director and the composer on a project that has been adapted to the film medium?*

The collaboration should ideally start as soon as the script is available. In the case of *Love Is Colder Than Death*, we began discussing the music before the script was even finished. Fassbinder could already tell precisely what the style of the movie was going to be and how it was to be underlined by the music. We then knew how to design ideas for the music.

Fassbinder offered clues, such as: the rooms where the action takes place should appear very cold, overly bright, super bright. The light should outshine everything else. So all the characters who act in those rooms vanish because they are driven out by the light pouring in from the windows. It was something I could instantly work with.

*What do such abstract descriptions of a movie's style suggest? How did you integrate this information?*

A situation can easily be articulated by sound. The coldness of a room can be expressed better with music than through visuals.

*Did Fassbinder himself make suggestions?*

He fortunately knew a lot of music. With *Love Is Colder Than Death*, I suggested Henze's music to Schlöndorff's "Young Törless," which is string quartet music. Before the film was available in its final cut, there was ample opportunity for change. For instance, he would say the music could be longer in this or that place, and we would make changes in the editing so it could run longer.

*Were there instances when you could not agree at all on the music?*

In *Love Is Colder Than Death* he had already shot a scene where two characters are together in a room. One of them puts a record on the turntable. But we had not previously discussed the music that should be heard. He imagined something that simply could not be produced in the studio with studio musicians.

*With Fassbinder's high-speed production style, shooting one movie after another in rapid succession, was his crew able to keep up with him?*

I always knew about a project in advance. I was able to start working in my head at an early stage. Then there were projects where he only needed to mention the title, as in the case of *Berlin Alexanderplatz*, for me to get going. It was more difficult with stories he had invented himself, such as *The Marriage of Maria Braun*. On the whole, it was fairly simple. We watched the movie together — i.e., an advanced rough cut — and then decided on the spot that this or that music should be inserted here.

In *Maria Braun* he had very specific ideas which wouldn't necessarily have come up while we were watching the movie. He thought of them while he was inventing the story. In the scene before Maria Braun goes off to apply for a job as a nightclub hostess, you see her in a derelict room full of old gym equipment from her childhood. She runs through a routine of exercises. Here, Fassbinder thought we should have music recalling themes from the Nazi era in a childlike manner, such as, "Oh, du schöner Westerwald," a brisk marching tune played on a xylophone. It was a good idea.

*What sort of ups and downs were there in your fifteen years of collaboration?*

It was one of Fassbinder's great talents as well as a dangerous weakness that he was able to pull a lot of things out of a hat. The moment he arrived on location, he instantly knew where the camera should be positioned, which special effects would be needed to shoot a scene under optimal conditions. This often was hard on the production department. It obviously is costlier for a production department to procure neccessary material at the last moment. It is a lot more costly than planning ahead and ordering everything in advance. That's why, during the first movies, we ran up an enormous debt, part of which was charged to my account. Fortunately, the artistic output was strong enough to make up for the loss. Otherwise our collaboration would not have lasted until his death in 1982.

*How did the two of you react to those debts?*

Somebody had to pay them. In legal terms, antiteater-X-Film was a private company, where people who placed orders on the company's behalf were held liable for the purchase.

My problem was that I had to use current income to pay off debts from previous movies. I could never get Fassbinder to agree to this principle. He always wanted to put all the money we earned into the next movie. It was a real problem. He felt the whole debacle was my fault because, as producer, I had not worked hard enough. Needless to say, this was open to debate.*

*How did you become the producer?*

By accident. We had started work on the first movie before answering questions such as who will be producer, who does cinematography, etc. Six hundred feet of material had already been shot. Ulli Lommel, one of the principal actors in the first movie, was so keen on making a movie with Fassbinder that he initially paid everything out of his own pocket; to the tune of about ten thousand D-marks. Then there was Thomas Schamoni, one of the young Munich filmmakers. He had leftover stock from a movie he had made which he put at Rainer's disposal.

*How did you end up reconciling with each other?*

Fassbinder was doing a production in Bochum while Peter Zadek was managing director. At the time, I was the in-house composer at Bochum, and I was doing the music for Fassbinder's production of *Liliom*. It's as simple as that. It's a moot question whether under different circumstances we would have gone on working together. Remember, though, that at the time Germany did not have a vast choice of movie composers, nor does it today.

---

* In 1991, a legal battle between Peer Raben and Liselotte Eder (later the Rainer Werner Fassbinder Foundation) was settled before the Oberlandesgericht of Munich. At issue was who had been the producer of the first ten Fassbinder movies, especially *Katzelmacher*, which had been produced under the label of aniteater-X-Film. Peer Raben's claim that he had been the sole shareholder of antiteater and that, in particular, he had paid off antiteater's debts were refuted. It was proved that it was Fassbinder who had paid debts in the amount of about DM 200,000. Hence, there is no doubt that RWF was legally the sole producer of all antiteater films. (See also the discussion in the interview with Liselotte Eder.) J.L.

*Is it possible to write political film music?*

It is, indeed. Look at a movie like *Lili Marleen*. The audience instantly understands what's going on when the sweet corny tune is juxtaposed with harsh, dissonant sounds.

*How does a composer deal with the insertion of existing music, like popular hits?*

It is a challenge that can only be met in collaboration with the director. You have to decide to what extent this other music should be referred to in the film music. Since it affects other scenes it cannot be totally ignored. This was the case with the cheerful country music in *Veronika Voss*. I suggested we draw attention to it by using country instruments like the hillbilly guitar.

*How do you pick a familiar theme from the wealth of musical history that will work in a movie?*

The problem is to pick exactly the right thing. When a familiar theme is placed in a different context, the audience must be able to follow it to this other level of perception.

*Can you explain Fassbinder's relentless production, his extraordinary speed?*

It's hard to explain. Only an experienced psychologist could do that. Even minor pauses in the working process caused him depressions which, in turn, accelerated his working mania. He needed to work; he could not live without it.

*How did this relentless productivity affect you?*

If my work had not been hitched to this high-speed steam engine, I never would have written as much music.

*Was there a price to pay for that speed in performance?*

That's not possible in music. When you enter the studio where an orchestra is assembled for a recording session, the music must be finished down to the smallest detail. There is no other way. An orchestra is a very sensitive instrument.

*Did Fassbinder ever fail to use your work after it had been finished in the studio?*

Preproduction discussions were so detailed that everything tallied in the end. Even in gigantic projects like *Berlin Alexanderplatz*, everything had been agreed upon between us, so there could be no misunderstanding. Everything had been discussed before we started shooting: the characters, their interaction, the conglomerate of visual and acoustic expression — the collage-like aspect which was clearly defined in the novel. This also had to be expressed in the music.

If there were misunderstandings, they were more of an anecdotal kind. In the case of *Jail Bait*, based on a play by Franz Xaver Kroetz, Fassbinder wanted me to compose some "popular music." I suggested something with guitars, trumpets, something I would call "consumer music." Instead of my music, he used his idea of "popular" music, which, believe it or not, turned out to be a piece by Beethoven!

*Since the days of silent film, there have been debates about film music, about whether the audience, consciously or subconsciously, should be aware of the music.*

By all means, consciously. No question about it. There is the danger, however, that things may become trivialized. People might say, "Ah, a piece from *Traviata*," and try to determine who sings it. That gives the wrong slant to the whole thing and becomes a diversion rather than an enhancement.

*Where would you say that the collaboration between you and Fassbinder, between music, pictures, and story, came together?*

In the movie *The Stationmaster's Wife*, based on the novel by Oskar Maria Graf. Fassbinder wanted the music to come from a recognizable source. He imagined that Herr and Frau Bolwieser had a favorite record which they played over and over again on the record player. I persuaded him to choose a Mozart minuet, an unknown one, which later I used as a theme further along in the movie. Since it is constantly changing, it underlined the changing relationship between Bolwieser and his wife.

*Fassbinder was constantly developing and refining his style and skills. Is there a parallel development in the music in Fassbinder movies?*

It reminds me of the movie *Chinese Roulette*. He filmed scenes where the characters moved as though they had been choreographed for a ballet. I wrote ballet music for it. It complemented the film so perfectly that he later wanted to do it over and over again. There is a scene in *Querelle*, for instance, which was filmed while the music track was running.

*Was the music for "Querelle" written specifically for the shoot?*

I knew what he had in mind. He had worked on the scene with a choreographer. The music had to be ready before the shoot.

*Martin Scorcese has the music written before he starts shooting; he inserts it during the shoot.*

It is a very difficult method. Since music determines the length of the setups and the camera movements, every element of the film loses its individuality. Movies combine contrasting elements such as speech, music, and visible images. The fun is in recognizing the edges of all these elements. It is like a dish which only tastes good if you can discern the ingredients that have gone into it.

*Was Fassbinder that kind of a "chef"?*

He definitely was. That's why he accepted actors with specific manners of speech; that's why he paid such close attention to the lines, in case an actor's speech might not be completely up to standard.

*Today, long after his death, discussions about German movies inevitably mention Fassbinder. How would you describe his loss?*

His was an incredibly powerful combination of work and personality. Fassbinder and his movies must be seen in the same context. His artistic work and his personality should be perceived as one entity.

*You have written film music for other directors, some of them Fassbinder's contemporaries, others his juniors. Where do you see specific differences?*

Fassbinder had this extreme openness about him. It always is a major event when music is added to a movie. It can even be a traumatic event. It changes the movie in a certain way. Fassbinder's attitude to this change was always open and curious; he was never afraid of it. There are directors who become extremely anxious when music is added because they dread the change. Fasssbinder was naturally interested in controlling the change; modulating it, for instance, using it dramatically, making it very soft or very loud in certain places.

*Did he respect your work?*

Fassbinder was quite old-fashioned. He would say, "I don't know anything about music. I'm sure what you're doing is right. If I don't like it, I will tell you."

*Were you in a unique position, or did this also apply to other areas?*

It was similar in cinematography. Ballhaus, for instance, did things where Fassbinder said, "This isn't right but it looks great, so let's have more of it."

*Have your views about Fassbinder's filmmaking changed over time?*

His movies are still valid, precisely because they are rooted in their time. I daresay *The Niklashauser Journey* is the only existing valid document about life in the late sixties, even though the movie is not set in the sixties but in some German middle ages.

*Do you consider your music on a par with Fassbinder's work?*

The music in the first movie wasn't terribly successful. I wanted the music you hear on the record to contrast with the film music. The record was to play the pop title "Lady Jane." Unfortunately, we didn't have the money to buy the rights. Instead, we were stuck with the pop music our studio orchestra was able to perform.

*Have you missed Fassbinder in the past ten years?*

Yes, I have missed him as an artist. Particularly in the movies. Too many directors make films for aesthetic reasons alone, not because they need to expose specific social conditions. Fassbinder combined both aesthetics and socio-politics. This synthesis requires enormous cinematographic skills and an unerring eye for social problems.

*What about Fassbinder's dark side? How much of it did you witness on the set?*

Most of the time, working on a Fassbinder project was like being at a country fair. Fassbinder knew exactly when to say, "Now we're gonna have pretzels, now we're gonna have beer and wurst." His motto was, "Work must be fun." There are people who never realized that he was working all the time, because it looked like so much fun. Curiously enough, he was more relaxed during a shoot than he was at other times. He always seemed free and playful on the set.

The actors can tell you better than I how he put pressure on people. His problem was that he really enjoyed being cruel. It often was hard on the actors. He went so far as to actually put obstacles in their way to make a scene more difficult for them. To some extent, he satisfied his yearning for a family on the set. There he was the great super-father, demanding proof of love from all his children. Woe to the progeny who stepped out of line!

*Did you yourself have such an experience with him?*

No.

*Do you consider it as a compliment or a stigma when you are labeled as a Fassbinder composer today?*

It's a fact. It is not just an idle remark but refers to a specific way of composing. In his *Handbook of Film Music*, Jürgen Schneider defines a Fassbinder composer as an historical phenomenon.

*How might Fassbinder's work have continued after 1982 in a culturally and politically different climate? Or had Fassbinder completed his cycle when his intuition told him he would not live much longer?*

It's hard for me to imagine that his work would have ever ceased as long as there was breath in his body. He might have taken an unexpected turn, perhaps into religion. He always had strong leanings in that direction.

# INGRID CAVEN

B*orn in Saarbrücken, Ms. Caven met Fassbinder and Peer Raben at Action Theater. She was married to Fassbinder from 1970 to 1972. In 1978, after having played parts in movies by Fassbinder* (Gods of the Plague *and* Mother Küsters Goes to Heaven, *among others*), *Daniel Schmid (including* Shadows of the Angels), *Jean Eustache, and Werner Schroeter, she started a career as chansonette (lyrics by Hans Magnus Enzensberger and Fassbinder, among others, music by Peer Raben) at the Théatre au Pigalle in Paris. Since 1977, she has lived in Paris. The interview was conducted by Camille Nevers for* Cahiers du Cinéma *(No. 469, June 1993).*

## CURIOUS IN THE PRESENT

*You first met Fassbinder during the transition period at Action Theater.*

I went to see a play Peer Raben had produced — a version of Sophocles' *Antigone*. Raben had transformed it into a dramatic collage about Antigone. I thought it was stunning. I was familiar with the principle of collage in painting, but here it was in the theater! I'd only heard of such experiments. So this was all new to me. I had an intense talk with Peer, Kurt Raab, and Ursula Strätz after the performance. Fassbinder sat in a corner, saying nothing. He was at the same time excessively shy and immensely curious. I went home. A few days later, Rainer rang my doorbell. That's how it all began.

*What were you doing at the time?*

I had given up on actual theater. I wanted to do something "serious." So I trained to be a teacher. Enter Rainer. He brought me back into the theater.

Rainer knew what he wanted. You were instantly aware of his presence, of his enormous curiosity in the present. Neither he nor Peer Raben had any use for nostalgia. Both were completely modern. Rainer came from a middle-class background, he had a middle-class upbringing — but his movies showed a completely different sensibility. He had all the characteristics of a sophisticated intellectual and he used them. He was chiefly interested in the present with all its pain, all its ugliness.

*No delayed gratification for Rainer.*

Rainer and I soon became very friendly. We went out every night. We thrust ourselves into the midst of things. We never thought about tomorrow. To us the next day didn't dawn even at sunrise.

We traveled a lot to Paris on weekends, just the two of us. We had this tiny room at the Hotel de l'Univers. There was a bar across the street with a small jukebox on each table. Rainer always got up early, went over, sat down at a table, fed the jukebox, and wrote his plays. *Bremen Freedom*, for instance, was written there. We acted out individual scenes in the café before he even wrote them. He would say, "You are ugly, look at yourself, who do you think you are? Your intelligence is my intelligence..." We acted out all those platitudes, all that everyday trivia. That's what fascinated me. I can't separate acting from the rest of life. Rainer was the same. Acting was something existential. Soon we no longer knew where acting ended and life began.

Rainer loved Brecht and Chinese tradition; masks, Kleist, puppets. That approach was basically what brought me to my profession. Trying to appear "natural" in front of a camera would have seemed simply grotesque.

*What gave Rainer this special force with actors?*

He was like an open wound, a fact he tried to hide, to camouflage. But it was why he instantly sensed people's weaknesses in their gestures and their voices. That weakness was his great strength, and it became a powerplay he thoroughly enjoyed. He liked to see how far he could go with a person. It was more than just a game. A mere game would not have satisfied him.

*How did the vision of a project come into focus?*

The moment he found a subject for a movie, whether on the street or in a newspaper or a fairground, he instantly saw the structure, the entire movie, right before his eyes.

*Did he write with certain actors in mind, or did he cast the parts later?*

He had a core of four actors: Irm Hermann, Hanna Schygulla, Harry Baer, and Kurt Raab. And there was Peer Raben, who was part of the writing process as well as being in charge of the music. Much of what Rainer wrote in those days was greatly influenced by Irm Hermann: her manner of speaking, the way she moved, her somewhat hysterical, very cool style. And by Hanna, who was Irm Hermann's exact opposite. His casting was always absolutely perfect. Later he turned actors into puppets. And you had to accept being turned into a puppet.

*How did he do that? Fassbinder must have been able to manipulate his actors, in the sense that he breathed life into his puppets.*

It was his forte. During rehearsals, before he started shooting, he would force actors into a kind of isolation. Some became frightened, others hysterical, and some were turned off. Hanna was the exception. He always said to her, "You are the most beautiful, you are the best." That's how he built her up for the parts he wanted her in. The rest of us were under constant siege.

*How did things change when you moved in together?*

We both felt somewhat ashamed of our privileged positions, he as the director and I as the actress. I was to play a major part in the tour of a Büchner play. I don't know why, but I felt embarrassed. So I refused, saying, "Let me be the prompter!"

I was production manager for *The Merchant of Four Seasons*. We had very little money and I had to take care of just about everything. At the last minute, he suddenly decided to write a part for me, which had not been provided for in the script. The character I was to play was called The Great Love. He let me do it entirely on my own, especially the funeral scene. I refused to be dressed in black, and he thought that was very good.

*Did your wedding reception get recycled into a film you were doing with Rainer?*

Yes! In *The American Soldier*, I sang an English song with lyrics by

Ulli Lommel. The scene was filmed on our actual wedding day in the very pub where we had just been celebrating. Rainer built everything into his productions — our travels, everything. But as soon as he started filming, he got it out of his system. I did the same; it made me feel better in our relationship.

*Was the movie an extension of living?*

Precisely. Everything was important. Yet he did not mean to turn life into a movie. Life was important in itself. And when he started taking drugs, it was because life was beginning to bore him.

*Was the theater more than just a means of getting into movies?*

Rainer was genuinely interested in the offbeat New York theater scene — in the happenings. He liked ordinary things, but he also liked very stylized, ritualized events with musical tendencies. On the other hand, he was somewhat bored with the theater, except for the work of Peter Zadek and Werner Schroeter.

*How about his own work in the theater?*

He wanted things to be done very fast. Working on a play for a long stretch of time was not for him. He was part of the pop generation, Warhol and rock 'n' roll. He had no use for the nineteenth century, for pseudo-psychological artifice, classicism and all that.

Our generation in Germany is skeptical about the culture of the past. All that German culture accomplished didn't prevent people from turning into murderers. That's why there's all this denial. We had to find new ways of expression. We needed to recognize that German culture is unthinkable without German-Jewish culture. Germans, whether they are Jewish or not, must understand this. That the Jews were persecuted and murdered is part of it. To us, it was impossible to simply go on as before, to forget what had happened.

*Does this denial also include prewar culture?*

We had a kind of erotic relationship with the present. We had to examine everything all over again. We were fascinated by everything that was new in the world and in everyday life. It was a worldwide movement. At first, it made for a happy, lively atmosphere. People didn't mind giving offence. You never asked, "Will I be able to live up to my own expectations — and do I have the right to apply them to others?" Courtesy didn't count for much in those days. At the same time, people invented clever games of seduction. There was no fear of intellectual kitsch. We were convinced that we had to start over again from zero. It can't be done, though. Each person has his own upbringing, his own background. But we believed we had to make a clean sweep.

*There was this image of a kind of noble savage?*

Yes, we played with that. The gangsters with their molls. We felt like gangsters in search of expression. We stole from everybody. Yet we never were part of the group who actually took up arms — that is another, a very sad story.

*Fassbinder shot an episode for* Germany in Autumn, *a movie that shows the reaction to the death of the Baader-Meinhof gang. Was he attracted to the violence of those people?*

Not at all. If he defended them, he did so as an intellectual — as Heinrich Böll, Peer Raben, and I did. He soon realized that those people were slipping into a very dangerous situation, that they were taking up arms against people they considered their enemy. We knew some of the RAF members from earlier days, but we were no longer in touch with them.

*In theory, Fassbinder was opposed to marriage as an institution. Many of his movies deal with that subject. Yet you and he were married for two years.*

We were, indeed. It would take a very long time to explain that. But remember, part of his family was very middle-class, and he never wanted to break with them. Besides, he thought I wouldn't stay with him unless he married me. Ours was a love story in spite of the marriage. He always felt free to contradict himself in every respect. Consistency was not one of his aims.

*In his book about Fassbinder, Yann Lardeau writes primarily about his relationships with men and about the role they play in his movies.*

Rainer was a homosexual who also needed a woman. It's that simple, and that complex. He was in love with Günther Kaufmann and later with Peter Zadek, neither of whom are homosexual. It would fill an entire book to explain that fact. When I knew him, he often hung out in the men's rooms of certain clubs. I never found out exactly what he was doing in there.

*A love story is a love story, whether it is between two men or two women, or between a man and a woman.*

When it comes to touching, in the broadest sense of the word, men and women have the same problems.

*How do you explain that so many people have accused Fassbinder of being anti-woman, anti-homosexual, anti-Semitic?*

Because he was seductive. People resented that this man, who was far from being handsome or classically beautiful, was so damn seductive. That's how it started. That's why he aroused so much jealousy. And there was the fact that he could be ruthless and that a lot of people who worked with him allowed him to get away with it. They gladly kowtowed to him because he had helped them to an existence. And he exploited that. Then those same people later became his worst critics.

*His play* Garbage, the City and Death *was denounced as anti-Semitic and was eventually banned. What was that all about?*

That was a great shame. There was a scene where a young neo-Nazi businessman says that not enough Jews were burned. And Lily, the whore I acted in the play, just weeps and says nothing. People in Germany claimed that this scene reflected the author's opinion. They insisted it should be rewritten and that the man should wear an armband, bearing a Nazi emblem. Rainer refused. He said that those aren't Nazis, ordinary citizens are saying such things today. It actually was the subject of the play: the taboo about the Jews. After the war, when Rainer was a child, he had often been told, "Be nice, this person is a Jew." So this was the subject. The principal character in the play is the rich Jew. Certain people did not approve—people who had gone to great lengths to prove they were not anti-Semitic. But when you raise this kind of subject, you must expect problems. I wanted the play to be revived, but no one would touch it. It is actually a love story, you know.

# HARRY BAER

Born in 1947 in Biberach, Mr. Baer was a member of antiteater since the 1967 production of The Beggar's Opera. He played his first major movie parts in Gods of the Plague and Jail Bait. As an actor — and occasional production manager and assistant director — he took part in many Fassbinder movies until the very end. Examples of his work with other directors are Hitler — a film from Germany, by Hans Jürgen Syberberg, 1977, and Palermo oder Wolfsburg, by Werner Schroeter, 1978–79. After Fassbinder's death, he acted in movies by Mika Kaurismäki, Jeanine Meerapfel, and Bernhard Sinkel, among others. He also worked as production manager on a number of movie productions. In 1992, he was the co-initiator and chief organizer of the Fassbinder Workshop in Berlin. The interview was conducted by Herbert Gehr.

## HAD EVERYTHING

During the turbulent time around 1968, you were highly politicized...

...politically engaged.

Did you imagine the theater could revolutionize the world?

Not at all. Acting in the theater was merely a convenience. With the university on strike, there was nothing to do during the day. But at night, we could earn a little money by acting in the theater: one D-mark for a beer and bratwurst. It was as simple as that. I'm sure it had occurred to me that somehow things might be moved through the theater,

but that wasn't the reason why I went into it. I would never have imagined that our tiny group could become a breeding ground for the German revolution. Nor do I believe now that the theater can ever achieve
or trigger social changes.

*Had you ever heard of Action Theater as a political stage before you started
working there?*

All I knew was that it was located on Müllerstrasse. I wasn't around
in the Action Theater days. I was elsewhere, probably on the street.

*Who did you get to know first, the people or the theater?*

The people, because two guys from my high school—Gunther
Krää and Rudolf Waldemar Brem—were acting in the theater. Since I
played drums, I once substituted for someone who got sick during *The
Beggar's Opera.* I spoke three lines. We were paid a few D-marks a night,
depending on whether there was enough of an audience. If there
weren't, we went without pay. Whenever we had money we spent it on
booze or playing the pinball machines.

*Did Fassbinder make a special impression on you?*

He was sitting with Hanna Schygulla one night, highly amused by
the way I struggled through my three lines. I sputtered a lot and stood
stiff as a soldier. Then—bingo—I was out again, hiding behind my
drums. It was my protective cover. That first time I saw him, he struck
me as someone who was laughing at my expense. I didn't like it.

*Who approached you to join the cast of* Katzelmacher?

Kurt Raab, who was miffed, by the way, because he wanted to play
the part himself. At any rate, he called me and I got paid for those few
days. I had never seen that much money before. It was cool. Real big
money. Taxes? Who cared about taxes when there was a revolution
going on? We just blew the money. After that, things developed sporadically. And then—ah, man, there was such confusion, such anarchy, I
hardly knew how to keep things straight.

*Had you seen* Katzelmacher *on stage before?*

I'd read the screenplay, which I liked. The entire action took place
by this staircase railing in the backyard. Behind the fixed camera was

[Dietrich] Lohmann with this cumbersome Arri [movie camera of Arnold & Richter Company with sound-proof casing], this blimp they hardly dared to move because it weighed a couple of tons. The stairway with its railing was somewhat like a stage, and that was it. There were very few stage directions. "Speak your lines and sit down," or "Speak your lines and get out of the picture," or words to that effect.

*No discussion about how to interpret the character?*

Are you kidding? You weren't even aware that the camera was present. The interior shots, with the lighting and all, that was different. When I was told to speak my lines, kneeling, stark naked, before Elga Sorbas, I knew it was different. It was more stressful, because indoors things moved more slowly on account of the camera and the lighting. It was a real production.

But it didn't turn me on. I found it utterly boring. It took forever to get from one setup to the next. The directions still consisted of, "Take your clothes off, kneel down, speak your lines, and—bingo—cut." In the first movies, that's all it was, even in *Gods of the Plague*. At one time Rainer got me so mad, I told him to go to hell, I was quitting. For two days, I holed up in my apartment, having a great time. Then he appeared, saying he hadn't meant it. He had driven me to the limit—not to coax a better performance out of me, just to annoy me, to drive me into a rage, so I would hit him. I got so close to the Franz Biberkopf character, the lethargic gangster type I was playing, Rainer didn't have to give me any specific directions.

*Did you know at the time how prominently the character of Franz Biberkopf figured in Fassbinder's biography?*

No, I didn't.

*When he needled you, did it occur to you that he was not struggling with you but with the character in the novel?*

Maybe so, but I wasn't aware of it. Döblin wasn't part of our high-school curriculum. Later I understood what our *Alexanderplatz*-Biberkopf was all about. I thought it was cool that I appeared so much in the picture. Even then I understood that if you appear in a picture often enough, you are playing the lead. Not that it went to my head. I don't much care about those things. I wasn't jealous, whether I was cast or not. I'm vain, all right, and sometimes I badly wanted to be cast in a certain part. But when I wasn't cast, Rainer's choice was so perfect that I realized I would have been wrong for it.

*What were the major shifts in your work with Fassbinder?*

In *Rio das Mortes*, I realized for the first time that Rainer was fully in charge as director. He stylized Hanna and Günther Kaufmann not just on film but right there in real life. The way those two acted—nobody talks that way and nobody walks that way. I finally understood that he used this artificiality as a tool. That was something special.

Then there was the dissident movement—"the great revolt." You see, all of this money came pouring down on us. After *Katzelmacher*, we were deluged with money from high places. All of a sudden, we were the talk of the town. Rainer went car crazy. Günther Kaufmann wrecked a few cars. Rainer thought that was cool. The more wrecks the better. The rest of us were jealous. Sure, we were busy and sure, we made a lot of money, but we couldn't see why we needed to buy a Stingray right away and why, if we wrecked it, a new one had to be parked in the driveway the very next day.

*It sounds as if Rainer was playing Hollywood tycoon with Hanna and Günther as his co-stars.*

They had nothing on their minds but glitz, money, and bacardi. There were thousand-mark bills bulging from his leather jacket. He threw money around like crazy. The rest of us were grumbling, "Isn't this supposed to be a commune? How come one guy calls all the shots and spends all the money?" Sure, we were getting something out of it, too—or were we? There was a minor revolt, headed by Michael Fengler. I was all for it. Hanna was somewhere in the middle. She wanted a revolution too, but she didn't quite dare, and there were others. In short, there was envy, revolt, dissidence, and a call to return to our roots.*

*What was the atmosphere like at the villa they shared?*

I can't tell you that, since I never lived at the villa where they all shacked up together. Not that I minded Sodom and Gomorrah, but I preferred my own commune.

---

* Michael Fengler, co-producer of several Fassbinder movies; co-director on *Die Niklashauser Journey* and *Why Does Herr R. Run Amok?*

*You did not succumb to the lure of this great ideal of communal living?*

No way. Not under the same roof. Fortunately, I was able to keep those things separate. I liked to work with the group and I liked to carouse with them, breaking windows and stuff, when we were stoned. It was fun, but I knew where my home was, unlike Hanna, who was neither part of Feldkirchen nor part of carousing. She always remained completely detached. She floated above everything like some Holy Virgin.

I created my own space, which is probably why the thing between Rainer and me lasted as long as it did. I must have had a guardian angel.

A great number of people were dropped over time. Needless to say, not everybody could stand Rainer's relentless speed, this continuous frenzy of "let's go, let's go, let's go!"

*When you worked with other directors — Werner Schroeter and Hans-Jürgen Syberberg — did he resent it?*

Quite a bit. It started with *Eight Hours Don't Make a Day.* I just thought it was too wimpy, not nearly leftist enough. So I quit for a while. He really resented my criticism of the film Many people thought it was cool. But I felt this granny character in it was just too cute. Pandering to the establishment. I had to prove to myself that I was still a leftist. To my mind, the thing had no depth.

*Did you think of yourself as a movie person at this point?*

Those leading parts eventually started going to my head. The lead in *Jail Bait*, the lead in *Ludwig II.* I thought it would go on forever. But then it didn't go on. The money ran out. I went to Filmverlag der Autoren, working with Uwe Bradner. I worked as assistant director, though at first I didn't have the slightest notion what an assistant director was supposed to do.

*The first ten Fassbinder movies were . . .*

. . . ecstasy, total production ecstasy!

We had money, we worked, we were drunk all the time — it was absolute ecstasy and absolute hell. No sooner had we wrapped one thing, with everyone thinking of going on vacation, than another project was scheduled for the following week. It completely sidetracked me from my studies. I never even thought of the university. I thought it would go on forever. I had been caught by a wave and didn't even know I was being swept away. Oh, I remember Willi, despair in his eyes, standing before a table in Feldkirchen, saying, "Here are the bills that need to be paid." A three-foot mountain piled up on the table. Willi was the first to see that things were bound to backfire. It was only a matter of time. No one else realized that certain dues needed to be paid. No one knew and no one cared. In those days, who would have thought that video rights or cable channels would exist one day, never mind the entire satellite business. Or replay rights, a term I first heard fifteen years later.

It was utter madness to keep on producing as though health insurance and the department of taxation didn't even exist. Our funds had been regularly replenished by higher authorities, by the top agencies of the republic. Each time the money would be put into the next project. And, predictably enough, things were costing a huge amount of money. A blind person could have seen it coming. The mountain on Willi's table kept growing, more cars were being wrecked, and one movie after another was produced. It was totally insane. We didn't need any speed in those days. All we needed was a dose of Fassbinder.

*What was your peak experience with Fassbinder?*

*Whitey* was the greatest experience. It was cool. The script was completely cockeyed, but never mind. We were in Almira, where we had a hotel entirely to ourselves. We shot during the day, and we danced and boozed in the lobby at night. It was anarchy at its best, the most wonderful time of my life. I'll never forget the things that went on.

*How did you decide what was to happen in the movie?*

There were no discussions. Nothing. We had the script, that was all. Before one movie was wrapped, Rainer had the script for the next one already written in his head. He may have discussed the music with Willi. But with the actors? Forget it. It all just poured out of Rainer like nobody's business.

*Tell me about your job as assistant director . . .*

Are you kidding? In Rainer's early movies, there was nothing for the assistant director to do. The first projects were shot in sequences of eight to ten minutes. A movie like *Why Does Herr R. Run Amok?* or *Rio das Mortes* had half a dozen setups. Eventually we realized that movies could have a couple hundred setups. A lot of mistakes could be made under those conditions, and I was allowed to make them. That's how I learned to be an assistant director: paying attention to continuity, watching over the chronology of the script, scheduling the actors, things like that. And organizing everything in the proper order, a process which borders on production work, where you say, "I figure Rainer will shoot this in x number of hours. Hence, that day we can shoot another thing or two." This sense of formula eventually enabled me to go into production management, because I had learned how much work can be expected from any individual.

Of course, no one in the world made movies the way Rainer did. In some respects he was quick, but he wasn't always predictable. Once he really let me have it. The script showed just two lines for a certain scene. He announced he was going to shoot it in seventeen setups, just to prove to me that it is irrelevant that there are only two lines in a script.

*Were all seventeen setups already in his head when he appeared on the set?*

He started drawing little pictures, storyboards, which minutely described the setups. He sketched those early in the morning or the night before. I had been pretty sure that a two-line scene could be shot within an hour. Then I opened his book and saw those seventeen sketches.

I stayed aloof from Feldkirchen, yet I wanted to be part of it at the same time. I played it cool, learned a few little things besides acting, learned to be an assistant director, picked up something about production management. After *Berlin Alexanderplatz* it all added up to "Harry Baer, artistic director." In *Alexanderplatz* I was completely on my own, I could do whatever I wanted. I knew what Rainer wanted. I finally told him I didn't want to do this kind of thing anymore. I was no longer interested in continuity. I wasn't in the mood to rummage around in archives for a year, looking for a certain precious scene. We needed a script supervisor for that and a continuity girl to look after our chaotic shooting schedule. So he had the brilliant idea of making me artistic director. This created a painless division of labor and eliminated those stupid jealousies where people do nasty things to each other. A very clever move on his part.

*Did you ever wonder how Rainer could be satisfied with so few takes?*

It's not that he was satisfied. It's that he was impatient. One of his lines was, "You can only learn from mistakes if you are constantly working." He couldn't allow himself to repeat a take umpteen times, just to be able to say, "This is it!" He was panting for the next scene that was already spilling out of his head.

There was the time in *Gods of the Plague* when he made me shoot a setup seventy times! I'm not sure whether it was because the damned slot machine refused to come up with the 777s it was supposed to, or because he wanted to drive me up the wall, or because he wanted to prove that the production manager was an incomparable asshole. Because a technical device — which the production manager had declared to be too costly — would have allowed us to do the whole thing in five minutes.

Rainer never did any mastershots from which things later could be assembled. On the contrary, it was clear from the way a scene was conceived that the rhythm from frame one to frame x would essentially be what would later be edited in the studio. Rainer always cut right into the camera.

*Tell me about the games Rainer played.*

Many of his games were designed to test how far he could go with a person. Sometimes he played them to perfection, other times it was more prurient. But it always worked. He did have this fiendish gift of playing people against each other for no reason whatsoever. And he made use of this gift. There are actresses who, when told to cry on camera, will say, "Just a minute," turn around, and cry snot and water by the time they face the camera again. There are others who burst into tears when you twist their nipple. For each actor, he had his own method.

*Do you think Fassbinder may have found a kind of surrogate family in the crew he worked with on the set?*

I sure do.

*Did he torment people so the movies would turn out the way he wanted it? Or did he make the movies so he could torment people?*

If only one could tell in retrospect. There were so many factors involved. It's a job for the psychoanalysts. I certainly believe that much of how he used people was a search for some kind of surrogate family. "Work must be fun," was one of his tenets. And it was fun. If all that early excitement and the madness of shooting ten movies in a year and a half hadn't been fun, it would never have worked. The relentless frenzy was possible only because this superman was at the helm, telling everybody how beautiful everything was and how glorious, and that we should all have a drink.

*He initiated that camaraderie?*

You bet he did. And, of course, it was contagious. Just think of it, if we had shot those movies in a bad mood, half the crew would have quit within the first month. I certainly would have quit if this maniac, who thought of nothing but work, hadn't made it so much fun. There was a jerk on every project, the guy who always gets mercilessly kicked in the ass. The others picked on him, and there he was, the poor bastard. In some ways it was o.k, in others it stank, as it is bound to, when ten people gang up on the eleventh and do it all over again the next day. Yet if this guy happened to do the right thing, Rainer had a way of praising him in such a way that for days on end he became the greatest.

*There was a kind of hiatus late in 1970 until August 1971, when he filmed* The Merchant of Four Seasons. *Did he use that time to take inventory of himself?*

Maybe he should have. I don't know. I remember the trip we took to Africa with El Hedi ben Salem. I had taken the same trip three years earlier as a student. This time we covered in three and a half days what I had managed myself in two months. Completely nuts. We tore across the countryside at 130 mph, from Fez to Casablanca, then to a town beyond the Atlas Mountains, where allegedly El Hedi was born, and back again to Marrakesh at breakneck speed.

*Doesn't sound like much of a vacation.*

It was like, "Let's see how fast the car can go. Scenery? What scenery."

*What sort of progress was Rainer making professionally?*

*The Merchant of Four Seasons* still had some flaws. However, compared to his previous work, it had reached a climax as far as the way Rainer told the story was concerned. *Recruits in Ingolstadt* was total chaos. That movie is a mess. *The Merchant of Four Seasons* is told completely straightforwardly; the story really jibes. The editor of this awful reactionary paper in the movie was modeled on one of Rainer's relatives, a real-life editor on *Bayern Kurier*. I feel the contemporary reviews were right on track: it is one of the best and most beautiful movies of the postwar era.

*Your break with Fassbinder came with* Eight Hours Don't Make a Day?

It wasn't just because I had criticized the ideology. All kinds of other things were being whispered around about people getting tired of Fassbinder movies, stuff like that. Jealousy and ennui, like, "The German cinema should not be represented exclusively by Fassbinder." And so on. And I was right in the middle. It was the beginning of a long hiatus.

*Until* Maria Braun *in 1978.*

Suddenly he appeared in Berlin. He had parted company with his production manager and a whole lot of other people. Things had been chaotic in Coburg, where they had been filming, because he hadn't properly assessed certain scenic elements in preproduction. Maybe nobody had been able to decode his half-finished sentences. Who knows? You remember this attic with the crazy elevator, where the trial scene is supposed to take place? Surely the art department must have offered him a variety of scenery. But he dismissed all their suggestions as boring. He didn't like the look of the bar where Hanna applies for a job. So Rainer said, "Not in my film," turned on his heel and went home.

*Wasn't Kurt Raab the art director at the time?*

Kurti had bowed out after *The Stationmaster's Wife*, when it became obvious how badly Rainer had messed up his finances. He was always incredibly generous, but this time Kurt had gone too far. Bavaria took Rainer to task. Perhaps it was just as well things did not continue the way they had been.

*Hence, an era where members of the established "family" were replaced, one by one, by officers of production firms or television companies.*

That's true. Kurt Raab is the best example. He had designed the sets of almost every Fassbinder movie to that time. But never again. I happened to be in Berlin for the Film Festival because Wolf Donner, the director, had invited me. There I ran into Rainer, who told me he had just fired half the team in Coburg. He was going to shoot the rest of the movie in Berlin. They were resuming work in two weeks. Why didn't I pack my gear and join him? I moved into Hotel Schweizerhof, where I found to my horror that the phone units were 60 pfennigs apiece. Not what you want to hear, when you're going to spend three days entirely on the phone. To get everything organized—the crew, locations, the whole bit—I was on the phone day and night. For some reason, everything went like clockwork. I was back on the team as though nothing had happened.

*And money was no longer a problem?*

I never said that! At one point, Fengler showed up with a suitcase full of money, something like 40,000 D-marks [about $160,000 at the time]. In cash. Rainer kicked him out, I don't know why. Fortunately, I caught up with Fengler at the elevator and made him give me the money which, yes, we badly needed. There was still a gap in our budget, though a minimal sum compared to the overall budget. Yet it was there.

Hanns Eckelkamp* lent us the money, in return for which Fengler gave him a disproportionally large number of distribution shares; a method bordering on blackmail, which, unfortunately, is frequently used in the business. This marked the end of the long-term Fengler connection to Rainer. It was obvious that Albatros was not going to produce *Alexanderplatz*. It also meant that Bavaria would have to pay Albatros for its preproduction work.

*Was* Berlin Alexanderplatz *planned as a television series, or had Fassbinder initially conceived the material as a feature film?*

It's hard to tell. Looking at his movies, back to *Gods of the Plague*, where the character of Franz Biberkopf first appears, I imagine he had always thought of it as a feature film. But when he went back to the book, he may have realized that it couldn't be properly presented in a movie. Apart from the superhuman effort it would have required, the same actors could not be cast in both a movie and a series. The movie, for which a screenplay exists, was to have had an international cast, with Charles Aznavour or Gérard Depardieu as Biberkopf and Isabelle Adjani as Mieze. The series with a cast of German actors would be shot on the set in the daytime. Then, everybody would go home, except for Rainer and a few die-hards, who would stay behind and shoot the feature film at night. With the international cast it obviously couldn't have worked. Not even Fassbinder could have pulled off such a feat. It would have required more green tea than is grown around the world. Besides, after *Maria Braun* it became obvious that Bavaria, not Albatros, would produce *Alexanderplatz*. Once that was settled contractually, the plan became a television series with a view towards a possible feature down the line.

But the real blow in the *Alexanderplatz* deal came from Peter Märthesheimer. Rainer had finished the script as a nine part series. One day Märthesheimer appears, saying, "Hold everything. ARD and ZDF

* Hanns Eckelkamp, co-producer of *Maria Braun*.

have changed their program schedules. You can't shoot nine times an hour and a half. The trailer can run an hour and a half for the first part, but the subsequent episodes must run fifty-eight minutes each." Rainer would have to sit down again and rewrite all the arcs, a gigantic job. I saw him turn pale, in total shock. And then he did it. And we did it. It was the first series in the history of German television. It was also relatively cheap, considering the number of air minutes we produced for fifteen million D-marks.

*Was Fassbinder more tense than usual?*

It definitely got to him. Starting with the casting. For a while there, Rainer ranked Klaus Löwitsch as the greatest living German actor. Everybody else was trash by comparison. Now came the question of who would play Franz Biberkopf. Of course, Rainer felt only he himself could play him, possibly Reinhold. I don't remember what made him decide on Günter Lamprecht who, when you look at *Alexanderplatz*, is ideal casting.

*Did Fassbinder see the old version of* Alexanderplatz *by Phil Jutzi?*

I am sure he did. During preproduction, everybody was assigned required viewing, so to speak, things like *Mutter Krausens Fahrt ins Glück [Mother Krause's Journey to Happiness]*, so-called socio-revolutionary movies.

*There is his famous line after the wrap-up of* Alexanderplatz: *"O.k., now I have mastered this craft."*

*Alexanderplatz* amounted to two hundred and fifty days of shooting. After part thirteen, there was a six week break especially requested by the production manager. The story time in *Alexanderplatz* stretches over a little less than four years, which meant there were four times four seasons to prepare for. Minx spent weeks on the shooting schedule. He became increasingly desperate, because he could never get hold of Rainer. Eventually I was at the end of my tether. Everyone was. There was a time when we could barely stand the sight of each other. At one point Rainer wanted to fire me, but Minx said, in effect, that if I went, he went too.

We had been cooped up together much too long in far too cramped a space — one room where I had witnessed him in every kind of condition. There were times when he couldn't stand Gottfried John or Günter Lamprecht, or couldn't stand the "Biberkopf Room" set, where he had spent two months. He no longer knew where else to point the camera. He would come into our studio and lie down on the floor, completely beat. I mean really: shut the door, boom, flop down, and snore. Maybe just for five or ten minutes. Then he'd get up, as though reborn, full of energy, and on he went again. It was only normal that, after a year's work under these circumstances, he should have said, "I can't stand your guts." After this project, with all its stress and torture, nothing could ever faze him.

We worked well together. On sets like the pubs or outside locations he never appeared without me. He never bothered about extras and such. That's why my job on *Alexanderplatz* lasted so long. Everything had to be historically authentic: the street fights between stormtroopers and Communists, the unemployment, all those details. He trusted me blindly in those respects, 99 percent of the time.

*With this central opus off his back, did he calm down at all, slow down his pace?*

Well, yes, movies like *Despair* with the international cast had a different dimension. *Lili Marleen* was a ten-million-mark project. He had reached the top. Money was coming in from sources that hadn't been available earlier. In those days, [Luggi] Waldleitner* or [Horst] Wendlandt in the case of *Lola* were the most powerful backers of the German movie industry.

*Considering his status after* Alexanderplatz, *could he do what he wanted with regard to subject matter and style?*

You'd think so. But there were always setbacks. His adaptation of Zwerenz' novel *Die Erde ist unbewohnbar wie der Mond [The Earth Is Uninhabitable Like the Moon]* never came to fruition, nor did Gustav Freytag's *Soll und Haben*. Missing from his list is *Hurra, wir leben noch [Hurrah, we're still alive]*, which Peter Zadek made into a movie. It would have fitted nicely into Rainer's overall presentation of the history of the German Federal Republic.

*Were there bouts of despair early in 1982? Any moods that would alert you to his imminent demise?*

I don't know what went on in his head between the time he wrapped *Querelle* in March and when he died in June. I simply don't know. Maybe he really had overdone it. He was working on *Rosa Luxemburg* while he prepared *I Am the Happiness of This Earth* and tried to wrap up *Querelle*. He could easily have collapsed even earlier. Why after *Querelle*?

---

* Luggi Waldleitner, producer of *Lili Marleen*.

In May 1982, we attended the Cannes Film Festival together. He was as exuberant and cheerful as ever. He was not exhausted. He was also very exuberant on his birthday, which we celebrated — with all the trimmings — in Munich at Deutsche Eiche. Ten days later he was dead. Crazy.

I was location scouting in a pub in the east end of Munich. I talked to him on the phone half an hour before he died, telling him the pub was perfect for the shoot. He sounded completely o.k. on the phone. And then, lights out, finished. Was it because he had taken on too much, or had he simply been driving himself to it for years with the idea, "Give me thirty-seven years, I'll live them to the hilt and I'll have had everything"?

# MARGIT CARSTENSEN

B orn in Kiel, Ms. Carstensen took drama classes in Hamburg and, in 1965, began acting at Deutsches Schauspielhaus of Hamburg. From 1969 to 1972, she was part of the Bremen theater ensemble. Then followed engagements in Darm-stadt, Hamburg, Berlin, Stuttgart, and Munich. After they met in 1969, Fass-binder became a determining factor in her life on stage as well as in movies. Between 1969 and 1976, she worked exclusively with him. He created the major female characters of his plays specifically for her. Her performance in The Bit-ter Tears of Petra von Kant won her the Film Prize of the German Federal Republic. In 1981, she began an extended collaboration with Hansgünther Heyme in Stuttgart, Essen, and Bremen. Since 1992, she has been working with Leander Haussmann. The interview was conducted in Munich.

## YEARNING TO BE LOVED

*Rainer described you as the first professional actress he'd worked with.*

That is a flattering description but an error of judgment on Rainer's part. I was a novice. It's true that, for a year, I had played the usual classics in provincial theaters but I had hardly had an opportunity to gain suffi-cient stage experience to qualify as a professional. I was already rather turned off by the theater. Then I went to Bremen, where a young, revo-lutionary theater had recently developed under Kurt Hübner. I was cast in Rainer's adaptation of *The Coffee House*. We had spent weeks trying in vain to find an approach to the play with a traditional director. We needed Rainer's advice. He arrived surrounded by his entourage and preceded by an alarming reputation. He inspired trust rather than anxiety. I instantly felt confident in his presence and readily revealed what my imagination told me about my character. There was a mutual understanding, though we never felt a need to discuss it.

*What was this mutual understanding based on?*

Rainer was the first person who wanted to see me the way I was. He made me aware that the character I was playing was also about myself. He let me know that I should trust myself. I began to understand my own personality and to bring it into my acting. My encounter with Rainer marked the beginning of my life. It was the beginning of my professional life but also of my personal life. Neither before nor after him did I ever find a person who took such pleasure in using me exactly the way I was.

*What do you mean by "using"?*

Making use of a person's specific qualities. What better for an actor? What more could you wish for than to fully assert yourself with everything you have? In order to bring out the essence of his actors, Rainer, in some movie projects, distributed a new, unknown text shortly before the shoot began, so there would be no time to study or memorize it. There is the actor on the edge of despair, completely at the mercy of the camera. At this existential moment, he or she is not in a position to fake anything. Rainer liked to cut on the first take, so as to preserve as much spontaneity and sensibility as possible. He actually "used" the actor's individuality.

*Rainer told me that you were less prone to headaches in those early days. Is that true?*

I enjoyed myself so much that I sometimes forgot that I was suffering. Now, there were also times of enormous stress. It was inevitable. There comes a point when one feels reduced to a few specific traits and it is humiliating to be used in this reduced state. You can't identify with the image you have of yourself anymore. We have all faced this dilemma. But in the end, a true actor must recognize himself as material a director can rely on.

*And you relied on him too?*

Many qualities lie dormant inside a person, wanting to be discovered. I hadn't met anyone who wanted to see my own qualities. On the contrary, people wanted to cure me of my quirks and peculiarities. Rainer, on the other hand, supported and nurtured them. He took an interest in them and made them blossom in the movies as well as on stage.

He invested a great deal of love in every one of us. Some people felt that his generosity entitled them to his undivided attention, which naturally generated all kinds of jealousy and bitterness. People made more and more selfish demands on him. They became increasingly dependent on his favor. Yet he wanted emancipated actors, actors who could share the burden of decision making or, at least, share his concerns. He would have felt secure in a group where people genuinely shared responsibilities. Instead, it soon became obvious that all creative impulses were coming from him and they had to be carried out by him. As a result, his decisions were followed blindly. Later, if anyone joined who was in the habit of contradicting, his days were numbered. Rainer showed him who was boss and made him assume the role he had been assigned; he set boundaries. He basically wanted to prove that utopias are just utopian. I believe his dream of the cooperative spirit finally ended in 1975 at TAT [Theater am Turm].

*When I met Rainer, I thought he was a free spirit, with no hangups and no desire for a middle-class lifestyle.*

Now and then, middle-class values caught up with him. It was hard to tell whether they attracted or repelled him. When he felt tempted to play little games with us, his favorite game was "pater familias." He criticized, praised, and corrected. We often sang folk songs together. He tested our proficiency in Latin and gave us grades.

After he finished a movie, he used to distribute pieces of paper with the names of all the participants. Each of us was to rate — from one to six — the performance of the other members, then fold the paper and pass it on. Then the next person would write his evaluation, again fold the paper and pass it on. In the end, a long row of figures appeared under each name. The sum total showed who was "best."

*How did you see him change over the years?*

He was changing even while I was still working a lot with him, though it became more evident as the years went by. He became calmer and more tolerant. He eventually abandoned his utopian idea of the extended family. Shortly before we started working at TAT in Frankfurt, in the summer of 1974, he told me he was going to stop interfering in other people's lives, in their development. I felt sorry for him because to me that meant he was becoming more detached and indifferent. Soon after that he started hiring more professional actors from outside.

*Did you see his attitude towards you change?*

When Rainer was planning his movie *The Niklashauser Journey*, he summoned me to Munich to join the group in the house at Feldkirchen.

*You were still married at the time.*

Rainer explained to me that for a life in the arts I had to be free and independent. He felt I was repressed in my marriage. My husband offered me the choice to either stay with him or separate and go with Rainer. Feeling somewhat insecure, I asked Rainer whether I could count on him if I had no one to turn to some day. His answer was no. It opened my eyes. Taking a giant, emancipatory step forward, I told him, "I'm coming with you," and I separated from my husband. It was my first move toward independence. Rainer was introducing me to the subject of female emancipation, which I would later play again and again from a variety of perspectives.

*What were the circumstances you found yourself in when you joined the group in Munich?*

Rainer had sprung me on them out of nowhere. And there I was playing major roles. Needless to say, this caused tension. While he protected me and never allowed any confrontation, I remained, as a result, an outsider. It took me a long time to make friends. I stuck close to Peer Raben who was a very good listener. Whenever I asked too many questions, Rainer referred me to him. If I needed to find out exactly what motivated my character, Rainer would tell me to talk to Willi.

*This referred to your work on stage. But then more and more movies were being made.*

My first important movie with Rainer was *The Bitter Tears of Petra von Kant*. I had recently worked with Peer Raben on the stage play for Experimenta at Frankfurt and was able to draw on that experience. Yet Rainer's film adaptation was what first made me aware of the subject's personal character.

Rainer and I loved to present people's shortcomings, to disclose their psyche, their sentimentalities, those multi-faceted aspects which arouse sympathy. It was what bound us together. We never needed to discuss anything. During a shoot, he never indicated how a character should be presented or how certain results might be achieved. Sometimes he surmised that a certain expression of mine had been sparked by accident in the heat of the situation. I don't think he always knew how carefully I had worked up to such accidents!

*And he encouraged such "accidents"?*

He allowed every one of us to blossom by his side. In his movies, he treated everyone with the same tenderness and total concentration. You were aware of the reverence with which he laid bare the actor's soul. None of us could have been memorable without that loving look from his eyes.

*Did he demand submission?*

What he demanded was love, or let us say, voluntary submission. Yet a growing number of people were just out for profit, even at the price of unmitigated groveling. If he was aware of it, he played the despot and let them lick his boots. He enjoyed the power game on every level. He never missed an opportunity to find out how people would react. But he also allowed himself to be deceived. His yearning to be loved made him blind to certain things.

*And how did you react?*

I kept my distance. I saw how far people would go in their expections of him; how they wanted him to attend to their own well-being; how they pressured him and held him responsible for their personal fortune or misfortune. I felt embarrassed, lest I myself might be suspected of harboring false pretenses. I became more and more isolated from the group. Work alone could no longer make up for the discomfort I felt.

*What about the famous game of truth?*

The idea was to tell the truth no matter how painful. Whoever happened to be the victim was cornered with specific questions until the truth came out. Rainer did not exclude himself. In 1976, during the shooting of *Chinese Roulette*, the game was not only played in the movie but also after work. At the time, we were living on location at the castle near Stöckach.

By then, the tension between Rainer and myself had become unbearable. It was time for a showdown. He provoked me and tormented me daily with his snide remarks. Finally things came to a head. During one of our nightly games of truth, I asked him — perhaps more bluntly than I should have — if he wanted to stop working with me. After a slight hesitation, he replied, "Yes." I asked him why, and he said I did not seem sufficiently interested in him. I felt misunderstood, but said nothing. Perhaps I should have made greater demands on him, been submissive, asked more of him.

*Definitely not! He couldn't stand that.*

He often sent word to ask me to come back, but I couldn't ever again become dependent on Rainer and be at the mercy of his benevolence. I limited myself to a few minor appearances in *The Women*, *The Third Generation*, and *Alexanderplatz*.

*If you'd gone back, you're not sure you could have escaped his influence again?*

He planned a career and a future for every one of us. By giving us regular work on his constant schedule of projects, he also provided us with a regular income. We never needed to go out and find jobs ourselves. On the contrary. He prevented us from working for others. And if anybody dared to take even a brief fling, he resented it for a long time. We were definitely not encouraged to leave the nest... Not a happy situation.

I saw Rainer only rarely in the last years. They were brief encounters but I noticed the change in him. I found him calmer, more thoughtful.

*He had turned into a wise man with an enormous amount of energy.*

You sense this intellectual energy in his last movie, *Querelle*. This movie is more radical than all his earlier ones. At the same time, it is more reasonable, more human, more humble. The more he revealed of himself, the more he gained in substance.

*How would you describe your relationship with Rainer?*

Our relationship was loving, and, in the final analysis, that was all that mattered. The truth is that he was serious and responsible, especially in situations which affected you deeply. Whenever Rainer was asked to pose for a photograph with one of his female stars, he always assumed the same poses. He either leaned heavily on her often fragile shoulders, or he stood behind her and leaned forward, burying his head in her shoulder. An expression of submission, refuge, and erotic power.

# PETER MÄRTHESHEIMER

Born in 1937, Mr. Märthesheimer studied sociology at the University of Frankfurt, then joined Westdeutscher Rundfunk at Cologne as a dramaturg. He transferred to Bavaria Studios at Munich in 1977, where, as a dramaturg, he was responsible for a number of feature films and television movies. From the start, he scouted cinematic talents for television. He produced Eight Hours Don't Make a Day *with Fassbinder, one of the first television mini-series. He won several awards for his dramaturgical work, among them the Adolf Grimme Prize and the Prix Futura. After 1981, he worked as a freelance author. Together with Pea Fröhlich he wrote screenplays for television productions and for several Fassbinder movies, among them* The Marriage of Maria Braun. *He has also published books on media theory and current political problems. Since 1994, he has taught screenwriting and drama at the Film Academy of Baden/Württemberg in Luwigsburg. The interview was conducted in Pullach near Munich.*

## HE TURNED OUT MOVIES LIKE OTHER PEOPLE ROLL CIGARETTES

*In what capacity did you meet Rainer?*

In 1970, I was editor of television dramas at Westdeutscher Rundfunk. It wasn't an easy assignment, considering that I was not all that interested in mainstream writers and directors of television. Young filmmakers, on the other hand, were not interested in television. They wanted to make movies. Now, this guy Fassbinder had first caught my attention when his picture appeared in *Stern* magazine next to a car he allegedly had wrecked in an accident. He was standing beside the wreck, proudly looking into the camera. He was supposedly a writer and a movie director, but I had never seen or read anything by him.

Then, one day I saw *Katzelmacher*, a film he had made, and I thought, this guy has talent. So I got his phone number and arranged to meet him.

*I always thought your first contact with Rainer had been in connection with* The Niklashauser Journey.

I had an idea for this series about workers, and I wanted to talk to him about it. That was in 1970. When I first met him, he was probably already planning to film *The Niklashauser Journey* but he needed the money for it. Smart as he was, he grabbed the opportunity to suggest that I could have him, provided I'd see to it that WDR funded the movie. And he managed there and then to extract that promise from me.

WDR had a slot in those days called "The Monday Television Play" at 11:30 on Monday night. Everybody knew this slot was only offered to a few of the country's chosen. It was reserved for what you might call the up-and-coming geniuses of the arts.

*And the reaction to this film shown late on a Monday night?*

As you know, the film touched on some highly controversial subjects. There were rumors that *The Niklashauser Journey* was meant to be an open call for class struggle. I was called to testify before the employers guild. As the representative of Westdeutscher Rundfunk, a legitimate public institution, I was summoned to show the film in a house on the banks of the Rhine in Cologne, the seat of the Federal Alliance of the German Employers Associations. Four minutes into the movie, the film ripped. Needless to say, the audience was convinced that this was a conspiracy. Then it turned out that the film was so tightly twisted inside the projector that it could not be disentangled fast enough. Fortunately, the delegates did not insist on a second showing.

*Rainer gave me the impression that you gave him his first major break.*

I never gave anyone a break. At least, not intentionally. I saw my job as making good movies with good people. I thought this guy had talent, so I used him.

*And the head of the drama department gave his blessing to everything?*

Even better — wherever possible, he said nothing at all. He let people be. He was like some country squire. There are the farm hands who bring in the hay and feed the cows. Every now and then, the farm hands get into trouble. Then the country squire steps in and bails them out. We only saw the producer when a program came under serious attack. The first thing he would say, was, "Let's keep cool, young man!" Only then did he look at the program at issue.

*What was your training to be an editor?*

I was trained as a sociologist from the Frankfurt School. I had a critical attitude toward culture, but I didn't know a thing about producing plays. For some reason, Werner Höfer, who was then director of television — another stroke of luck for our station — thought I would prove a talented dramaturg. After he hired me, I had to look up the definition of a dramaturg in the dictionary.

*And what is it?*

It is the art of telling a story in the proper rhythm, while faithfully following the actual story line. For instance, with *Eight Hours Don't Make a Day* I spent a few days sitting at an editing table with this Herr Fassbinder and his film editor, looking, minute by minute, at the rough cut of the workers series. Now and then I would stop the film and say, "Here I find it a bit too slow, or here it's too fast." Dramaturgy is primarily a matter of instinct, the intellect merely justifying the instinctive response.

*Did Rainer allow you to intervene?*

Remember he was not yet a national monument in 1972. He was a young man who had been offered five hundred minutes of prime time by Germany's largest television station. He knew that a lot of trust had been invested in him. So he, in turn, trusted that this editor who sat with him at the editing table did not mean insult or harm but simply thought the story was a bit slow. Then he and his film editor would examine the sequence to see if something was indeed askew. Sometimes it would turn out that something quite different was the matter. Everyone understood that my aim was to improve the work and not to censure or humiliate anyone. At any rate, it was always up to them whether to adopt my suggestion or to come up with a counter proposal. Sitting in that editing room, I was

Herr Fassbinder's first audience, and he always took audiences seriously. It was to the audience, after all, that he was telling his story.

*Five times one hundred minutes. That must have been a frightening prospect in the days before serialized drama.*

I think he must have felt very anxious. But he had this way of making a frightening situation manageable by preparing himself down to the smallest detail. Here's an example: he was determined to get Luise Ullrich for the part of the grandmother. But Luise Ullrich wasn't all that interested. She had misgivings about the production in general, and specifically about this wild young man in his leather jacket. The initial contacts had been made through her agent, and I was ready to give up, but not Fassbinder. So we sent word that we would like to call on her in Grünwald. Before we set out for her villa, we stopped at the Grünwald florist shop to ask which were Frau Ullrich's favorite flowers. Then we arrived at the villa. Fassbinder, in a special effort, had squeezed himself into a dark suit — which made him look like a high school student at graduation — and he handed Frau Ullrich the bouquet of flowers. "But those are my favorite flowers!" Frau Ullrich exclaimed. Fassbinder performed something like a bow and said, "Frau Ullrich, anyone who knows your movies also knows your favorite flowers." As it turned out, he had not only seen all of Luise Ullrich's movies, he also remembered every single setup. He had prepared himself meticuously.

*How in the world did Rainer manage to get the WDR production team on his side when he had never worked with a production team he didn't know? And his own crew had never been anywhere near that size.*

He just made sure to prepare himself even better. In those days, Westdeutscher Rundfunk called a so-called production conference at the start of any new production — maybe they still do. I had advised Herr Fassbinder that he could get everything he wanted, provided he gave us a list at this conference and not at some later date. He arrived with me and his cinematographer, Dietrich Lohmann, at this windowless, neon-lit, fully air-conditioned conference room, where we were met by about twenty well-dressed businessmen. The heads of all the various production departments were convened: lighting, stage management, set design, all experts in their field. All of them were obviously skeptical; they were fully prepared to spend a long, disorganized afternoon with this mad artist. As I was introducing him and the project, Fassbinder interrupted me, saying that, if it was all right with everybody present, he would prefer to get right down to business. And he was off. On the first day of filming, there would be a somewhat intricate train sequence, for which he needed a dolly and, of course, the necessary tracks. "How many yards of track, Dietrich?" And Dietrich Lohmann told him precisely how many yards of track. The suits were stunned and started taking notes. "And because the sequence is intricate, we also need somewhat intricate lighting." And so it went. The gentlemen were charmed. A bird of paradise had flown into their conference room, but he sure knew what he was talking about. After the first week of shooting, he had won their respect. Each day, he either kept to the schedule or finished ahead of time.

*He was cutting down filming time even then?*

Look at in the daily reports in the WDR archives. We had anticipated 105 days of filming and he wrapped after 97 days. He was incredibly disciplined. It was his personal obsession to come in under all of WDR's budget projections. WDR's head of production had a sign on his desk that read, "Anyone who talks about art in this room will be kicked out!" Fassbinder's greatest triumph came the day this man visited him on location to have his picture taken with him. To Fassbinder that was like a mini Nobel Prize.

Rainer knew just how to cater to the WDR crew. Everybody loved him: his pace, his precision, the power of his artistic expression. After a few weeks, a slogan began to circulate, "This guy knows exactly what he wants." That is, of course, the highest praise a production team can pay a director.

*There must have been some problems.*

None, absolutely none. There was one change in casting for which I was also partly responsible. It happened right at the start and was quickly resolved. Initially, Hanna Schygulla's part had been cast with another actress. We looked at the rushes with the other actress, and he saw right away that the part had been miscast. So we quickly replaced her with Hanna Schygulla.

*How were the ratings?*

It was a great success as far as the audience was concerned. The ratings were very high, on a par with murder mysteries. The critics, on the other hand, treated the series badly. Once critics make up their minds to pan a production, they do a proper job of it. In those days, they were still able to work Fassbinder over. He was not yet the established, all-around genius but an arrogant young man. Here was the perfect opportunity to kick him in the ass. Of course, the dramaturgical concept lent itself to a kick in the ass.

*The next project you did together was* World on a Wire. *Had you suggested the novel by Daniel F. Galouye to him?*

He read it overnight, as he was apt to, and the next day he told me that he was extremely interested.

*Didn't anybody say, "Whoa, let's wait and see what else this guy is going to produce in the open market. Let's give another director a chance"? The administration must have been shaken by the reviews, no?*

Not at all. We knew what he was worth to us. We took a rather snooty attitude toward critics in those days, in retaliation, so to speak. We were annoyed by their ridiculous panning, yet somehow we felt honored to have made so many enemies. As far as the work was concerned, Rainer and I were in complete agreement.

*Where did you come by all that self-confidence?*

The three of us were quite a match. Westdeutscher Rundfunk enormous self-confidence, Fassbinder was self-confident, and people used to say about me, "Watch out! This guy has read Marx in the original!"

*That bit about Marx must have made a tremendous impression on Rainer.*

Fassbinder was always impressed by middle-class education. He insisted that I explain the theory of surplus value to him. He was totally fascinated that the awareness of people in a society could be judged by the economic conditions under which they lived. He was well informed in many areas of life. He was totally familiar, for instance, with Sigmund Freud and with Nostradamus and, of course, with the history of film.

*In 1978, WDR helped produce Rainer's feature* In a Year with 13 Moons.

We simply owed that much to Fassbinder. As you well know, he was in bad shape in 1978, and the small amount of money we contributed was the least a television station could do for someone who had gained that station so much recognition.

*How do you account for his amazingly prolific output?*

People used to say, "This guy turns out movies like other people roll cigarettes." He had this incredible curiosity about the world. Since he had very definite attitudes toward whatever outraged or delighted him at the moment, he had to give instant expression to his feelings. He was extremely belligerent; and he loved to argue, but whenever possible — and somehow he always made it possible — he answered the world with an artistic production. Schiller kept scribbling non-stop in his notebooks. Picasso didn't say on Friday night, "That's it! I'm off for the weekend." To Rainer, continuous work was the natural way of life. He felt good as long as he was able to work. He was happy or charming or obnoxious, but he was in a predictable state of mind, because he was being productive.

*A major hiatus occurred in Fassbinder's life around 1976–77. Have you any example of that shift?*

Perhaps I can best describe it by way of *I Only Want You To Love Me*, the last production we worked on together. I had asked him to read the text of a sound tape, which a team of writers had collected under the title *For Life*. For his story, he had drastically changed the material, focussing on what interested him, i.e., the protagonist's childhood, its circumstances and its anxieties. He had interpreted the material in a very personal way, which accounted for the movie's quality. In our discussions, I carefully avoided saying anything personal about his script. Instead, we both pretended we were just talking on a dramaturgical level. He even accepted my title, *I Only Want You to Love Me*, a line from the recorded tape. He made a typical crack, like, "Do what you need to do." We had always communicated in an easy, playful way. With *Despair* that adaptibility, that ease suddenly vanished. I could no longer reach him. I was no longer able to talk to him. People were no longer allowed to enter his hotel room unannounced.

*Despair was the script by Tom Stoppard, based on a novel by Vladimir Nabokov. For the first time he was working on a script written by somebody other that Rainer Werner Fassbinder.*

That certainly was an important factor. He was extremely interested in the Nabokov novel. But he was unable to absorb it through the usual channel of writing it out, since the script had already been written by Tom Stoppard. Of course, Stoppard's adaptation had been done with the full support of Herr Fassbinder. Nothing ever happened without his agreement. But getting his agreement somehow was not the same as get-tig his blessings. It was also the first time a project did not run under his auspices but under the auspices of the movie industry, which only hap-pened one other time, in the case of *Lili Marleen.*

*Despair* had all the makings of an international success. The author of the novel was well known worldwide; the author of the screenplay was an international celebrity ; the cast, with Dirk Bogarde, Andrea Ferréol, and Bernhard Wicki, was international. The movie was to be filmed in English.

*Even the film editor had been imported from England.*

And he was exported back again shortly thereafter. Fassbinder recut the whole film in one night with the help of a certain Juliane Lorenz. And it is important to remember clearly how this film was made. Herr Fassbinder and Herr Märtesheimer, in his capacity as Bavaria pro-ducer, traveled to London to meet Mr. Stoppard. We met in an elegant hotel for an elegant lunch and had a very superficial discussion, partly due to the language barrier. Then we returned to Munich—and did nothing. This was in basic contrast to the old days. Neither Rainer nor I felt the urge to meet and discuss the story. We didn't need to convert it into a script, since all that was supposed be done by Stoppard. In due course, Stoppard's first English version arrived, and we had it translated. When the first discussion took place, it was not in one of our offices or in Fassbinder's kitchen but in a conference room at Munich's Hotel Vier Jahreszeiten.

*Hollywood made in Germany.*

The script was almost an hour too long. We knew it would require a considerable amount of work. Tom Stoppard himself said he was sorry the script had gotten too long and that he wasn't quite happy with this first version. But Fassbinder said, "No, it is an excellent script. I am going to shoot it kind of boulevard style, the dialogues in ping-pong rhythm, the whole thing at a very fast pace. I'll cut some dialogue here and there." With that pronouncement, he relieved everybody of their responsibilities. Stoppard was excused from his responsibility to revise, which Fassbinder took upon himself. Everybody was looking to Fassbinder. Everybody thought he would eventually get this thing into reasonable narrative shape. I, however, felt it was already too late.

*The next movie you did together was* The Marriage of Maria Braun, *where his narrative is very clear and precise.*

There he had a decent script...

*I am delighted to hear you make this self-congratulatory remark.*

...although the movie lacks perfection in spots, where the script just ran too long—the same thing that happened in *Despair*. He had edited on line. And cutting isn't just a snip here and there. It is a process that requires close examination. The scene which may appear too long still contains certain vital emotions and information, which must be respected.

*So you don't think of* Maria Braun *as perfect?*

No, I think it is a great movie, but I believe certain transitions that were made in the editing are not entirely successful. For instance, that scene in the first half of the movie, where Maria has a picnic on the grass in front of her house with Bill, her American beau, and the whole family, Betti and Willi (played by Elisabeth Trissenaar and Gottfried John). Originally, that scene was much longer. In the script I had built up an emotion, which, I regret to say, wasn't all that well written. Unfortunately, he only noticed the deficiency during the shoot. He probably hadn't had a chance to deal with it earlier. Most likely he dreamt up the new dialogue the night before the shoot. Unfortunately, his lines turned out even less inspired than mine.

*Not that there were any lack of problems on the set.*

I remember those problems vividly. I was the one who saw to it that his acting producer sold Bavaria the production rights to *Berlin Alexanderplatz*. When that trust began to shatter, I made every effort to force him out. With an author's vanity, I also wanted to protect *The Marriage of Maria Braun*. At the time, I was the only one who knew that this movie would revolutionize the history of German film.

*How did you happen to write the screenplay for* Maria Braun? *You'd never written a screenplay before.*

I didn't know I could write screenplays. Nor did Herr Fassbinder. Rainer had this story about Maria Braun in his head. He also had a rough outline of a few written pages. We had the central idea of the story, something like a news report. There is this great, everlasting love, which unfortunately can't amount to anything because of the war. Instead, the woman has an affair with a black man. This was Rainer's basic idea. I became the writer for a very simple reason. Being the dramaturg, Rainer gave me the rough outline and asked, "You think you can impose some order on this thing?" He basically wanted me to do a treatment. I carried out my job as a dramaturg and presented him with something. Whereupon he suggested I might as well write the script.

He had this refreshingly blunt way of steering a person toward his own highest capacities. As you know, he liked playing the role of the benevolent father. He paved my way by asking Michael Fengler to draw up a contract for me, and I wrote what I considered the first draft of the script. It was obviously too long. Yet he said, "No, it is o.k. the way it is. It is a beautiful script." He fixed up my first draft, which I didn't mind at all. I had so much respect for Fassbinder, the screenwriter. I just would have liked to write a second version, but that was not to be. Deep down I knew he didn't want to wait for a second version. But I did expect he would fix up my first draft before he started filming rather than cut it during the shoot.

*I know very few movies with a narrative rhythm as perfect and homogenous.*

*Veronika Voss* is much more perfect.

*He also made a few changes while filming in that one. And we made changes during editing.*

I am talking about the kind of perfection you find in some of the screenplays he wrote and particularly in their cinematographic conversions, such as in *Berlin Alexanderplatz*. I am talking about the difference between something that is perfect and something that is just very good. There is a fine line. Of course, I measure Herr Fassbinder by the fact that he was capable of perfection. He proved that early on with movies, such as *Ali: Fear Eats the Soul* and *Martha* and *I Only Want You to Love Me*.

We must, nonetheless, aviod the temptation of calling his entire oeuvre perfect, simply because he sometimes achieved perfection.

*You spent two days on location in Coburg. Were you aware of the situation during the shoot?*

I arrived the day Fassbinder went on strike, which was only a few days into shooting. He suspected his acting producer had siphoned off money from the original production budget. But he couldn't prove it, let alone nail him for it.

*Wasn't it odd that Rainer, who had had no problems with a large institution such as Westdeutscher Rundfunk suddenly got into trouble with a so-called "friendly production"? Maria Braun was his thirty-second movie. Rainer not only knew how to deal with large budgets but also with firmly established production systems.*

What was most odd was to see him conduct a strike the way they happen in real life. He was striking from a loser's position. The flier he had written was sweet but also pathetic. All I could think of was the king doesn't write fliers. The king kicks his servants in the ass — and *basta*!

*Your metaphor makes a lot of sense, but then even the king is a human being.*

He was helpless, and I felt extremely sorry for him. It was not at all his style. In this central phase of his creative life — by then, I had known him for seven years — he had become "master of the universe," at least that's how I saw him. He could direct the planets any way he liked. And now I saw to my horror that the master had messed up. Suddenly the "master of the universe" was as impotent as a child. He had allowed himself to be provoked by an acting producer, a man who is supposed to carry out orders. WDR had signed a contract with the acting producer's company, but it was clearly understood that they were investing all power and privilege in Herr Fassbinder.

WDR didn't give a hoot about whoever acted as producer for this "Fassbinder movie." I was ordered to step in as producer to keep *Alexanderplatz* from sinking any further into the quagmire. I only realized on the spot that Fassbinder no longer had the handling power I had hitherto credited him with.

He was helplessly floundering around, getting upset about some shit that should never have merited his attention. He dreamt up things just to annoy the acting producer, the way children do to annoy their parents. It wasn't malice, you see, but a case of aggressive despair.*

*As we know, you transferred the production to Bavaria. I assume the seller didn't suffer too great a loss, having received a considerable sum of money for the production rights.*

You may put it that way.

---

*In November 1994, the long-term court battle over Rainer Werner Fassbinder's share in the movie *The Marriage of Maria Braun* ended before the Oberlandesgericht in Düsseldorf. The verdict did not confirm Fassbinder as co-producer but granted him the contractual fifty percent share in the net profits. J.L.

*Can you explain why Rainer sometimes failed to confront the obvious weaknesses and stupidities of some of his earlier companions until it was almost too late?*

Rainer's principle was loyalty, a patriarchal syndrome you may describe like this: you kick a person in the ass now and then, or show a person the door, but when push comes to shove you stick together. Family belongs together, and the head of the family may be just or unjust, but he must be reliable.

*And then in the case of* Maria Braun, *the super-father, Peter Märthesheimer, who always addressed Herr Fassbinder by the formal "Sie," for the first time decided to intervene.*

We valiantly kept up that "Sie" business. But I was no super-father. That former close relationship no longer existed. Starting with *Despair*, there was nothing I could influence anymore. During this phase, his "Herr Märthesheimer" assumed a different tone and, like everybody else, I withdrew from this man who suddenly had become unpredictable and defensive.

*What about* Berlin Alexanderplatz? *Do you think the film is too dark?*

Not at all. Some shady characters kept shouting the film was too dark, but only because they couldn't see the dirty parts clearly enough.

*After* Berlin Alexanderplatz, *you and Rainer were talking again. And you worked together on* Lola.

By that time, the defenses had come down again. Herr Fassbinder told me that he considered my first version of *Lola* somewhat "banal." Banal, not a word more. I was so upset that I went home and wrote an entirely new version. That one he liked. As for me, I like *Veronika Voss* best of the three movies about women. I think, except for *Berlin Alexanderplatz*, it is aesthetically the most self-assured movie Herr Fassbinder ever made.

If Herr Fassbinder had made *Rosa Luxemburg* it would have been a truly great film, at least on a par with Bernardo Bertolucci's *1900*. The movie would have accurately conveyed what the character of Rosa Luxemburg was about. It would also have conveyed the artistic capacity of a mature Rainer Werner Fassbinder: a movie about a character who loses but, in actual fact, proves that she wins in the process.

*What distinguishes Rainer from other directors of his time?*

Rainer's movies brought an important element to the German cinema. Whereas many movie directors tend to present an overall view with their pictures, Rainer focused on the immediate effect of the individual frame. No doubt, the myth of some of his actresses, especially Hanna Schygulla, lies in the artistic quality of the individual artist, but more than anything, it relies on Rainer's cinematic timing, particularly in his use of closeups. There are not many closeups in *Maria Braun*, but they are very deliberate, precisely used, and lit in a very special way. Most of them are silent shots, filmed in just the right light.

*The psychology of the characters became increasingly important to him. And he conveyed that, for instance, through editing in a closeup.*

That's true. But it only gradually developed. In *Eight Hours Don't Make a Day* you still find a certain conventionality in the visual conversion and continuity. That's because he edited by dialogue — he filmed according to its rhythm. *Berlin Alexanderplatz* was about emotions and how to make these emotions visible.

Take *Eight Hours Don't Make a Day*. You know, the love scene between Gottfried John and Hanna Schygulla in the ice-cream parlor. There they sit, facing each other, and in the center of the picture is this bouquet of flowers. They move closer together, speaking dialogue for lovers. But then another element intrudes: a waitress behind the counter in the back. You have seen this character before and you have noticed that she has a dime-novel in front of her on the counter. Now this character turns toward the lovers. The lovers' emotions are being reflected through this character, who watches them, holding a cheap novel in her hand. This is how Herr Fassbinder enhances emotions. We, the audience, are watching with the yearning eyes of the waitress behind the counter. I am talking about thc step-by-step refinement of Herr Fassbinder's cinematographic language. When it comes to emotions, even in his earlier work, before he reached absolute mastery in *Berlin Alexanderplatz*, that is precisely what his movies are about. And that in barely ten years! Dear God, if he could have only had ten more. What treasures he would have produced!

# DIETRICH LOHMANN

*Born 1943 in Schnepfenthal/Thuringia, Mr. Lohmann has worked as a cinematographer since 1968. He was awarded the Film Prize of the German Federal Republic for* Gods of the Plague, Katzelmacher, *and* Love Is Colder Than Death. *After he broke away from Fassbinder, he collaborated with directors of the New German Cinema, notably Robert van Ackeren, Edgar Reitz, Volker Schlöndorff, and Bernhard Sinkel. Since 1986, he has worked mainly for American, English, and French productions with directors such as Carl Schenkel, John Schlesinger, Vera Belmont, and Chantal Ackerman. He won the A.S.C. Award and an Emmy nomination for the television mini-series* War and Remembrance. *He lives mainly in Los Angeles. The interview was conducted in Berlin.*

## LET'S SEE WHAT HAPPENS

*Do you differentiate between Fassbinder, the director and Fassbinder, the person?*

The person is often quite different from the artist, who frequently hides behind his work. I'm sure this was true in Rainer's case. I got to know Rainer Werner Fassbinder, the person, very well. After all, we worked together for three years on his very first movies. We began making movies together. He changed a great deal during his career, I can't say whether for better or worse.

*You yourself must have changed.*

I did, indeed. Everything in those days evolved from antiteater, the group that had formed around Fassbinder and, through him, left its mark on the theater. From it the movie scene later evolved. I never actually belonged to this group. I never lived with them. I was an observer. I never let myself become part of the scene. Should things become too intense or complicated with the antiteater group, I wanted to be able to make an easy exit. Eventually, I quit. After three years of intense collaboration, I saw that I wasn't developing in the way I had visualized. It seemed hard at the time, but I wanted to develop in a different direction.

*You were there in 1970, when Rainer made six movies in that one year. Churning out one movie after another must have been intense.*

I shot eighteen movies with him, including the television mini-series *Eight Hours Don't Make a Day*. He could turn out a movie in a week. Today that wouldn't be feasible; quality standards are different. We were strapped for money, so we had to move fast. He was always surrounded by a great many people who enabled him to work at that pace.

Fassbinder is always depicted as the great father figure who kept his group together. That may be true in the case of some people. But it certainly did not apply to my work or the work of Michael Ballhaus or Xaver Schwarzenberger. Our work with the camera made us more independent. His movies certainly became more and more professional and genuinely cinematographic. We were all very young in those early days; none of us had much experience. We had very little equipment. Our aim was to produce decent movies which differed from the traditional German cinema. That's what was important to us.

*There must have been a lot of talk about film aesthetics.*

Indeed, we talked a lot about film aesthetics. "Nouvelle Vague" was popular in those days, the so-called film noir, black-and-white and very evocative. We often tried to imitate the style, particularly in the early days, with *Love Is Colder Than Death*, *Gods of the Plague*, and *The American Soldier*.

*Did you watch movies together as a group or did you work from your own individual visual experience?*

No, we didn't watch movies together. We agreed on a style, based on our mutual cinematic instincts, although the style of *Katzelmacher* wasn't so much a stroke of genius as a result of technical and financial necessities. It was Rainer's forte to create something out of nothing, to inspire us to creative collaboration, so we could take pride in what we had done.

*There was a great deal more money available for* Eight Hours Don't Make a Day. *Did that make a difference; did it allow more room for experimentation?*

There was much more money and much more pressure. We had to shoot a fixed number of minutes, edited minutes, each day. Curiously enough, in those days the director was paid a kind of completion bonus. If you stayed under the scheduled time budget, you were paid some extra money. And we did stay within the schedule.

*In a way, you exploited yourselves.*

I wouldn't call it exploitation. This young, very inexperienced cameraman learned an awful lot in the process. I had the chance to gather invaluable experience around Fassbinder. I learned to react quickly to ideas and to convert them into pictures, light, and atmosphere. A good deal, I'd say.

*You were so eager to learn and experiment that it didn't seem like work.*

Any experiment is welcome, because the experiment forces you to reflect. We just pushed ahead, doing things we later called experiments. It was dilettantism — but not mere dilettantism!

*What most impressed you about Rainer?*

Above all, he was an extremely talented guy. He was also a very hard worker, incredibly active and creative, always full of ideas. His creativity was so inspiring, so compelling that it made us strive to be equally creative in our own field. He was unique in his precision — a spontaneous precision which picked up emotions and situations and immediately converted them into collaboration with his crew. Working with Fassbinder in those days helped my personal development. It also shaped my character. He taught me to cross boundaries, to be courageous, to be my own man.

*What was special about the productions you did with Fassbinder? Do they differ from the way you are working today?*

Productions were much more chaotic. When I think back on how we used to make movies — we were just disorganized. We said, "We want to make a movie, so let's make a movie." This would be impossible today, which doesn't mean that it is necessarily for the better.

*Which of his movies still affects you most?*

I saw *The Merchant of Four Seasons* again the other day. I was really impressed after all those years. I also recently saw *Bremen Coffee* again, which Fassbinder and I adapted for television from his stage play. We worked with an electronic camera and with the blue box, not knowing what we were letting ourselves in for. The bottom line is that we proved we were able to do it. There aren't many directors who will urge a cinematographer to be daring, who will say, "We are going to try something new, we are going to take a step forward."

*Why is Fassbinder's reputation abroad so different from his reputation in Germany?*

His movies were not specifically German in nature. The German public's negative attitude may have something to do with the fact that Fassbinder held a mirror up to the face of the German middle-class, shocking many people because they recognized themselves. For a long time, he was the bad boy who showed things in the movies that people didn't even dare mention in those days.

*What are you thinking of?*

In *Jail Bait*, for instance, a penis appears in a picture. That penis caused a tremendous outcry. Nowadays, it is totally accepted. Today people think there is something wrong with a picture if it doesn't show at least one penis. Many directors are trying to save a movie with such gimmicks. In the old days, it was considered a provocation. Even after the time of anti-authoritarian uprising, such things were considered provocative in the movies. Take *The Niklashauser Journey*, a highly political movie. At the time, television referred in subtitles to the works of literature Fassbinder was quoting from—Marx, Engels, Lenin. This was to inform the public that these were not necessarily the views of the television station!

*Do you think the history of the German Federal Republic can be reconstructed in Rainer's movies?*

I should think so. Especially in his early movies, which I personally consider his best, particularly *The Merchant of Four Seasons*, *The Niklashauser Journey*, *Recruits in Ingolstadt*, and, later, *Fontane Effi Briest*. These movies tell a great deal about the German Federal Republic, especially about its middle-class values, its inability to communicate, its hostility toward foreigners. All those elements have always existed in Germany, though not many people wrote or made movies about them. I believe his principal subject was the lack of communication between people.

# WERNER SCHROETER

$B$orn 1945 in Georgenthal/Thuringia, Mr. Schroeter grew up in Heidel-berg. At age fourteen, he became an ardent admirer of Maria Callas, which laid the foundation for his later opera productions on all the major interna-tional stages. Another woman, Magdalena Montezuma, became the inspiration of his early career as a movie director. Between 1969 and 1996 he made thirty-eight movies, among them Der Tod der Maria Malibran, Die neapolitanis-chen Geschwister, Der Rosenkönig, Malina, and Poussières d'Amour [Embers of Love]. He staged over forty theater productions, at Bochum, Cologne, Düsseldorf, Bremen, and Berlin, among others. Fassbinder predicted the history of film would place him somewhere between Novalis, Lautrémont, and Céline in literature. At present Werner Schroeter lives in Düsseldorf. The interview was conducted in Berlin.

## ON THE SAME WAVELENGTH

*When did you and Rainer meet?*

I met Rainer Werner when his play *Anarchy in Bavaria* was being per-formed at the Forum Theater in Berlin. It must have been in 1968–69. I remember telling him, "You'll end badly, if you keep on pretending that no one can love you." I felt he refused to accept love in order to prove that love did not exist. Yet, at the same time, he wanted to prove that it does exist. He and I were quite crazy in those days. We're talking 1968, the ex-citement of political "upheaval," the climate of that era, booze, drugs... I think booze, which burns up fast inside the body, was our major driving force. In those days, a regimen of yogurt, mineral water, an egg for break-fast, and ten hours of sleep would have been inconceivable in his life and mine. We were in a perpetual state of euphoria over discovering new things, which—with the help of other substances—kept us at work around the clock. Rainer Werner and I had this terrible gift of relentless energy.

*Do you remember being in the pub, Deutsche Eiche, when you said something to Rainer about Salem which really hurt him because, as you know, he took you seriously?*

It was a simple story. Salem had hanged himself in jail. I blamed Rainer for that. I told him that people assume responsibilites for one an-other. I believe that in the hectic, creative life he led, it was inevitable that he would hurt people. These are things for which I blame myself just as much as I blame him. I blamed Rainer because I felt he had let down a friend who, to a certain extent, was not his equal. Salem was not an educated person; he was not at all sure of himself. Of course, rage came into it, too. I know I myself make mistakes of that kind all the time. I blamed Rainer, knowing perfectly well that the same could happen, and often had happened, to me.

*How do you feel about responsibility turning into patronage?*

The problem doesn't exist between partners who are on the same wavelength. I don't blame Rainer for anything in our relationship, and there is nothing he would have blamed me for. We were equals who lived and shaped our own lives with great energy. When it comes to depen-dence, people should be careful not to let it turn into patronage. On the other hand, you can't drop a person for fear of encroaching patronage, ei-ther.

We knew each other for almost twelve years in varying degrees of intimacy, distance, and friendship. That definitely makes him an impor-tant person in my life, and I assume I was also important in Rainer's life. Our lives touched through our way of thinking, our attitude toward work, and our attempts at friendship. Those things leave their mark on two partners, no matter how alien they may be in other respects.

# WIM WENDERS

Mr. *Wenders was born in 1945 in Düsseldorf. After brief periods of study in medicine and philosophy, Mr. Wenders found his way to the Academy of Television and Film in Munich. He produced his first movies and, in 1971, became one of the founders of Filmverlag der Autoren. In 1975, he established his own production company, Road Movies. With movies like* King of the Road, In the Course of Time, *and* The American Friend, *he became one of the best-known and most successful directors of the New German Cinema. Between 1978 and 1982 he lived in the USA, where Francis Ford Coppola commissioned him to film* Hammett. *In 1982, he was awarded the Golden Lion in Venice for* The State of Things, *which allowed his next movies,* Paris, Texas *(Golden Palm at Cannes, 1984) and* Wings of Desire, *to break into the international market. At the time of the interview in Berlin, he was preparing his most recent movie,* Lisbon Story.

## WITH HIS FISTS

*You and Rainer started making movies at the same time. Both of you were born in 1945, Rainer in May, you in August.*

And we are both sons of physicians.

*Did you always want to make movies?*

Actually, I wanted to become a painter. Even while I was at the Film Academy, I still wasn't at all sure that I wanted to make movies. In fact, I very much doubted that I was able to make movies, whereas Rainer knew all along that he would make movies.

*When you were awarded the Bavarian Film Prize in 1994, you said in your address that the era of authors' movies was coming to an end. I was shocked to hear you say that, but I admired your courage in spelling it out so clearly.*

The author's movie is finished. It was a model we adopted from "Nouvelle Vague" in the late sixties. The idea was that we would develop our own projects, write our own stories, do our own productions, from idea to screenplay, from shoot to final cut to presentation, taking full responsibility for the whole product. That's why we founded Filmverlag der Autoren, which was initially conceived as both a production company and a support group, so to speak. But we soon realized that there was no point in making movies that nobody was going to distribute. In the initial stage, no distribution company was willing to take on our movies. So we eventually added a distribution company to the production company. As a result, the people who had earlier produced now focused more and more exclusively on distribution. Gradually, the distribution company lost its original mission. In the end, distribution was all that was left of Filmverlag der Autoren. The distribution company ran into problems, because an increasing number of productions required more and more distribution. Movie-making within Filmverlag der Autoren became obsolete.

*What happened to all the incoming money?*

The money from sales was used for further distribution. The few money-making movies were primarily Rainer's and mine and movies by Hark Bohm. The money we were entitled to as founders, we left in the company. Of course, we hoped it would be available to us for our future films. But that wasn't so. The money flowed in other directions outside our control, and we received nothing.

Bear in mind that Rainer and I had been the ones who had financed the whole thing. Our movies were the first to be sold in the international market. We were the ones who produced the most and kept the market going. Sometimes, when Rainer and I met, we wondered why we hardly ever saw any money. The first international sales were often closed outright, i.e., without a time limit, without percentage interest. A disaster! We were glad that our movies were distributed, but we couldn't understand why other people were raking in the profit. We never really understood what was going on.

*I remember Rainer giving the same reason for his resignation. You mean you never looked at the contracts?*

At first, I was simply and stupidly too trusting. It took me a while to catch on. But we were being cheated right and left. Later I paid more attention. But in the final analysis, I left several hundred thousand marks in the former Filmverlag der Autoren. When at last it dawned on me what had happened, I just wanted out. We paid dearly for our learning experience.

*May we assume that you began studying your contracts more carefully?*

After I resigned from Filmverlag, I studied my contracts very closely. I realized that you need a solid contract right from the start, even more so when you are working with friends. In cases where no contracts existed, there always was trouble later on. Of course, there never is trouble when a movie is a flop. Trouble only comes with success.

*How did you feel about Rainer's productivity?*

His work was a tremendous challenge, an example almost. And as to his speed, I simply realized that his working style was completely different from mine. Rainer delegated much more than I did. He was surrounded by this clan of efficient people. Besides, he didn't fuss around as much as I do.

Yet I also worked with the same people. It would not have occurred to me to consider a cameraman other than Robby Müller, an editor other than Peter Przygodda, a sound engineer other than Martin Müller.

*What's changed for you since those early days?*

In the early seventies and toward the end of that era, I made a movie every year. Rainer, as we know, made quite a few more. All of us were prepared to take risks. And we found the same readiness to take risks on every level, in government support as well as in television. There were people like Günter Rohrbach of Westdeutscher Rundfunk who was interested in us and allowed us to make movies for television which today nobody would have the courage to do. Whoever finishes a movie nowadays needs three or four years before he can launch another one. I fear the projects we did in those days would not be taken seriously today.

And the methods of distribution have changed. In those days, when an American movie opened here it was shown in one large movie theater.

In a large German city today, an American movie is exhibited simultaneously in as many as ten movie theaters. As a result, a German movie hardly has a chance to get into a movie theater. The distribution system was much more open, more fluid and not nearly as centrally manipulated by a few large distribution companies. At Filmverlag we were still able to select our movie theaters. One phone call and we got into the movie theater of our choice.

*Was it that easy?*

Pretty much. Meanwhile, a great change in marketing has taken place, which has advanced the film medium to a different level of experience. Nowadays, no movie finds an audience without a publicity budget. All we could afford back then was a set of display cases and a few hundred posters, which we ourselves pasted onto the advertising space. As a rule, the entertainment sections of the large papers kept us alive. Today that would be inconceivable. If I tried to launch a movie with just a few favorable reviews in the entertainment sections, no one would show up. You have to attract the public through advertising. This was true when Rainer was alive. His last movies reached a much larger public than did his earlier ones.

*Rainer finally reached the point with* Maria Braun *where he knew he was going to make a movie that would be of major importance to him. Then came the breakthrough, financial success. However, the profits didn't come to him, but to the man who called himself the producer.*

I know, that was a sad chapter. In those early years, I felt Rainer had always slugged away and pushed ahead, while others who were riding on his coat tails had siphoned off the cream.

*Initially, the story was based on an idea which Rainer had conceived for a television series under the working title* The Marriage Of Our Parents. *Back in 1975, he wrote down his thoughts about it. Eventually, it ended up as a script by Peter Märtheseimer and Pea Fröhlich.*

That's correct. It was going to be about the marriages of our parents. He told me that, too.

*Depicting the history of the Federal Republic of Germany through characters' personal development had become one of Rainer's major inspirations. He wanted to use the film medium to illustrate political, sociological, and psychological con-*

*nections. You differed from him in this respect. You were more focused on pictures than on people.*

Except that from *Maria Braun* onwards, Rainer was increasingly interested in pictures as well. My interests have become focused on history and dramaturgy. Rainer gradually learned to appreciate pictures through his craft. I felt he didn't much care what his movies looked like in the early days. Toward the end, his pictures became regular puzzles.

When we were hanging out at the Bungalow, the pub on Türkenstrasse in Schwabing, we heard the news that Rainer had produced a feature film! The rest of us were still at the film academy, barely having produced a short. We were all in shock. We called ourselves the "Sensibilists" because of the movie reviews we wrote to earn a living. And here was Rainer Werner, who had made a movie while the rest of us were still dreaming. His movie had suddenly appeared out of nowhere. It changed our entire relationship. The Fassbinder group had made a movie. It proved to us that there were other ways of doing things, that there was an altogether different approach to making movies.

*Did you watch his movies when they came out?*

Not all of them. I saw *Katzelmacher*, when it first came out. But there was a time when I did not look at anything for fear of being influenced. Solidarity didn't come until later during our time at Filmverlag, when I saw every one of his movies. That was also the beginning of our friendship. In 1981, we met in Los Angeles during the Academy Awards. At that time I was going through a bad phase. He told me, "We'll have to get you out of here." I was working for Coppola, making *Hammett*. I can see him now, in his tuxedo with the bow tie, determined to stand up for me, with his fists, if need be.

*Shortly before he lured you into his studios, Francis Coppola asked Rainer if he wanted to do something with him. Rainer was adamant. He said he didn't know what he would do in the States, that he would have to live there for a while to be able to tell stories from America. In those days, he felt he still had plenty of stories to tell in Germany.*

He was right about that.

# GÜNTER ROHRBACH

.

Born in 1926 in Neunkirchen/Saar, Mr. Rohrbach studied German literature, philosophy, and psychology and wrote a Ph.D. thesis on Christoph von
Grimmelshausen. In 1957, he started out on a career as a theater and movie
critic. In 1961, he joined Westdeutscher Rundfunk [WDR]. In 1965, he was
appointed head of WDR's department of television plays, which later included
entertainment and family programs. From 1979 to early in 1994, he was head
of Bavaria Film Studios in Munich. Meanwhile, he worked as a freelance producer. He met Fassbinder when WDR produced his movies, which paved the
way for Fassbinder's later collaboration with Bavaria. The interview was conducted in Munich.

## WITH GREAT CONSISTENCY
## AND DETERMINATION

*What was your first encounter with Fassbinder?*

It lasted about three quarters of an hour. During those 45 minutes
he smoked thirty cigarettes and drank half a bottle of whiskey.

*Had he brought that with him?*

No, he didn't bring it. We offered him a drink. We didn't expect him
to drink the bottle. The meeting obviously made him uncomfortable,
which I understand better today than I did at the time. Entering Westdeutscher Rundfunk, across that huge lobby, along those long corridors,
past one door after another, with not a soul in sight. What an oppressive

experience! And this television exec, whom he met in his office, must have struck him as alien and powerful. He probably compensated with excessive consumption and bravado. I had a similar experience with Wim Wenders. The first time Wenders came to my office, he carried a bag, which he put down by his side and which he reached into from time to time. Suddenly I heard music in the room. At first, I didn't know where it came from, until I connected it with the gestures he made toward the bag. He had brought a tape recorder. I presume music had a similar function for Wenders as whiskey had for Fassbinder.

*And what happened when the first film was finished?*

*The Niklashauser Journey* was a disaster. It was a movie no one really liked. I believe even Fassbinder didn't like it.

*Did he tell you that?*

No, but he approached us several years later to do a remake and shoot additional footage. The unusual thing about Fassbinder was that he didn't care at all whether he did something for the movies or for television. He just wanted to make movies, and he made them for whomever paid for them. Above all, he wanted to make his movies right then and there. He did not want to wait for years, which sometimes is the price of getting a specific constellation of talent together. It was not as though we, the television industry, were the givers and the filmmakers were the takers. On the contrary. We feared that television might disintegrate into a mediocre, aesthetically boring medium, its subject matter watered down by too many restrictions, while a lively, wildly exciting movie culture sprang up at the same time. Under no condition did I want to have television lose out to those filmmakers. I did not say, "We've got to do something for the movies." I said, "If we get hold of those filmmakers, they're going to do something for us, for television."

*How would you describe Rainer's productivity and his development?*

He not only produced relentlessly — always finding and inventing stories — he also had this drive for moving things ahead. I'll never forget how *Germany in Autumn* was made. All those guys got together and decided, "We're going to make a movie about the current political situation. Each person will contribute about ten to twelve minutes. Let's meet again in a week, see what ideas we have, and coordinate the material." When they met again, some had an idea, others had a script. Rainer had a complete movie. That was classic Fassbinder. If he wanted to do a project, it was as good as done. Nowadays we spend weeks on end doing test shots. He always started at tremendous speed, like a pole vaulter, with great consistency and determination. He was a master at casting, finding the right people for the right parts.

Now, there were exceptions. There was the Simmel novel, *Hurra, wir leben noch [Hurrah, We're Still Alive]*, which he wanted to adapt for the movies. We never reached an agreement with him, because we would not accept the script and the concept. Yet his suggestion for the leading actor was sheer genius. He wanted Goetz George, who was somewhat forgotten at the time.

*By late 1981, however, you were unwilling to represent the direction that Rainer was heading?*

I never felt that at all. He was, of course, prone to a variety of moods. He was also full of surprises. Let's just say, he went through various phases of discipline. I remember, a week before he was to start shooting *Alexanderplatz*, Horst Wendlandt asked me if I'd hired a deputy director. I said no, why? Because, said Wendlandt, everyone knew it was unlikely that Fassbinder would be able to stand the strain for more than two weeks.

*Had Horst met Rainer at that point?*

I doubt it. Wendlandt lived by rumors, as does the television industry in general. In those days, Fassbinder was considered a sick man. Many people thought he could not last through that long and complex a production.

I can't say I was without doubts myself. It was no small undertaking. I'll never forget the moment he arrived on the set—not with whiskey, not with cigarettes, but with a bicycle. He was in very good spirits. He had arranged regular soccer games and God knows what kinds of athletic activities he had scheduled. He set up a recreation program to help the team physically master the long stretch of work ahead.

*Do you miss him personally?*

Yes, very much. You wouldn't believe how often I think of Fassbinder, how often I wish he were with us today. He was a force that had meaning not only for his own movies. He constantly brought us new ideas on what else could be done and with whom.

People of outstanding talent simply don't come in large numbers. Fassbinder was a great master, a true genius. Today, we have good movie directors, some very good ones, as well as the inevitable bad ones. You can't expect one genius followed by another like on an assembly line. Wim Wenders was awarded the Golden Palm, which Fassbinder never received, because he never had the perseverance to work toward it. That kind of thing requires a certain amount of planning. It needs to be staged. You have to be there at the right time with the right movie. He found it boring to think in such self-promotional terms. His attitude became quite obvious when he made movies. When he was launched by big distributors, even Wendlandt, who was a major supporter, said, "This guy makes too many movies. I cannot promote four Fassbinder movies a year."

*Horst Wendlandt offered him a million marks to do nothing for a year.*

There you are! He simply refused to abide by the laws of the market. And the laws of the market dictate that you launch, at the most, one movie a year by one director — but not four!

# MICHAEL BALLHAUS

$B$*orn in Berlin, 1935, he began his career as a photographer's apprentice and later turned to stage photography. In 1959, he started working for Südwestfunk as a camera assistant and, within six years, rose to chief cinematographer. During that period he met Peter Lilienthal, whose early movies he filmed. Between 1967 and 1970, he taught at the Film and Television Academy of Berlin. The movie* Whitey *marked the beginning of his collaboration with Fassbinder. Eight years and fifteen movies later,* The Marriage of Maria Braun *marked the end of their collaboration. Since the early eighties, Ballhaus has filmed mainly in the United States with prominent directors such as Martin Scorsese, Mike Nichols, James L. Brooks, Francis Ford Coppola, and Robert Redford. He has also made music videos for Prince, among others. He is about to direct his first feature film,* Lotte Lenya. *Michael Ballhaus lives in Los Angeles, New York, and Berlin, where the interview was conducted by Herbert Gehr.*

## A NEW KIND OF REALITY

*When you and Fassbinder first met, you were already an accomplished cinematographer with well over ten years of working experience. The first meeting between you and Fassbinder must have seemed like a professional meeting an amateur.*

Yes, you might say that. But Fassbinder had a different approach to movies. I was intrigued by the analytical manner in which he built images.

*How did you two first come to work together?*

It happened almost by accident. Carlo Saura's cinematographer had initially been chosen for the job on *Whitey*. But he wasn't available or they didn't have the money to pay him. Ulli Lommel, who was a friend of mine, took me to see Fassbinder. On the one hand, it was obvious that Rainer was a little intimidated by me; on the other hand, he tried to pin me down on every single point I made. I was not precise enough for Fassbinder. Once, we were discussing a location, and I remarked, "With a location as beautiful as this, we should try to really 'sell the scene.'" It was an accepted term in those days. But he looked at me and said, "What's this you want to sell?" as if I were talking about a real estate deal. He needed to be very precise with regard to language — and also with regard to images.

We had a lot of problems with *Whitey* from the start. For the first three or four weeks, I didn't unpack my bags, because I figured, "This won't last; the guy is going to fire me." There was constant friction between us. He had his own ideas, which he was determined to bulldoze through. He said to me once, "The camera should be here." So I said, "Just a minute, that changes the axis." And he said, "Changes the axis? How?" I said, "Well, the guy is looking from right to left, and suddenly he looks from left to right." At which point he summons Peter Berling, demanding, "Fire this guy; he refuses do what I want." That's how it went all the time. And he wasn't joking. Everyone knew it. He was highly impulsive, and he had fired a lot of people.

Gradually, things loosened up a bit. He realized that I enjoyed his approach to things, the way he let me know what he had in mind. There was a fist fight scene, for instance, quite a violent scene, which, under existing rules, would have been put in several shots, meaning one master shot, then cut to a closeup here, a face there. But he said, "Nope, that's not what I want. The brutality of a fist fight is more exciting, more explosive, if it's shot with a wide-angle lens. That way you see everything. Nothing is faked, everything is real." He would shove actors into situations which were far from make-believe. There is a scene where Katrin Schaake slaps Ulli Lommel for two solid minutes. It was real, and the audience knew it. It was a new approach, a new kind of reality. And so we gradually felt our way toward each other — though I never dreamt there would be a follow-up to this first movie.

*Were both of you — director and cinematographer — aware that you were trying something new which might eventually become valid, or was there initially a lack of understanding between yourself and Fassbinder?*

There was no lack of understanding. It is hard to make rules in this business, since the nature of film is constantly changing. There are no set rules. At the most you can say that one person sees things one way, another person sees them another way. Both views are valid. What matters is the narrative style of the director. Fassbinder made movies the way other people make newspapers. His movies were close to whatever was happening at the moment. He read a lot of newspapers. A great deal of topical material went into his work. Watching some of his movies today, you sometimes feel you are reading a thirty-year-old newspaper.

It was fascinating to work with him. Even with all his problems, he was a fascinating person. He was incredibly dynamic. But we had our arguments and disputes. He was very authoritarian. Our collaboration was never without friction, because I always asserted myself. I could afford it because I was more independent than the rest of the group. I could walk out that door and earn my living without him the next day, and he knew it. The others in the group needed to cater to their lord and master. Being fired would have meant the end of them. He resented my working with other directors between films. But I was not enamored of being identified as a "Fassbinder cinematographer."

Every time we started on a scene, he knew I would have ideas about it. It was like playing tennis. The better the partner, the better you yourself become. We egged each other on. That was how the 360 degree drive in *Martha* developed. I thought it would be great to start at one point of an ellipse and return to it in the end. So he said, "Why don't we take it a step further, drive around twice and make the actors spin around as well?" He always wanted to go one better, which, of course, was stimulating. You always got something in return. Or, let's say, most of the time.

*How did the creative process develop during your collaboration? Did you have detailed discussions after he finished a script? Were there storyboards? Did Fassbinder have definite ideas about the sequence of scenes? Everyone knows at what speed he produced. Was there time for rehearsals, or were decisions made on the spot?*

On the spot. He did not like lengthy preparations, which he left to the production designer, usually to Kurt Raab, or occasionally to me. Fassbinder needed a certain tension born of spontaneity. He didn't appear on location until the day of the shoot. He decided right there and then how a certain scene should be done. He never arrived with a preconceived idea only to realize that it wouldn't play in reality.

He did make preparations, of course, but they were on another level. We often watched movies together and discussed them later. He never had much time for experiments because he was such a workaholic. He was a director who pushed, sometimes even pursued his team through a movie. *Petra von Kant*, a two hour and ten minute movie, was filmed in ten days. He was not a man to put off or avoid decisions. There are directors who put off decisions because they don't dare decide. There are gifted directors, good directors, who suffer from decision-making anxieties. He was not like that. He was incredibly driven. But there was never much time for reflection.

*Working at that pace, did you sometimes look back and feel we could have done better here, we should have tried again there?*

Yes, of course. Watching a movie on the big screen, I often thought, "Oh man, I wish we had done that differently, that wasn't good, not good at all." When I watch those movies today, I am sometimes shocked at how primitive some of our methods were.

*I've never quite understood that. How did he reconcile his enormous ambition to the blunders he made?*

There were certain things he couldn't be bothered about. When a spotlight showed up in an upper corner of *Petra von Kant*, that really irritated me. It should not have occurred — but Fassbinder didn't really mind, since it didn't divert from the scene. A few people might notice, but most people wouldn't even see it. Technical perfection simply did not matter that much to him. What mattered was the timing of a scene, the correct rhythm. That had to be right at all times. That's what he always had his eye on.

And he was greatly concerned with the accuracy of the pictures. During *Petra von Kant*, the second movie we made together, we had a huge fight. We had thought up a final shot, a rather complicated pan, covering almost the entire space and ending in a closeup of Irm Hermann. We shot the setup and he asked, "Was that o.k.?" I said, "It wasn't quite the way we had planned it. I didn't quite get the timing." Looking at the frame through the viewer, he said, "That's not what I wanted." Said I, "At that moment, it was impossible to do any other way." This led to quite a fight. He said, "I want precisely the pictures we discussed before. And if you don't do them, I'll look for someone else." So I said, "O.k., you look for someone else." And I left. I wasn't just going to cater to his wishes. We patched it up in the end. But there were constant arguments. There was always this friction.

*In 1970, you did a documentary,* Fassbinder Produces Film No. 8.

I wanted to get a grip on his working methods. I was so involved in production that there was little chance to reflect on or even observe what was actually going on. So I had this idea of doing a portrait of him. At the time, he was planning *The American Soldier* with Dietrich Lohmann. I wanted to observe him during the film and learn a little of what his work was all about. I approached Westdeutscher Rundfunk and asked if they might be interested. They said yes, they liked the idea very much. We were given DM 30,000 for this forty-five or fifty minute movie. But I needed a guaranty for the money. In those days, none of us had much money. Rainer was the only one who always had some funds tucked away. So I asked him about the guaranty, and he said, "Sure, I can give you that."

But as soon as we started, he did everything to boycott the project. He banned me from the set, refused to let me interview him. At first, he thought he could control what I was doing. Then he found that he no longer could, because I was interviewing Hanna Schygulla or Peter Berling or whomever. So he became suspicious. He was afraid somebody might say things he didn't like. So he torpedoed the whole thing as much as he could. The portrait turned into something in which he barely figured at all. His personality was encompassed by other people's reflections. In the end, however, the film did reveal something about him, perhaps more than if he had actually talked about himself.

*How about his work with other cinematographers? How did you decide when to work with him and vice versa?*

There were a variety of reasons. When he was planning the television series *Eight Hours Don't Make a Day*, he wanted me to sign on. I said, "That's a long committment. Find a job for my wife, who is an actress, so we can be together." He thought about it and told me, "I see your point, but in that case I'll make the movie with Lohmann." Or, another time, I had an offer to do *Summer Visitors* with Peter Stein. Now and then, projects overlapped. I would have liked to do *Effi Briest*, but that coincided with another project. Sometimes it simply didn't work out.

*After 1975, in movies like* Satan's Brew, Chinese Roulette, The Stationmaster's Wife, Despair, *and, finally,* Maria Braun, *Fassbinder's movies started to be more accessible to the audience. Did this development express your own interest in shaping and interconnecting pictures? Or did he just allow it to take its course?*

He never allowed anything to just take its course. He was far too interested in the process. But by and by, a strong mutual understanding developed between us — which doesn't mean that we always agreed. It's just that our relationship graduated to another level. We no longer had these constant confrontations. We knew what we could accomplish together. Three movies evolved in that period, which are interesting with regard to our collaboration. One was *Chinese Roulette*, a movie which I find impossible to watch today but which had a special meaning for us then. There the camera turned into a person, an actor, so to speak. We developed a very precise and interesting visual language. I learned an incredible amount while we shot it, and our work was surprisingly harmonious. By the way, only three months elapsed between the idea and the finished product — the fastest work of my entire career.

Rainer had been given a grant. So he said, "Let's make a movie. What shall we make?" We first chose the actors and decided on the locations. I told him, "We own this house in Franconia. We might do it there. It's quite a beautiful location." Rainer went to Paris for a couple of weekends and returned with the script. We decided to shoot the movie in our house, and I realized that this was bound to end in disaster. Rainer, who goes out every night, who constantly needs to be surrounded by people, in a place where there was no entertainment for miles. The nearest bar was in Schweinfurt, and it was very boring. I thought it was going to be awful but it turned out to be the exact opposite. We were all together in that house, we lived together, ate together, spent every evening together playing Chinese roulette. Of course, we also tore each other to pieces. But Rainer felt he had a family, and in the end he didn't want to leave. A lot of crazy things happened, but he felt at home and never even left the house. It was a strange experience.

The second movie of that phase was *The Stationmaster's Wife*, one of my favorite movies apart from *Maria Braun*. We had perfected a style which was highly artificial but very interesting. We were trying to write a subtext with the camera; the camera would express what the actors did not say. The camera told the story on its own, conveying to the audience an emotion that had not derived from the dialogue but could be a counterpoint to what was being said. In *Bolwieser* this came out quite beautifully. We also had very good actors. Aesthetically and structurally it may have been the most interesting movie of that era.

The problem came with *Maria Braun*, the last movie we did together. Originally, Rainer hadn't wanted to make the movie. He had written the scripts for *Berlin Alexanderplatz*. For three months he had churned out text at the rate of twelve hours a day. Suddenly he wasn't in the mood to make this movie anymore. He procrastinated, delayed over and over again, until Michael Fengler told him, "If you won't make it, I will." Next day Rainer appears on the set. He simply could not let that happen. Rainer put the brakes on in the most incredible way. He dismissed every location as shit, just to gain time. He offered no objective reasons, and there weren't any.

We were somehow coming to an end with *Maria Braun*. When it was over, I thought we'd better leave it at that.

*How do you define the relationship between director and cinematographer?*

It would take a book to analyze the process. It is a combination of mutual understanding and the dynamics of egging each other on to greatness. One person says this, the other says that and, as a result, ideas are set in motion. Rainer rarely interfered when it came to lighting. But when he appeared on the set, he knew that this is the essence of the story, this is what I want to relate, this is what is important. But then there were also scenes he considered transitory. I learned in my work with him that there must be those moments that allow you to catch your breath. You can't just tack one major scene onto the next. In those days, we were much more limited in our resources than I am in my work in the States today.

During *The Stationmaster's Wife* we had a few very long pans and complicated setups, which would probably require twice the time and three times the money today. There were times when I felt his pressure and passed it on to the team.

It taught me to be extremely precise, meticulous, and quick, which later helped me a lot in the States. But it's hard to describe exactly how these things came about. There is a beginning, a thread you spin, which is always a combination of things. A great deal came from him, of course.

*You have known three "icons" of the Young German Cinema: Fassbinder, Schlöndorff, and Wenders. Where do you see the essential differences between the directors you worked with in the seventies? How does Fassbinder stand out?*

Fassbinder's great forte was that he was able to work with people as a group. Although, in retrospect, it doesn't seem all that clear whether this forte always produced cinematic works of art. Some of the films we did together, such as *Beware of a Holy Whore*, I find pretty awful when I see them today. I also find *Fox and his Friends* pretty awful. About ten years ago, at a workshop in Mexico, I saw *Petra von Kant*. That still holds up. Strangely enough, it still works because of the characters and the story. *The Stationmaster's Wife* also holds up. I never saw *Martha* again, which lately has been reissued. I am sure there is something vibrant left in *Martha*, which was incredibly intense work. Certainly, *Maria Braun* will prevail. So much for our collaboration.

He made quite a few beautiful movies in later years. I never wanted to see *Querelle*. Too sad for my taste. But I saw the others and recognized many things we had developed together. When you open a twenty-year-old newspaper, you still find interesting items which evoke that era. He very accurately reflected his time in his movies, perhaps best and most precisely in *Ali: Fear Eats the Soul* and *Maria Braun*. But then there are newspapers you open and say, "What a bore. It seems so dated. It has lost all interest because it happened so long ago." There are many movies, where I think, "Good God, did I make that?" At the time, Fassbinder was interesting, which doesn't mean that Wim Wenders or Volker Schlöndorff may not have made better movies. Since he made so many movies, he was fashioned into something that should gradually be brought down to realistic proportions. Of course, he was gifted and he made some very good movies, but he also made an incredible amount of junk.

He was a symbol of his time. Perhaps his work stopped when that time came to an end. To my mind, he had reached the end with *Querelle*. His life had come full circle. There wasn't much left, which is why his death had a certain logic. He had never lived like a normal person, wanting to live till eighty. He lived twice as intensely as the rest of us. Work was all he had in life. Everything else was of secondary importance.

# GOTTFRIED JOHN

*B*orn *in Berlin in 1942, Mr. John graduated from drama school in 1963 and immediately thereafter started to work in the theater. In 1972, Fassbinder hired him to act in the television mini-series* Eight Hours Don't Make a Day. *Their collaboration continued at TAT in Frankfurt, in the movies* Despair, The Marriage of Maria Braun, In a Year with 13 Moons, Berlin Alexanderplatz, *and* Lili Marleen. *At that time he also worked with other directors, such as Billy Wilder (in* Fedora*), Rudolf Noelte, Peter Beauvais, Michael Verhoeven, and Hans W. Geissendörfer. He lives in New-Moresnet in Belgium, where the interview was conducted.*

## SOMEONE WHO FINDS EASY
## WHAT OTHERS FIND HARD

*Did you have a special relationship with Rainer?*

Everyone who got involved with Rainer was convinced he had a very personal, very direct relationship with him and assumed that only he counted in Rainer's life. Besides, Rainer himself went through these abrupt changes. One time he would be a fat, ugly slob, the next time he would be trim and sparkling, like a young Marlon Brando. There were awesome changes.

*You first met in* Eight Hours Don't Make a Day.

It was our first collaboration. By then, I had worked in the theater for ten years. I had played the great classics, Richard III, Macbeth, Oberon,

Marat, etc. at a relatively early age. This set me apart from the other people around Rainer, who more or less had been made by him. But I never wanted to be in the theater. I wanted to be in movies. I was a product of the James Dean and Marlon Brando era. I landed in the theater because that was how you became an actor. But I really wanted to do movies.

I went to Bavaria Studios, the only address I knew. The casting director said, "Why do you want to be in movies? With your looks, you'd be better off in the theater." As an aspiring actor, I had heard similar remarks before. I flunked the entrance exams at Max Reinhardt Drama School in Berlin: not talented. So I went and had some coffee. Something told me I would get into the movies, deep down I just knew. Then suddenly this long-haired character came up and talked to me. "I hear you're from the theater and you want to do movies. I write film scripts, and we are looking for a leading man. Would you be willing to do a screen test?" So we did a screen test. He said, "You're from the theater. Forget everything you've learned. Forget art. You're not supposed to act at all." "If that's all," I thought, "maybe the camera will do the acting too." At the end of the session, he said, "Beautiful, excellent, you'll hear from us." A week later he called to say the screen test had turned out badly, that I had no screen presence, but he was convinced I was right for the part. Would I do another screen test? "Sure," I said. The second time I definitely did act but made sure the director didn't notice. That was it. "Great, beautiful," the director said. "Didn't I tell you not to act at all?" So much for the movies. It made me somewhat suspicious of movie directors, who evidently don't notice how actors create. At any rate, this got me my first movie part.

*And the movie got you an agent . . .*

And the agent calls one and said that there's this young filmmaker who's doing a family series who would like to meet me. One Sunday I drove out to the country, to some small village, where we were supposed to meet. But he wasn't there. I was pissed and ready to go back. Suddenly this rotund, pimply guy shows up, and I know that's him. I had seen his photograph. "Are you Fassbinder?" I ask. "Yes," says he. "Why?" "Listen," I say, "we had an appointment. I was about to go home." "Well," he says, "now we're here."

We went into the pub and there was the whole gang. Everybody looked at me in this distant sort of way. Then we argued a lot about whether I should have gone home and whether or not the appointment was important. He said that if he had been in my place, he would have gone home. So I said, "O.k., I'll go home. Makes no difference to me."

And he goes, "Would we be able to stand each other for six months?" "Don't know," I say. "Remains to be seen." So he goes, "O.k. then, let's do it." That was it.

We were off to quite a bad start. I had long hair and I was told that the workers in *Eight Hours Don't Make a Day* were wearing their hair short. "I wouldn't dream of it," I said. "Why should I cut my hair? These days, workmen have long hair, too. Tell Fassbinder from me that Jochen, the worker I am playing, wears his hair long." I remember being utterly amazed that a group who was working on a project about moral courage, about resistance against meaningless orders, would uncritically follow the orders of their master, as he was already called in those days. Hanna Schygulla was the only one who never took part in this group behavior. At any rate, the master accepted my long hair. But we didn't get along very well and had little to say to each other.

We were sizing each other up. I remember how he once passed me in the WDR building, looking straight ahead, while he stepped right on and over my foot. I thought he must be crazy. Then I saw him standing in a corner somewhere. So I went over and stepped on his foot. We looked at each other, laughing a little. That was it. Our first real contact. Never spoke to each other. At one time I said to him, "People always say you are a genius. How do you figure that?" So he goes, "Genius is when someone finds easy what others find hard." I liked that phrase.

Then the shoot began. I was terribly nervous. He never told me what I was supposed to do. He said that after all, I was the one who was playing the character, and that he could play it better anyway. If I was a good actor, I should know how to play the part. We were shooting in a factory shed. In one scene he blew his top but I couldn't hear what he was saying on account of the acoustics. Rainer had a low, muffled voice. So I raised my stage voice above all those engines, shouting that if there was something he wanted from me, he'd better come over and tell me. He sent word through his assistant that he would not have John shout at him. And I replied that I wasn't shouting at him, I just couldn't hear him. But he kept on escalating. Then the leading lady was re-cast and he said it had all been my fault. He had this idea that I was turning on the girls on camera. He wanted Hanna for the part, but Hanna didn't want to do it.

*According to Peter Märthesheimer, the other actress had been miscast.*

But he put the blame on me. We were off to a bumpy start. For a while we didn't speak at all, except through others. We would sit next to each other and I would say to the guy on my right, "Tell Rainer I find this such or such." And Rainer would tell someone on his left, "Ask Gottfried if he would do such and such in that scene." In those days, I considered him a ruthless despot, but I could handle that. I really liked the way he directed. I, too, had been raised in an orphanage. We had that in common. I always treated our fights like a game, whether with words or fists. He was a great partner. He always came up with something new.

*He wasn't exactly predictable, was he?*

No, and there was nothing traditonal about his way of directing, either. One day, for instance, we were shooting a tender love scene. Hanna and I are in bed, kissing and so on. So Rainer says, "The technicians tell me that you took this fat girl up to your room last night. Everybody but you knows she has V.D." "Who told you that lie?" I angrily snap back at him. "Last night, I was learning my lines for today's shoot." So Rainer goes, "Ah well, none of my business. Let's go back to the love scene. You two are in bed, kissing. I don't have to tell you anything about that scene." He didn't. Hanna loathed me, but I tried to be tender. The perfect lovers. He was determined not to get a routine romantic scene in bed.

It was his way of emancipating people, not letting them get stuck in clichés. To me he always appeared like a child in the playground, taking things apart, not because he is mean but because he wants to know what's inside. Children wreck a lot, but they also experience more and know more. Like artists who question everything, who take things apart and put them together again in another way. It's a question of courage, which has nothing to do with good or evil or traditional morals. In this respect, Rainer was more courageous than the rest of us.

*I still find* Eight Hours Don't Make a Day *an incredibly fresh, witty, intelligent series.*

Well, I think the basic idea behind it was supposed to be something about the positive side of anarchy, that with common sense people can emancipate themselves. With sufficient self-determination, everybody — the audience, the manager and, last but not least, the actor — can overcome authoritarian concepts and change himself and society. The idea was packaged in an ordinary family series: a feasible utopia, in a way, which made it provocative. I only remember bad reviews. They called the series unrealistic. Workers, who were interviewed, said, "Bullshit. There's nothing like that in our shop. We are decent workers." I remember a photograph of myself in a television magazine. The caption read, "Ugly is beautiful again."

*Did working with him teach you to emancipate yourself?*

I wouldn't go that far! At that time I thought, "Never again, not with this guy." The more I saw through these group games, the less I enjoyed them.

*Did you get offers after* Eight Hours ... ?

Not one! It was over, finished, the absolute end. I was toolmaker Jochen of the factory. People actually thought Rainer had discovered me at work in the factory. I was this Jochen — not an actor who had created the character.

I had been attracted to the idea of playing the boy next door. I had already played major stage roles. I had played two dramatic movie parts. But could I just be the boy next door? To my intense embarrassment, I succeeded so perfectly that it threw me and my career for a loop. I dropped out entirely. I went back to the theater in Hamburg with Peymann. Then Neuenfels, who lived in Frankfurt, asked me to work with him again and play *Liliom* with Elisabeth Trissenaar.

*At Schauspielhaus?*

Yes. I played *Liliom* and got involved in that artistic cooperative business before I realized that all those lofty political discussions were actually about small fries trying to play big shots. It was a total farce. I thought, this is no artistic cooperative, it's sheer madness. Then I hear that Fassbinder is joining TAT, and that he, too, is now in favor of a cooperative cult.

*They had collective management at TAT before Rainer arrived. But once he had adopted it, he took it seriously.*

Then I read in the papers that Fassbinder was forming an ensemble with Karlheiz Böhm *and Gottfried John*! It was news to me! "He must be crazy," I thought, "mentioning me as part of his ensemble." We hadn't spoken a single word since I left.

*He was very interested in you.*

Apparently. We met and he was charming; no, he was angelic. And

I said, "Listen. I'll join you at TAT, but I don't want to play more than two leads a year, and I want to direct." Says Rainer, "No problem. After all, it's a cooperative. People do whatever they want."

Rainer let it be known that he wanted Kurt Raab to be deputy-director. So, lo and behold, Kurt was elected by a landslide. I learned a lot about democracy in those days. The third director, Petri, was a city functionary, a political appointment. He was the schoolmaster, so to speak, who made the children behave. As the only fool who would always argue with Rainer, I was elected speaker of the ensemble. In order to be able to properly inform the ensemble, I asked to attend the board meetings. Rainer objected. We argued until four in the morning. I finally won and was allowed to attend the meetings, albeit without a vote.

This is how the first board meeting functioned: the two directors, Rainer and Kurt Raab, were summoned to Herr Petri's office. They arrived around ten. Herr Petri said, "Herr Fassbinder, as the artistic director you must..." Rainer sat down, plunking his boots on Petri's desk. Petri tugged at his necktie, saying, "I won't have you provoke me. I've been told that you are not in your office every morning at eight." And Rainer said, "That's a lie. The entire Socialist Party is lying. You're just pissed because you have to be in the office every morning at eight. Not me. I'm leaving. So long. I'm going on vacation." That was the end of the board of directors meeting.

*What were your other responsibilities?*

Each of us had about ten jobs at any one time. I was criticized for only having taken on five jobs: leading man, director, associate dramaturg, press chief, and head of poster pasting. I wasn't earning my three thousand marks, you see. There were constantly big discussions about tiny issues and severe punishment meted out for every infraction. Reports were written, duties reassigned, people demoted from office. All this with productions in progress.

*You were part of the* Miss Julie *production.*

Rainer wanted a woman to direct it. I was disappointed personally but thought it was interesting. First, there was Frau Brocher, and eventually it was Ula Stöckl. Rainer was only going to act. He wanted nothing to do with directing. But, of course, he couldn't help himself. There was a costume conference. Kurt Raab dropped by and said, the last thing Rainer wants is to interfere, but he was thinking leather for costumes.

Wow, I thought, that's an idea. Miss Julie in leather! It made me think of the whole gay leather scene. Then Ula says, "Yes, that's a good idea. Jean is wearing this vest with little leather buttons." That's when I quit as dramaturg. If he says leather and she understands little leather buttons, these guys obviously don't see eye to eye. Two weeks later, Irm, Margit, and Rainer asked us, the associate dramaturgs, to drop by. The rehearsals weren't going so well.

We took one look and said it's the Firing Squad.

### *Firing Squad?*

The Firing Squad meant raking someone over the coals until he quit. Oh, the cooperative life could be brutal. Out of sheer mischief, I said, "I think this rehearsal is quite good but I find it too cinematic. It should be more theatrical." As a result, I was apppointed assistant director to Ula Stöckl, and got a little closer to directing. But arguments kept cropping up. In the end, Ula Stöckl was dismissed and I was appointed director. Voilà, I started directing like crazy.

Rainer hadn't memorized his lines. I told him, "I can't rehearse with you like this. Guess I'll have to rehearse with Margit instead." Margit was getting better and better all the time. He didn't like that. He took me aside and said, "Listen, Marlene Dietrich had Sternberg . . . if you have Margit take it away from me, I'll probably get sick. And if I do get sick, the entire production is going to collapse. In that case, none of the prominent directors who are supposed to direct here — Douglas Sirk, for instance — will come either." "I certainly don't want to be blamed for the collapse of TAT," I said. "Then the opening must be canceled," said Rainer, "You are the director; better break it to Margit gently." "No way," I said, "I want the opening. It's your fault. Tell Margit yourself." He didn't dare do that. So we went on with the rehearsals.

Then Rainer asked the ensemble to watch the play. This was supposed to be a firing squad aimed at me. Margit is upset and gets stuck in her lines. Rainer interrupts, kisses her hand, bows to the ensemble, as the great Gustaf Gründgens used to do. He regretfully shrugs his shoulders and leads her off the stage. However, the ensemble actually likes what they have seen so far. There is a vote: the opening is to take place; Gottfried is to continue.

Then comes the second dress rehearsal, and I think I'm dreaming. Rainer suddenly plays Jean as a queen! He plays a flaming queen throughout the entire performance. During the critique, I attempt to give Rainer a note, "Forgive me, Rainer, but I don't think Jean is a queen." "Who? Me a queen? My heart is bleeding on stage and and all you can say is that I am playing a queen." He calls the ensemble together and says, "I can't act with Gottfried watching from below..." The opening is about to take place, and all of a sudden the director is barred from attending the rehearsals. Moreover, the lighting still needs to be done. So I said, "I can't very well do the lighting, if I'm not allowed to attend rehearsals." I was dismissed as director and Ula Stöckl was reappointed. The posters read: Stage manager — Gottfried John. Director — Ula Stöckl. The critics called it an interesting, sensitive ensemble performance.

*He told me he felt terrible going on stage every day. He was scared of acting and scared of the audience.*

He was immensely talented, a very good actor. He was very direct; an extremely strong presence. He spoke his lines in such an immediate way; it was fascinating.

*People had high praise for your integrity..*

My bluntness, you mean. I was surrounded by constant chaos. But it was a very exciting chaos. I learned an awful lot. Not that we ever did art; we were too busy fully giving of ourselves, passing on ideas as they came into our heads.

*The TAT era was quite brief. Just one season, 1974–75.*

That's true. But the story isn't over. I continued directing and eventually even Rainer became quite enthusiastic. I was allowed to select a play, and I chose *Saved* by Edward Bond. But I couldn't seem to cast the character of Pam out of the ensemble. As a hetero, I found all the women extremely unattractive. When the ensemble met in conference, people said, "How is this guy supposed to direct if he finds all the women unattractive?" Hence, a vote: by a very slim majority, I was allowed to continue. Then there was another conference, which I did not attend. There it was decided — listen to this — that only pre-Fascistoid plays should be staged.

*"Pre-Fascistoid" plays?*

My question exactly. Rainer walked into his rehearsal of *Uncle Vanya*, in which I played the title role. "I suppose," he said, "you've heard about yesterday's meeting — sorry, only pre-Fascistoid plays." I argued with him. *Saved* had something to do with Fascism? My face must have betrayed grave disappointment. He pointed to my belly and asked, "Does that hurt?" "Yes," I said. Then he pointed to my heart, "That, too?" "Yes," I said. He pointed to my head, "That, too? I'm sorry," Rainer said, "let's continue rehearsing *Uncle Vanya*. Where were we? You were entering from the right." Yet I no longer remembered those steps, nor did I remember my lines, nothing at all. Rainer said, "I want you to sign a written promise that tomorrow you will know your lines." "Rainer," I said, "I'll sign anything but this really hurts. I can't remember a thing. I'm leaving." And I left. Rainer came to see me, "Don't think I don't want you to direct." "I said, "I believe you, but first you say *Saved* is not a pre-Fascistoid play, then you let me do it. But no date has been set for the opening. And we don't have a leading lady." Thereupon he: "That's no problem. We'll get you a leading lady, and we'll set a date for the opening." Rainer recommended a leading lady, and I started rehearsing. I had gathered together a pretty unruly ensemble. They were all fighting among themselves. But I managed to keep them more or less in line. "Rainer will try to do something to prevent the performance," I warned them. Rainer was furious. He said it was a colossal insinuation, and he would prove it false by going away until the day of the opening. So Rainer took off, leaving me feeling embarrassed. The day of the opening approaches, however, and the leading lady tells me, "I can't play on opening night. Rainer has sent me a wire. He wants me to play the lead in his movie, which happens to coincide with the opening." Rainer was right on cue.

*Did the opening take place?*

Yes, and the reviews were very good. But TAT no longer wanted us; we were too chaotic.

*Your story makes me realize how much Rainer changed. In later years, this kind of chaos no longer existed. But then the crowd around him wasn't the same, either.*

Rainer had a lot on his plate with this ensemble. Those votes alone — no sooner had we reached an agreement, than people would change their minds again. It drove him up the wall.

*But you continued to work with Rainer.* Mother Küsters' Journey to Heaven *was filmed in 1975, after the TAT era.*

I also had problems in *Mother Küsters*. There was a bed scene. I knew Rainer's male actors often performed naked.

*Whom was the scene with?*

He was directing a love scene with his former wife, Ingrid Caven. It took place in a loft bed which could only be reached by a ladder. He said, "Here is the setup: you two have slept together and now you're kissing. I'll show you." Rainer clambers up the ladder in his boots and leather jacket and pounces on Ingrid. I tell him, "Let me do it. I do that much more subtly. After all, I'm playing the part." "O.k." he says, "you do it." And I say, "Ingrid, I'm not going to take off my clothes, o.k.?" She says, "Neither will I." The shoot is about to start when I see Ingrid in her bra, one tit hanging out. I don't believe it. So I climb up the ladder in my underpants. Rainer says, "After you've kissed, the phone rings downstairs. Gottfried climbs down the ladder to answer it. Without his pants, of course. Remember, you've been sleeping together." I say, "What do you mean? The camera is down below, photographing me from behind while I climb down with my equipment dangling?" Rainer says, "What can I do? It's the situation." So I say, "There should be a cut. I won't take off my pants." And he: "Sorry, Gottfried, in that case I'll have to recast you and you'll be charged for the previous shooting days." "O.k.," I say, "I'll take that risk." He made the cut.

*A real stand off.*

Self defense. But there was something else this movie made me realize. Brigitte Mira had to leave the set briefly during rehearsals. Rainer spoke her lines offscreen. Here I am acting with him onscreen and suddenly I am seized by a laughing fit. Rainer has become Biggi. Rainer could be Hanna; Rainer could be whoever happened to be his leading lady. He actually became the beautiful woman — that was his emancipation. He identified with them. I finally understood how he structured his movies. To Rainer, those characters were objects of projection. He revealed the way he saw himself through them. He was always the other character, too.

He knew the psyche of his actors. That was his forte, and he used it to the hilt. I felt he was my negative alter ego, or the ego I rejected in myself. It caused friction between us.

I once told him, "Your view of the world is so negative. The way you approach the world is the same way the world is going to answer you back." I promptly found that line in the next part I was playing. He always inserted things like that. He enjoyed making actors play characters which revealed a part of themselves.

*Had he been a therapist, you might not have found that so frustrating.*

That's true. I didn't realize until much later how much strength he had given me, how much self-confidence, how much ability to reflect, how much daring. He dared me to come to terms with the negative aspects of myself. He was constantly changing your point of view. He could run circles around you.

*Reinhold in* Alexanderplatz *is one of the most beautiful characters you have played. Whose idea was the stammer?*

That's in the book. I managed to pull it off fairly well, perhaps dangerously well, because I'd had a stammer as a kid. I didn't get rid of it until I went to drama school. I revived my stammer for *Alexanderplatz*, but then I had trouble shaking it.

*How did the negative press campaign after* Alexanderplatz *affect you?*

It was ghastly. We were all very depressed. We knew the series was good. It was a work of art. The other sad fact was that I couldn't get any work after *Alexanderplatz*. The Fassbinder label simply counted against me, against all of us.

*What is important to you today when you think of Rainer?*

He was like a vast mirror. Dangerous, too, because he brought out people's negative sides. And, horrible as it may sound: he was right. In retrospect, I understand why he had this negative image of people. I didn't realize until later how right he was. My basic approach to people was always positive, because it made me feel more secure.

*Did he ever betray you?*

No, he never betrayed me. He tried to break me, it's true. But when he didn't succeed, he left me alone. He did try, though.

*How do you remember Rainer as a director?*

Oh, he pushed people in a certain way, to make them feel strong and tall. He told Hanna right from the beginning, "You are a star." To him, people were unique, the greatest, regardless of what they had done before. It was the essence of his personality.

*So you, too, felt like a star?*

Very much so. Rainer made me learn a lot about myself. I was always a little too arrogant for him, so, I frequently got hit over the head. It was a very exciting very creative state of tension. At a shoot, he insisted there would only be one slate, the first one: in other words, live right now, just as you never can repeat anything in real life. I learned that much from Rainer: keep your cool and remember there's only one chance, only one scene. It later helped me with American directors who shoot at a very fast pace.

*Are you asked about Rainer in your international work?*

Yes, often. Rainer has great prestige abroad, which gives me a lot of advantages. It's the red carpet I run on. I'm just sorry he didn't live to enjoy this enormous success. Many people still ask me today, "How did you stand it? That guy was such a tyrant. He used people." To which I reply, "If that had been my experience, I wouldn't have stuck around that long." Everything was a much broader question to Rainer, a question of freedom, love, loyalty, morals, politics. I think of Rainer as one of the most perceptive, couragous and lively people I've ever met.

# ERNST KÜSTERS

M*r. Küsters was born in 1930 in Düsseldorf, where he started his career as a gaffer. Beginning in 1958, he worked at Westdeutscher Rundfunk, rapidly advancing to head gaffer and, in 1975, to first lighting engineer. He was part of all the network's major television film productions until his retirement in 1993. The interview was conducted in Cologne.*

## TAKING YOURSELF SERIOUSLY

*Rainer respected everyone who knew and enjoyed his craft. And he thought very highly of you. You were said to be the "benevolent spirit" of the production department.*

He appreciated people who always gave their best. And he knew when they didn't. In our first collaboration, *Eight Hours Don't Make a Day*, he sized up people very closely. I had a colleague who was not all that interested in work. So Rainer said, "This guy just hangs around. Why don't you send him home?" He never missed a thing.

*When you first worked with him in 1972, you had already had many years of experience with established directors. Now here comes this young guy with barely three years of filmmaking.*

But he knew exactly what he was doing. He was better and quicker than the rest. It was fascinating to see, for instance, how he managed to shoot fifty-four setups in a day with no overtime or frenzy. He was the driving force and he carried the rest of us along. He would arrive on the set in the morning, open his script, sketch his little men, sketch every single camera position, every camera angle, the positions of the actors in relation to the camera. Then he would put a frame around it, hand it to the cinematographer, and say, "That's it. Let me know when you're finished." And he'd go off to play pinball.

When we were ready to shoot, we called him and the shooting would begin at once. There was only going to be one take and we knew it. As far as the camera is concerned, there are so many factors: the interaction between the cinematographer, the assistant who sets the focus, the dolly driver. It was a great effort for everyone to be at their best and totally focussed the very first take. Rainer was not only aware of this tension, he kept it up and passed it along to the crew.

*You worked with the first three of his cinematographers: Dietrich Lohmann on* Eight Hours Don't Make a Day, *Michael Ballhaus on* World on a Wire *and* Martha, *and Jürgen Jürges, who collaborated with Fassbinder on three pictures, the first being* Fear of Fear. *In* Fontane Effi Briest, *Dietrich Lohmann was the cinematographer of the first shooting phase; on the second one, a year later, it was Jürgen Jürges again.*

All three were outstanding. But Michael Ballhaus was an aspiring artist.

*How could you tell?*

It was obvious. In *Martha*, for instance, he asked the WDR production department to reserve outdated 16 mm conversion stock for him. He was trying to achieve a certain overall brown tone, particularly for the scenes in the villa, where Helmut Salomon and his wife move after their wedding. The brown tone was supposed to emphasize the story's mystical background.

Needless to say, the processing company kept trying to eliminate the brown tone from the material. When *Martha* was restored last year, because the color had faded, I had to explain to them that the color was intentional. Ballhaus wanted it that way.

*It seems to me that with* Martha *Rainer entered a new phase of visual perception and cinematographic conversion.*

There was a tendency, in those days not to use artificial light as long as daylight was available. Michael Ballhaus went the opposite way, supported and perhaps even inspired by Rainer. Ballhaus used artificial light even with available daylight. A red spot would later show in the window, which brought a certain excitement to the mood of the dark villa.

*How would you describe the collaboration between the cinematographer and the head gaffer?*

First off, you confer with the cinematographer who should have conferred earlier with the director. The head gaffer then sets up the basic lights. The cinematographer then determines the finer points.

*Did Fassbinder give a lot of directions?*

His directions were very precise, and we followed them.

*Did the crew still look at the rushes? After* Berlin Alexanderplatz, *Rainer only wanted to see the finished cut. Were you present when the rushes were shown?*

Every day. It was very important to him. It was also important to us, because each of us wanted and needed to see what had been shot at such speed and with so much fun. But he never let the actors see the rushes. He considered it inappropriate.

*In* Fontane Effi Briest, *Rainer was particularly proud that the camera change was not noticeable in the movie, from part one, shot by Dietrich Lohman, to the second part, shot by Jürgen Jürges.*

Jürges is a wonderful cinematographer. I particularly remember an interim cut we were supposed to shoot of Hanna Schygulla. We didn't have much money. We had to skimp in every area. We brought along all sorts of props. Jürges asked me to get some black felt and a glass table. When everything was assembled, we did some very elaborate lighting. The result was a picture in a slanted mirror which, through refraction, was reflected in the glass table. The reflection in the table magnified the picture, making it seem as though she was looking at a picture of herself.

*A typical "Fassbinder" setup.*

Though it was Jürgen Jürges' idea, who, of course, knew exactly what Rainer liked and considered important.

*What made you and Rainer become friends after working hours?*

That's hard to describe. He liked me and I liked him. We liked to meet in pubs, just talking about life. He was incredibly aware and knew exactly what the other person liked. Once he had a pinball machine delivered to me. I kept it in my apartment for several years. My wife and I and the children had a lot of fun playing it.

*I assume Rainer's habit of giving presents to his collaborators — which, incidentally, he kept up to the very end — was not common practice in the movie business.*

You can say that again.

*What do you find most special about his movies?*

He presented the audience with something new, unknown, and unusual. He made you see yourself as a thinking human being. He forced you to take yourself seriously. Very few filmmakers consciously intend to or are able to do this.

# MARGARETHE VON TROTTA

B orn in 1942 in Berlin, Ms. von Trotta studied German and French literature in Munich and Paris. In Munich she attended and graduated from drama
school. She made her first stage appearances in Stuttgart and Frankfurt before
going on to act in movies by Klaus Lemke, Volker Schlöndorff, Rainer Werner
Fassbinder, Reinhard Hauff, Claude Chabrol, and Herbert Achternbusch. In
1970, she began writing movie scripts of her own. In 1975, she and Volker
Schlöndorff filmed The Lost Honor of Katharina Blum. Since then she has
directed her own movies, among them The Second Awakening of Christa
Klages, The German Sisters, and, in 1994, The Promise. In 1978, she was
awarded the Film Prize of the German Federal Republic; in 1981, the Golden
Lion in Venice; in 1994, the Konrad Wolf Prize. She is a member of the Berlin
Academy of the Arts. The interview was conducted in Berlin.

## A SURE INSTINCT

*How did you and Rainer meet?*

I first met Rainer with Volker Schlöndorff who wanted him for the
lead in *Baal*.

*I was told Rainer had approached Volker with his two short films and had
begged him to let him play* Baal.

As far as I know, that's not quite true. Volker and I had seen *Anarchy
in Bavaria* in the theater workshop of Kammerspiele. Earlier we had seen
*Love Is Colder Than Death*, which had greatly impressed us, especially

Rainer's acting. When we met him, there was no question but that he would play *Baal*. Volker never even considered anyone else. He had good instincts about people and instantly recognized Fassbinder's potential. Rainer didn't have to beg him for the part. But he did try to wangle as many parts as possible for his antiteater friends.

*He tried that?*

Volker agreed to hire five or six antiteater people. Hanna Schygulla and Kurt Raab were among them; also Irm Hermann and Rudolf Waldemar Brem.

*What was your first impression of Rainer?*

He was sitting at a table and didn't say a word, but you felt something powerful churning inside. When we were shooting *Baal* I was fascinated by his enormous capacity for work. All the things he could do at the same time! As you know, Baal is the absolute leading role with a monumental text. Not an ordinary text, either. Those lines really must be memorized. He never made a single mistake.

He was an extraordinarily disciplined actor who, at night, edited his movie *Katzelmacher* and also wrote a radio play. All this while we were shooting from dawn to dusk.

When we were filming *Beware of a Holy Whore* in Sorrento, he would go on three or four hours of sleep. Like Pasolini. There are people like that — often people who freely, almost obsessively, give rein to their sexuality, without becoming intellectually or artistically drained. They derive special spiritual and creative power from their excesses. Pasolini wrote and filmed like a maniac all day, and went out at night in pursuit of male lovers. I sometimes wonder if those people know that their lives will be short and therefore need to burn their candle on both ends, frantically living for the moment.

*Were there similarities between Volker and Rainer?*

Volker is the complete opposite of Fassbinder who, from the start, filmed with the utmost economy, cutting in the camera, the very cut he has had in his head all along.

Volker always had doubts about himself. It is one of his basic characteristics. Whenever he shoots a setup he wonders whether it has been the right one, so he reverses the whole thing and shoots it from the opposite angle, only to discard it again just as fast.

*In 1969, Volker was the undisputed star of the German cinema.*

Rainer told me he had seen *A Degree of Murder [Mord und Totschlag]* at least ten times. It was probably the reason why he never hesitated to work with Volker.

*Was Volker the reason you became an actress?*

No. Like Rainer, he had seen me in a movie and, as a result, offered me a part in *Baal*. I only met Rainer two months after I'd met Schlöndorff. Actually, I always wanted to direct myself. I accepted small parts because I was interested in the directors. I wanted to see how they worked, and wanted to learn something from them. There was a lot to learn from Rainer, for instance, the way he focussed on the essence of things. His sure instinct in making decisions was not a matter of learning but of perception, such as his choreography in the course of a long, single setup.

*I have often heard that Rainer tried to prevent gifted people from getting to the top.*

Rainer often found that people he supported failed to deliver what he wanted. He believed in the abilities of his collaborators, such as Michael Fengler, Christian Hohoff, and Ulli Lommel, and helped them make their own movies. He didn't ask for proof but simply said, "Go ahead." This is unusual; normally, it is the reverse in our society.

*Was he vindictive when he found himself disappointed?*

He was very sure of himself and his dream. That's why he made it come true. That's also why he believed in others and allowed them to have their dreams. I often reassure myself with a quotation from Goethe, "Wishes are premonitions of abilities." Fassbinder attributed those abilities to many of his collaborators and he helped them realize them, although sometimes he was forced to admit that the power to make it come true was not as strong as the dream had been, or that there was not enough substance to the dream. Not everybody had Rainer's perseverance and discipline.

*Can you illustrate this tendency?*

In *Gods of the Plague*, the first movie I made with him, he let Fengler direct for days on end. This was more than a little confusing. We were committed to Fassbinder and there was a considerable difference in talent and imagination between the two. We felt abandoned whenever he wasn't around. There was no inspiration when he was away from the set.

*What was your sense of the group dynamic?*

Most people had a very tense, emotional relationship with Rainer. Since I was not, strictly speaking, part of the group, I was probably more independent. Without Rainer the group would have been lost. People depended on his strength and his imagination, but he also needed them. Without them, he would have been at the mercy of his loneliness, and that would have been hard on him.

Rainer could also be quite obnoxious. The more people depended on him, the worse he treated them. Maybe he needed their dependence, but he also despised them for it. He wasn't like that with me, nor with Hanna. She never allowed herself to be fully integrated. She and I were the only ones he treated with respect because he knew one nasty crack and we'd have been out the door. He had very sharp instincts. He knew precisely how far he could go with people, though he was particularly fond of those who depended on him and put up with his tantrums. "Despised though loved," was what his movies were about. I myself was rather scared of this subliminal game of power and helplessness, this spiderweb game. I think it was one of the reasons why I never wanted to be part of the group.

*What triggered this fear of closeness tied to the fierce desire to be part of the group which they all shared?*

Under normal circumstances, as soon as shooting starts an ensemble is formed — a particular group behavior. You don't want to go home at the end of the day or meet anybody who doesn't have anything to do with the movie. Nevertheless, everybody has a different background and a life of his own. During Rainer's early movies, the group also lived together after work. A lot went on among them which surfaced only sporadically, which was rarely expressed. Yet there was always something throbbing, like a power plant. Sometimes the tension became too much even for Rainer. He'd withdraw to preserve himself, to preserve his talent. It wasn't always easy to constantly be in the presence of such an enormously talented person. They admired him, but at the same time they resented him because he made them aware of their own inferiority or inadequacy. It wasn't his fault, yet they blamed him for their inadequacies, as though he were the god who had denied them greater gifts.

I experienced something similar in my own life. In those days, I was known as Schlöndorff's actress, not to mention his wife; I was "part of" him. Except for Fassbinder and Achternbusch, very few had the courage to deal with me, i.e., indirectly with Volker. They must have felt Schlöndorff's eyes were watching them over my shoulder. I am sure this same fear was palpable around Fassbinder: Fassbinder is watching, and he is a genius; maybe I'm not as good as I think I am, and I'd rather not put that to the test.

*You make very political movies. How did Rainer translate politics in his movies?*

The most successful example of how a personal testimony can be translated into a political statement is Rainer's episode in *Germany in Autumn*. He described an atmosphere which concerned us all and the fear that throttled us in 1977, the year of the witch hunt against Leftist sympathizers — it was not so much a documentary as a documentation of his own fear. It really was a shocker. He was not afraid to expose his fear.

*At that time he not only was afraid of what the German government might start in retaliation for the hijacking in Mogadishu, he also was afraid of what his failed personal relationship had triggered. His contribution tried to make both fears visible. When you knew him, was Rainer incapable of personal relationships, particularly with women?*

No, I never saw it that way. At one time, he even proposed to me, although I believe he knew he could safely do so because I wouldn't take him up on it. He certainly needed to rid himself of the women who clung to him.

*"When you love, you are nailed to the cross," Rainer once noted on a piece of paper. He quoted this line in the scene with Soul-Frieda in* In a Year with 13 Moons.

Maybe the free, independent love people always dream of doesn't really exist.

*Can you work without love?*

Of course not. Yet, people try to win love, each in their own way. I also try to be loved by the people I work with, not by playing them against each other, but by trying to enable them to be to be together and work together.

# THEO HINZ

$B$orn in 1931 in a Pomeranian village, Mr. Hinz often skipped school to go to the movies. He trained in advertising (early PR-movies for aviation), and in 1955 landed at Constantin, then a large motion picture company, where he soon became the head of its marketing department. In 1977, Rudolf Augstein appointed him executive director of Filmverlag der Autoren, a position which he held until March 1996.

## THE ORIGINAL

*At what point did you intersect with Rainer's career?*

By the time I became involved with him, Fassbinder was already well known. I had been linked to the New German Cinema very early on and, in those days, had many friends among filmmakers who were working in Munich: Schlöndorff, Alexander Kluge, Edgar Reitz.

Originally, Constantin had been something like a department store. When I joined it in 1955, it was one of many motion picture companies. But then it became a leading distributor. In those days, American movies played a minor role. They were given whatever slots happened to be left. Obviously, Constantin mainly took care of the New German Cinema. The first time I saw a movie by Rainer was at the Mannheim Film Festival in 1969. I also met him, but he didn't mean anything to me and I meant even less to him.

*At what point did you get turned on to his work?*

The first movie I really took in was *The Merchant of Four Seasons*, which deeply affected me. I was also greatly moved by *Why Does Herr R. Run Amok?* which Rainer co-directed with Michael Fengler.

*Did Filmverlag der Autoren already exist in those days?*

It has existed since 1971/72. But I had nothing to do with Rainer until after he left Filmverlag der Autoren. In 1972, when I left Constantin, I turned down Augstein's initial offer to join Filmverlag as executive director. I wasn't eager to join another...

*...chaotic outfit.*

It was a chaotic outfit alright. Almost everything was decided on a democratic basis. The co-owners, the former associates, were always mad at whoever was having a success at the moment. They only got along so long as they were all unsuccessful.

*Was anybody financially successful in those days?*

Sure. Hark Bohm, for instance, in 1975, with *North Sea, Murder Sea [Nordsee ist Mordsee]*; Bernhard Sinkel, in 1974, with *Lina Braake*. Wenders would say, "If those people gave my movies the attention they are giving to Bohm's and Sinkel's movies, my movies would be hits too."

Meanwhile, Horst Wendlandt and I were planning to set up something similar to Filmverlag, that is, distribution and co-production for German movies. Suddenly Augstein agreed to everything I had demanded, including that we stay in Munich. I thought, if they find the right person to manage Filmverlag, I would have created my own competition. While we were still negotiating, I heard that Fassbinder, whom I had regarded as one of its pillars, was pulling out of Filmverlag. I told him, "I am coming here as executive director and you are pulling out. Why are you doing that?" He said he no longer wanted to have anything to do with all those pseudo-artist-bureaucrats; he'd never had any influence nor had he wanted it. I said, "But it looks as though you are leaving because I'm coming in as executive director." "That's bullshit," he said, and I said, "O.k., it's bullshit, but I don't like it." He thought we could continue working together without his being an associate. I can't say we were friends, but we respected each other. I admired his work and his creativity.

*How did your collaboration with Rainer work?*

The first movie I made with him was *In a Year with 13 Moons*. I met him in Frankfurt at an apartment in the red light district. He had extracted

150,000 D-marks from Mengershausen at WDR, and he wanted Filmverlag to match it with another 150,000. "O.k.," I said, "in that case our Project Film will do a fifty/fifty production with you." It worked out relatively well.

*I still remember how stunned you were when the first rough cut was shown. You were absolutely flabbergasted. Tell me about the evolution of* Germany in Autumn.

Well, it turned out to be an unusually radical movie. The movie actually happened by accident. In the fall of 1977, Schlöndorff had submitted *Knife in Hand*, a project by Reinhard Hauff, to the Film and Television Commission. But WDR asked Bioskop to withdraw the film, because "under the circumstances" [the police raid against terrorists after the Schleyer assassination], it would be unwise to make a movie in which a police officer misbehaves. "Shit," I thought, "News blackout, film censorship — the damage that will do!" There were news blackouts on a variety of matters. Television did not cover the events. Nothing was heard on the radio. People with long hair got into trouble riding through the countryside and stopping at some country inn.

There was this ominous mood, even among filmmakers. I told Schlöndorff, who was working on *The Tin Drum*, "Now is the time to make a movie about the whole situation, something like *The Lost Honor of Katharina Blum*, which had targeted Bild Zeitung. But Schlöndorff couldn't do it. And the others, including Rainer, were also otherwise engaged. Then Schlöndorff and I had the idea of doing something collective, calling together all the authors and directors we knew in Munich. If this was to be a collective effort, we had to move fast; there wouldn't be time for a competition. So I phoned around to ask who might be available. Next day we met and agreed that whoever was interested could participate. Present were Rainer, Sinkel, Brustelli, Steinbach, Kluge, and Schlöndorff, who had brought Katja Rupé of *Rote Rübe*. By then Schleyer had been found. A memorial service had been scheduled in Stuttgart for the coming Friday; the Stammheim terrorists were to be buried in Stuttgart later the following week. Both events were to be documented. There was no way we could wait for a written script. Schlöndorff, Trotta, Kluge, and a few cinematographers were given film stock and sent to Stuttgart. The others were supposed to coordinate their efforts, so people wouldn't duplicate. We agreed to meet again a week later to look at the footage they had shot in Stuttgart. Rainer asked, "You think you can get me a camera and some film stock today?" That was Friday night.

By the following Monday he had shot his entire film. While the others were still thinking about their stories, Rainer had finished his thirty-seven minutes. They were shown at the Arri Cinema. He said, "Look here, I've done my part. Maybe I'll cut it a bit," which he did all by himself the night before the opening at the Berlin Film Festival. The others were getting increasingly nervous because his contribution truly surpassed everything. We soon agreed to run Rainer's piece at the beginning. Rainer was fuming because the others were taking so long. He argued that whatever wasn't finished should not be included in the film. Yet he never criticized a colleague and, on the whole, approved of what the others finally did.

Waldleitner was approached. Somehow it irked me that Wendlandt and Waldleitner had suddenly emerged and were doing something with Rainer. Of course, he was proud that these people, who only recently had told him to get himself cleaned up, now wanted to work with him. He was impressed that they were patting him on the back, which was understandable.

*He may have been impressed by the situation, but he certainly wasn't impressed by Herr Waldleitner, though he had a good relationship with Horst Wendlandt.*

I'm not against letting other people lose their money developing a project, and then stepping in, saying, "Now it's my turn, now we'll make something big." In Rainer's case that was *Lili Marleen*, a melodrama, which was his specialty, after all. He was allowed to pick the actors, and then this product emerged in a hundred copies, the highest rate at the time. On the other hand, I was glad that Wendlandt approached me after the second film, *Lola*, which was not a great success, at least not with foreign audiences, when Rainer was planning to do *Veronika Voss*.

*Horst Wendlandt did not like the story.*

A black-and-white movie, of all things! He called to tell me, "We are still short DM 400,000. I'm only going as far as such and such, no more. And I am not going to distribute the movie. You can be co-producer." I told him Rainer would pitch in with his Tango-Film. In those days, he also wanted to support Thomas Schühly,* and there was another party involved.

---

* Thomas Schühly, production assistant in *Berlin Alexanderplatz*, later established his own production company. He was production manager in *Lola* and executive producer in *Veronika Voss*.

*Maran Film.*

That's right. I said, "Should I come in as a fifth party? How much would that leave? How much do we need? 400,000 D-marks? Just a minute, let me make a few phone calls. I'll pledge a minimum." In record time, we raised almost a million D-marks over the phone. The film became a great success.

*So* Veronika Voss *was a success?*

Good box office, many awards, Golden Bear.

*In fairness to Horst Wendlandt it should be said that he did not want Rainer to produce so much. That was his main concern. And it isn't quite true when you say that Wendlandt did not want to take risks. For one thing, he offered Rainer Pitigrilli's novel* Kokain, *for which Rainer wrote the script. Even though Rainer was already known in those days—at least to foreign audiences—you must admit that it took courage for Wendlandt to suggest such a story. Having been able to raise a million marks by phone, you must have realized that he already had a certain market value in those days.*

That's true. But during *Lili Marleen*, Luggi Waldleitner showed up with *The New York Times*—the New Year's issue—which had a photograph of Hanna in *The Marriage of Maria Braun* as "Woman of the Year" on the front page. Waldleitner asked, "You know how to get in touch with Schygulla. She is to play Lili Marleen." *Lili Marleen* had been one of Luggi's pet projects for years. He had had the script rewritten severals times. "Let me warn you," I told him, "you won't get her without Fassbinder as director." Said Waldleitner, "Then I'll take him too."

*Hanna made that condition.*

I had warned him earlier that he could only get the two as a package. But I never imagined Luggi Waldleitner would do something with Rainer or vice versa. Especially since Manfred Purzer was on the project as screenwriter and dramaturg. Everybody knew about Rainer's run-in with Purzer. But then I understood: things always worked that way. After his modest success with *The American Friend*, Wenders defected and allowed himself to be bought by Coppola. He went to the States, planning to make a movie over there. Schlöndorff dumped his *Coup de grâce [Fangschuss]* on Filmverlag, but *The Tin Drum* went someplace else.

Now Augstein was complaining: "You must be doing something wrong. The blockbusters always go someplace else." I don't know if you remember, but when you and Rainer were living at Clemensstrasse, I once sent over a bushel of tomatoes for his birthday.

*Those tomatoes came from you?*

Yes, and each one had a small label that read "traitor."

*Let's go back around the time of* Veronika Voss.

There were new plans in the works. We talked about *Martha*, about what chances there were of bringing it into the movie houses, about the problems with *Beware of a Holy Whore*. We were reorganizing our business relationship. But then there was the strange behavior of Eckelkamp and Fengler during *Maria Braun*. Rainer was furious that we were to be kicked out despite the fact that we had co-financed the project.

My last encounter with Rainer was at his birthday party at the Eiche. We had discussed his part in *Kamikaze*. I had seen the movie a few days earlier and had told the producer, Regina Ziegler, whom I greatly admire, "I don't believe I'll be producing this one." People had told Rainer that I had rejected the movie. When I said goodbye, he asked, "You don't like my movie?" And I replied, "Would you take it, if you were me?" And he said, "Probably not, but I am so good in it." A few days later he was gone. I was deeply shocked by his death, although I did not belong to the group.

*I don't like the word "group." What you mean is the circle around him, to which you most certainly belonged.*

I was more like a satellite, useful for certain things, but not part of the core. I truly miss him personally. There is no one to take his place. When you look at his complete oeuvre, Rainer created something unique. He was an uncontested original. He set a standard for his colleagues and for the movie scene of his day. There were people who made movies in defiance of Fassbinder, after the motto: "This is not the way to do it." Others tried to make movies like Fassbinder and failed or, in taking issue with him, found their own style. After he departed, the New German Cinema underwent a complete change. Somehow everything became more pleasing, less relevant. Just look at our domestic and foreign policy today. What about Communism and Socialism? How did they disappear overnight? What movies would have been made if, for instance, Rainer or anyone one with similar dynamism and similar genius were around?

⌒⌒

# LISELOTTE EDER

M<sub>s.</sub> *Eder's mother was born in 1922, met her future husband, Helmut Fassbinder, in 1942 at the University of Munich, and married him in 1944. Their son, Rainer Werner Fassbinder, was born a year later. She worked as a translator whenever her frequent bouts with lung disease permitted. Divorced from Fassbinder's father in 1951, she married Wolff Eder, a journalist, in 1959. In addition to her job as program director of a research institute, she also acted as business manager for Tango-Film from 1971 until 1978. After appearing in* Gods of the Plague, *she acted in twenty Fassbinder films, culminating in* Lili Marleen. *In 1986, she established the non-profit Rainer Werner Fassbinder Foundation to protect and manage Fassbinder's artistic legacy. In 1992, she transferred the management of the Foundation to Juliane Lorenz. Liselotte Eder died in 1993. This interview took place in Berlin during the 1992 Fassbinder Exhibition. It was conducted by Professor Wallace S. Watson and Juliane Lorenz.*

## MY SECOND JOB

*I assume you had the poet Rainer Maria Rilke in mind when you named Rainer?*

No, actually I just liked the name. But his father insisted that we name him Rainer Werner, in case he became a businessman who didn't like having a poet's name. This way, he could legally choose either name.

*Tell me about Helmut, Rainer's father.*

He was a very unusual man, brilliant in some ways — he knew a great many poems by heart — but he was disturbed and difficult to live with. He wanted to be a writer and considered his medical practice merely a means of making money. But he was not a bad doctor. He was too clever for that.

People say he was an alcoholic. I don't know where they get such ideas. He never drank, he never smoked. *I* was the one who liked to smoke! He'd tell me: "Smoking is bad for you; it turns your lungs black."

*Were you aware that Rainer felt mistreated or unhappy growing up in your crowded household?*

True, there were a lot of people living in the house with us. But they formed a kind of extended family, which is supposed to be healthy for a child. Rainer got a lot of love and care. He was a sweet child and everyone in the house spoiled him. He had a good life until Helmut and I divorced when Rainer was six.

*What did he say to you about his father? Was he angry when you and Helmut divorced?*

I don't know. He hardly knew his father. The divorce itself wasn't that important to him. It was the collapse of the extended family that really mattered. At the time of the divorce, my mother, brother, and father also left. Rainer and I were alone. The first Christmas Eve he and I spent alone together — I wasn't feeling terribly in the holiday spirit myself. But I decorated the Christmas tree nonetheless and arranged all the presents around it. Rainer said to me: "What? Just the two of us?" It was like being stabbed in the stomach.

*At age six, he was put in a home?*

Only for half a year. The extended family was breaking apart. I was hospitalized sporadically with tuberculosis. Later, he went to boarding school whenever I was in the hospital. Tuberculosis is a very changeable condition.

Now I'm saddled with another disease: cancer.

*Did Rainer have trouble dealing with your illness?*

He was having a terrible time in school. I took him to a child psychologist who gave him some tests. Rainer was supposed to draw a picture of his family. Where the father belonged, he drew his uncle, my brother. This uncle became the model for the protagonist of *The Merchant of Four Seasons*.

*He is treated very sympathetically in the film.*

Yes. It's astonishing how much Rainer understood at his age. He was only eight or nine years old when these things happened. The film is based on our family, but it doesn't tell the true story. My sister-in-law has never cheated on my brother! But Rainer said, "I needed it for dramatic reasons." I was the one who had to explain these reasons to his aunt.

*Did Rainer ever accuse you of not being a responsible mother?*

In the days of the antiteater he came to visit me one day and said, "You know, when I see what kind of mothers the others have, I think I've been pretty lucky having you." Much of what has been written about me is no doubt what the writers thought about their own mothers — not what Rainer thought about me.

*Were there indications in Rainer's childhood of his future artistic life?*

He made wonderful drawings and paintings which I still have. He wanted a tape recorder, so I bought one for him. Between the ages of nine and twelve he rounded up his playmates to put on radio plays; he also wrote stories.

*Did you encourage his writing?*

It made me very nervous. Remember: the entire Fassbinder clan — his father, his father's brother, his brother's children — were all writing poems. And they all sounded like Rainer Maria Rilke! If you went to visit his uncle and his children, you would be presented with original verses by the children. And I said to myself, "Oh, God — not Rainer, too! I can't put up with that." It was naturally all quite amateurish. I kept giving Rainer soccer shoes, building blocks, anything to divert his attention from poetry and art. I encouraged him to do things with his hands. The last thing I wanted was for him to become one of those amateur poets!

*It has often been reported that Rainer had a difficult relationship with your second husband, Wolff Eder. In his book, Raab says that Eder despised Rainer, and that your son was only allowed to visit you when Eder was out on his Sunday afternoon walks.*

First of all, Eder never took Sunday afternoon walks alone. Once he even refused to go to a men's get-together at a bar because he couldn't bring me along. Eder was seventeen years older than I. He was not authoritarian, yet there was a natural authority in his demeanor. That's a good thing to have when you are trying to raise a young man. Wolff Eder always said that women do not know how to bring up boys.

*He worked for a newspaper?*

When I met him he was a free-lance journalist. He had worked earlier for the *Süddeutscher Verlag* and occasionally for the *Spiegel.* Kurt Raab really got it wrong! He imagined that the character he played in *The Merchant of Four Seasons*, the protagonist's brother-in-law, was based on Wolff Eder. He claims Wolff wrote for the *Bayernkurier,* a right-wing paper. Actually the Raab character was based partly on my brother-in-law who did write for the *Bayernkurier.*

Wolff Eder was a dyed-in-the-wool Socialist, a dedicated Social Democrat — by no means a right-winger. He had experienced the Weimar Republic, the entire Nazi period, and then naturally the Adenauer period with open eyes. He didn't agree at all with Adenauer's politics. Rainer, in fact, once gave an interview to the effect that his political awareness came from Wolff Eder.

*But they didn't get along very well personally?*

Well, of course, there were problems. Wolff Eder took away the last human being with whom Rainer had a primary relationship. Children are always jealous when their parents remarry. That's normal. I started living with Wolff Eder soon after I was released from a two-year stay in a sanatorium. Rainer was at boarding school and visited us on weekends.

*Was there a problem between Rainer and Eder concerning Rainer's homosexuality?*

When Rainer was about fourteen, he said to me, "I'm homosexual." I was perplexed. It thought it was a sickness, and I said we should send him to a psychologist to be cured. Wolff Eder said, "It's not an illness. It's probably just a phase he's going through." I was worried about Paragraph 175 — homosexuality was against the law in those days. But Wolff Eder and I always entertained Rainer's homosexual friends. Wolff said, "They are his friends, let him bring them along."

*Raab wrote that when you and Wolff Eder came to the antiteater premières, he sat through them grim-faced, and that he left without ever uttering a word.*

I wouldn't say Wolff was all that grim-faced; both of us did leave the theater without comment because we didn't know what to say. Wolff Eder was in his early sixties during the heyday of the antiteater. We were really out of our depth, like many others of our generation. The productions were extremely avant-garde. Ten or more Fassbinder films were shown before Eder's death, and he saw all of them with me. Our tastes changed somewhat during that time.

*Did Rainer actually come out and tell you that he was unhappy in school?*

When he was about sixteen, he told me he no longer wanted to go to school. I didn't know what to do. Wolff Eder said that if he didn't want to go to school anymore, he should learn a trade. When we asked him what kind of work he wanted to do, he answered, "I don't care. It makes no difference."

*That was in the sixties.*

The child psychologist had predicted that he would become a great painter, because the pictures he made were so unusual. When we suggested that he go to a school for art or graphics, Rainer said again, "I really don't care." Then Wolff Eder suggested he might get a job in a theater as a set designer. Since Rainer didn't want to go to any school, Wolff said I should at first apprentice him to a house-painter so he could learn the basic skills. To that suggestion also Rainer replied, "I really don't care."

*You played many minor roles in your son's films, usually as a secretary or a mother. Some critics have concluded that in casting you in such subservient roles Rainer was subjugating you and getting back at you for neglecting him as a child. Any truth in that?*

I don't think so. I had a full-time job at a research center in Munich. The only time I could act in his films was in the evening or during vacation. It would have been impossible for me to play more significant roles. I didn't mind playing small parts. It was fun. I didn't feel ill-treated.

*Just before Eder's death, you started out in a new profession.*

I learned computer programming in 1969. And my professional life took a completely new turn. I helped establish a professional library for a company that did research into radiation, and co-published their professional magazine. Then I became a member of the workers' council. It was all very interesting for somebody who hadn't done anything much until age forty-nine.

*I beg to differ. You'd done some important translations.*

I translated some short stories by Truman Capote. One of the stories was "A Tree of Night."

*That was the story on which Rainer based his first screenplay. He wanted to make the film, too.*

When I explained to him that if he wanted to make the film he'd have to pay for the film rights, he started to make up his own stories! One of those stories became *Only a Slice of Bread*.

*You were involved in his work in other ways than acting.*

When Wolff Eder died in 1971, I had more time for Rainer. After his divorce from Ingrid Caven in 1972, there were so many things to take care of. So I did them — someone had to! The others were all interested in making art, but nobody was interested in putting things in order once the film was finished — taxes, all those things. I did them until 1978, for almost six years. It became my second job.

One day, Rainer came to me and said, "People are saying that when things get complicated, I send my mother to straighten them out. We have to change that, don't we?" Then he met Juliane Lorenz, and she took over.

*What else did you do?*

I typed scripts — *Berlin Alexanderplatz*, for example, which he had dictated into a tape recorder.

*In the film* Germany in Autumn *(1977), we see Rainer dictating* Berlin Alexanderplatz *into that recorder. There is also a much-discussed sequence between you and Rainer at his kitchen table. Many critics have interpreted this as your son's ultimate humiliation of you — goading you on camera into making extreme political statements in response to the murder of the pilot of a hijacked airliner by terrorists in 1977. True?*

I was not tricked into saying those things on camera. I was genuinely very angry after that murder. I thought that the government ought to kill one imprisoned terrorist in Stammheim every time the hijackers in Mogadishu killed one of the passengers, as they said they would if the German government didn't free the Stammheim terrorists. It was only a fleeting idea, and I was ashamed of it later. But a number of people were talking the same nonsense. Then about two weeks later, Rainer asked if I would come over to his apartment and repeat those things for a film he was making. So I did. But not as me. As a character. I was just playing a part in one of his films. People who think Rainer would make that film only to humiliate his mother don't understand his attitude toward his work, his unbending honesty, and the atmosphere in West Germany at that time.

*You found Armin's body shortly after Rainer had broken off their relationship.*

Rainer cared a great deal for Armin and he suffered greatly because of his death. But it had been a very difficult relationship, and he was really desperate when he wrote a goodbye letter to Armin on May 2, 1978. The official police report, after the autopsy, said that the probable cause of death was general paralysis caused by an overdose of pills, but they couldn't conclude whether that was intentional or accidental. What can I say? Armin drank a lot and took a lot of pills.

*Towards the end of Rainer's life, you were seriously concerned about Rainer's health; about what he was doing to himself—the overeating, the constant smoking and drinking, the drugs.*

Rainer didn't invent cocaine, and he wasn't the only one to use it. Why does anyone use drugs?

He used to say you have a choice of living a short, intense life or a long, boring one.

*He had been thinking and talking a good deal about death toward the end. Is there any chance that his death was suicide?*

No.

*It was an accident?*

No one comes into this world, or dies, by chance. Rainer didn't count on getting old. When he was in his mid-twenties, he said to me, "Anyway, I'll die before you."

*Tell me why you established the Fassbinder Foundation.*

To take care of Rainer's legacy. You have no idea of the difficulties we have had, unbelievable difficulties, with *Beware of a Holy Whore*, for instance.

*What was that about?*

Two former associates of Rainer's changed the music and shortened the film in order to get it into theatrical distribution. Rainer had used songs by Leonard Cohen, The Rolling Stones, music which meant a great deal to everyone. But he didn't have theatrical film rights for the music. The film could only be shown on television. These two men substituted a lot of music from Rainer's other films and shortened the film by fourteen minutes. They managed to really botch it up. Then they tried to market it outside the country, but I was able to stop them by going to court. All that costs a lot of money.

*Some people, including Peer Raben, Peter Berling, and Michael Tengler claimed that they had the rights to some of the early films. Can that be true?*

Nonsense. Rainer did not relinquish rights to anyone. After his death, a lot of people said, "He promised me this, that and the other." But they had nothing in writing. No real proof. They brought along friends who said, "Yes, I was there." It was dreadful, dreadful.

*You fought long and hard to become independent from men.*

Ah, independence! It used to be that whenever a man was half-way reliable, I started to believe everything he said. My desire to trust someone had become so powerful. I wanted to trust someone at any price. I guess, as a woman, I could not have enough trust in myself. It took me a long time to outgrow those feelings. Bagwhan says that his German followers were his favorites because they were so easily influenced. I spent my youth under a dictatorship; it didn't disappear in 1945. It's continuing now in a more subtle form.

# DIETER MINX

Mr. *Minx managed numerous productions of Bavaria Studios in Geisel-gasteig near Munich, where he works as chief producer today. In two Fassbinder movies,* Despair *and* Berlin Alexanderplatz, *he was production manager. Serene and even-tempered, Minx — whom Fassbinder called "Mockelchen" — greatly contributed to the successful production of these movies. The interview was conducted in his office at Bavaria Studios in Munich.*

## AN ALMOST MYTHICAL EXPERIENCE

*How was Rainer to work with?*

As time goes on, it becomes increasingly difficult to say anything negative about him. But we shouldn't make the mistake of looking upon our work with Rainer as the golden age. We won't be truthful if we romanticize him. Rainer was not an easy person and he did not always give us an easy time. He demanded top quality performance. He seldom made allowances except with members of his so-called inner circle, even though the friends he had worked with for a long time were made to feel his anger.

*Rainer liked you a lot.*

Because everything worked. Fassbinder initially approached every-one with reservations. Once you established a working relationship with him and he saw that you accomplished things he had not expected to work out, he gave you his trust. At the start of *Berlin Alexanderplatz*, I pulled off something he may have intended as a test: I traced an actor who had gone away on vacation without leaving an address. Rainer was determined to cast him in a minor part.

*You are talking about Karlheinz Braun.*

That's right. It was basically a hopeless undertaking. No one knew where he had gone and there were only four or five days left before we started shooting. When I finally tracked him down, I persuaded him to accept the part. Rainer was impressed. Whenever, on future occasions, I told him that something was impossible, he accepted it. He knew that if there was the slightest chance, it would be done. It was the basis on which we worked.

*Weren't there difficulties on* Berlin Alexanderplatz?

The construction expenses got somewhat out of hand, which led to a lot of arguments. Rainer refused to believe the figures. We were desperate to find ways to save money. Rainer suggested that we cut five or six weeks off the shooting time. And it was true: the studio shoots were going so smoothly that we always finished our daily schedule by four or five in the afternoon. But while it was very pleasant, it didn't gain us much financially. It was very nearly an impossible mission, especially in a production of that size. Existing contracts would have to be curtailed, actors made available at different, earlier dates, and an entirely new schedule worked out. To make matters worse, all the thirty-five actors from parts one through thirteen were to appear once again in part fourteen at the end of the schedule.

I didn't believe it would work, but I wanted to give it a try. Many German theaters gave us generous help — we had a cast made up of virtually all stage actors. It worked, because I always started this way, "Hello, greetings from Rainer Werner Fassbinder. We are wondering if you would..." Without Fassbinder's name, we wouldn't have gotten anywhere. The whole manoeuvre was so labor-intensive, it was almost insane. But it paid off. We cut down the schedule by about six weeks and the financial savings kept the movie almost within the planned budget. Of course, Rainer was very proud, since it had been his idea. But he also respected my achievement, which gained me an extra bonus.

*How did you two first meet?*

It was in 1969, during a television production called *Al Capone in a*

*German Forest.* Rainer was the third or fourth supporting gangster and I was production manager. One day during the shoot he told me that from now on he'd be producing his own movies. I thought he was joking. Then he explained that he'd be doing it with his theater group. "I'll show you a budget," he said. Two days later he came up with a budget. It was a piece of paper, the size of a page from a note book, with a few columns on it. It ended with a sum which, even then, seemed so ridiculous that I almost burst out laughing. I kept that piece of paper for years. It should have been framed: Fassbinder's first home-made budget. Of course, I just smiled because this guy, who played a minor part in our production, whom nobody knew except for a few theater insiders from Munich, this guy actually thought this was how he could shoot his first movie, on 35 mm film, of course, and for the real cinema. A year and a half later, I learned to my amazement that he had produced the movie. Much, much later, in the middle of *Alexanderplatz*, he reminded me of that budget. "You looked at my budget with such disdain, as if it were a figment of my imagination. But, you know, that only boosted my determination to make my first movie, just to show people." He showed us, all right.

*How did your first movie with him,* Despair, *come about?*

Rainer had filmed *The Stationmaster's Wife* at our company. He had a terrible fight with the production manager and the stage manager. In the end, both were banned from the set. When word got around that *Despair* was to be filmed and Fassbinder would direct, the number of Bavaria people available for the project dwindled considerably. Some people felt they had been shortchanged in the previous production. Others fled from the start. The job came to me by default. A terrific production. First off, we had sufficient funds at our disposal. Then there was that incredible re-cut episode. That was about the greatest thing I ever experienced in the business, when you and Rainer re-cut the entire movie in a single night.

It was also the first time he dealt with a genuine international star, which Dirk Bogarde was at the time. And it was probably the first movie for him which was actually produced with a solid amount of money and designed for substantial commercial marketing. What's more, Rainer had only been hired as the director. He had nothing to do with the production or the organization, not even with the script.

Logistically, it was a very difficult movie, moving from one end of Germany to the other. We started shooting in Interlaken, then went to Berlin, to Mölln, to Lübeck; we filmed the fair near Hannover, the studio scenes at Bavaria in Munich. There also was that problem about the candy factory, the color of which had to be mauve. So part of the Sarotti chocolate factory in Berlin and the interior of a marzipan factory in Lübeck were painted mauve. I still can't believe that in those days the owners cooperated all the way.

*What was Rainer's great strength?*

At one time or other, he had done almost every job himself: sound, editing, camera, set design, organizing the entire production. He had largely financed his student and training years out of pocket and at great risk. It was to his advantage that he knew his trade when he started making his big commercial movies, when big business finally came to him. It began with *Alexanderplatz*, where, for the first time, he had a large amount of money at his disposal.

*So there weren't any major run-ins with you?*

Well, once during preproduction of *Alexanderplatz*, I was in Berlin while he was filming *The Third Generation*. I called on him at his large apartment in Charlottenburg, where the production office was located and half the team had been put up. I never managed to get in to see the "master." I returned without having accomplished anything. A few days later I flew back to Berlin and we were able to discuss everything properly. The previous incident was never mentioned. Rainer never said, "Sorry, I didn't feel well that day," or "I was busy with something else." The day simply did not exist. I learned to live with it. I could have gone back with anger in my belly. But that wouldn't have served any purpose.

He did other crazy things. For instance, when we were shooting *Despair*, he organized a gigantic birthday party for himself. He took over an entire restaurant. Yet Rainer Werner Fassbinder, the birthday boy, never showed up.

*Was he more reliable on the set?*

He was highly disciplined in his work, especially in *Alexanderplatz*. In the early days he had always been described as undisciplined, though we were shooting an average of more than six film minutes a day. The film ratio was minimal, about 1:3. Two days after the shoot, the complete scene was shown in its final cut. He showed up every morning — though not always on time.

*But, my dear Herr Minx, it was just a matter of half an hour.*

Your memory may have embellished that a bit... But it was of no importance anyway, since no matter when he appeared, he always finished the daily schedule by evening, often with extremely complicated pans which made great demands on the cinematographer. It was largely to Xaver Schwarzenberger's credit that those superb pictures were achieved. Problems only arose when Rainer arrived on the set in the morning announcing, "This is not what I had in mind." He never liked to look at motives. Sometimes it took a lot of persuasion to lure him to a location. He rarely looked at set designs or blueprints, which led to certain arguments during *Alexanderplatz*. Arriving at Franz Biberkopf's apartment, he took a look at the set and said, "Is this where I'm supposed to shoot for four or five weeks? I'll exhaust all the camera positions in three or four days." The only question he asked was, "How many days have we scheduled for this, and how many days do you need to rebuild the set?" So we enlarged the apartment by half. A loft was built into it, an old printing press was installed, and a closet with a window added. The whole thing became visually more interesting. The reconstruction cost us nearly three shooting days, but he nonetheless finished filming the apartment on schedule.

*How was the morale among the crew during the shoot?*

He knew how to motivate the team. We even had fun during off hours. Someone was in charge of the entertainment program. We had bowling and a movie show once a week. We watched many of his early movies.

Once a week we had soccer practice. That was the most important day, since we had our own soccer team. Rainer was a total soccer fan. We managed to pick eleven acceptable soccer players from our not very large crew. At first anybody who could halfway handle a ball was made to play. On soccer night, we took extra care to wrap on time. That night was sacrosanct. We would take off for Kühler Grund, where we practiced on artificial grass at SCC Charlottenburg.

Shortly before the end of the shoot in Berlin, Rainer came to my office and wistfully remarked that the good times were over now that we were all going back to Munich. "Why should the good times be over?" my wife asked. "Well," he said, "up till now, we've done something together practically every night. When we get back to Munich, you'll see: everybody'll go home as soon as possible after work."

Believe it or not, Rainer was on a health kick in Berlin. He'd bought himself a racing bike, which he once rode from our office in Charlottenburg to a performance at UFA in Tempelhof. At first we smiled in disbe-lief. But he actually stuck it out for quite a while.

*Many people have told me that the* Alexanderplatz *shoot was something very special.*

It certainly was special. First off, it was quite unusual for a production of fifteen hours airing time to be filmed in one piece and in a relatively short period of time with a high film-minute schedule per day. That is very labor-intensive. People felt that Fassbinder was really up to some-thing special, his lifetime oeuvre, and that — in spite of head colds and the flu — he was giving it his all. And since there weren't any boring rushes, just the final cut of a whole scene two days after the shoot, each member of the team constantly experienced some success, which was highly moti-vating.

*Were you ever scared of this mammoth production?*

No. I had known Rainer in *Despair,* and I knew *Alexanderplatz* had a special meaning for him. Besides, I had assembled the best people avail-able, since a production of that length and size can only survive with a first-rate crew. The amount we filmed in this relatively short period of time was crazy. I'd be called insane if I planned anything like that today. But Fassbinder pulled it off, though he could not have done it without the excellent team he had. Everything worked to perfection. Over the years, it has turned into an almost mythical experience.

# RUDOLF AUGSTEIN

Born *in Hannover in 1923, Mr. Augstein began his career in 1946 as editor of* Hannoversche's Nachrichtenblatt, *transferrring at the year's end to the news magazine* Die Woche. *After the departure of the British press officers, he was appointed its publisher and editor-in-chief. On January 4, 1947, the magazine appeared for the first time as* Der Spiegel, *whose publisher Augstein remains to this day. He met Fassbinder while he was shareholder of* Filmverlag der Autoren *[from 1977 to 1985]. Rudolf Augstein, who lives in Hamburg, answered these questions in writing.*

## A RELIABLE PARTNER

*In which year and under what circumstances did you meet Fassbinder?*

I don't actually remember when I met him. As shareholder of Filmverlag der Autoren, I occasionally had business with him. I preferred his mother. Fassbinder was not a very likeable character.

*If you were to explain the subjects of his movies to a young person today, how would you describe them?*

I can't answer that. Young people should develop their own judgment.

*Can you remember your thoughts and feelings when you watched Fassbinder's first movies?*

To my mind, *The Marriage of Maria Braun* is Fassbinder's best movie. At any rate, it was the movie which spoke to me most.

*You were a shareholder of Filmverlag der Autoren from 1977 to 1985. It was quite a disaster financially. What made you come to Filmverlag's rescue in those days?*

I never lost money with Fassbinder movies. In those days, I had a variety of reasons for going into the movie business. It was a favorable moment.

*Could you say anything about the political and economic idea of collective management at Filmverlag? Why did the concept fail?*

There were various reasons why this method of movie sponsorship did not work in the long run. When you think of the American movie business, it is obvious that, in the face of that powerful an industry, we had little if any chance at all.

*How were Fassbinder's films received by Filmverlag?*

Fassbinder was a reliable partner.

*How would you describe the socio-political impact of his movies at the time?*

I believe his movies reached a certain group of intellectuals, though hardly the majority.

*How are his movies remembered today and what is their impact?*

Even today, only a small group of movie buffs and Fassbinder fans are interested in his work. I still admire the intensity with which he carried out his projects. If he revealed an idea on a Saturday, the finished concept, sometimes even a finished treatment, was on the table by Monday. It was remarkable.

# BARBARA BAUM

M*s. Baum grew up in East Germany. During the early sixties she came to West Berlin where she learned dressmaking, in preparation for her career as a costume designer. She worked with Fassbinder for ten years, beginning with* Fontane Effi Briest *in 1972 and ending with his last film,* Querelle. *She also worked with Peter Lilienthal, Wolfgang Peterson, Hans Jürgen Syberberg, Volker Schlöndorff, Bernhard Sinkel, and Bille Augus. Today, she is Europe's foremost costume designer. In 1988 she received a prize for best costume design at the Venice biennale. In 1993 she was given the Bavarian Film Prize for Life-Time achievement, with special emphasis on* The House of the Spirits *and* The Movie Teller. *Everyone who worked with her on Fassbinder's films remembers — among other things — her irresistibly infectious laugh. The interview took place in Berlin.*

## EVERY FILM A CHALLENGE

*When did you first work with Rainer?*

I first worked for Rainer on *Effi Briest* in 1972–73. I did not imagine then that it would turn into such an intense, wonderful, collaboration lasting ten whole years. The first time I met Rainer was in Munich. I had just done the costumes for a film which Reinhard Hauff was shooting at the Bavaria in 1970–71. It was the story of a legendary poacher: *Mathias Kneissl.*

Rainer and Ursula Strätz played a peasant couple. I fitted him for his costume, and that was it. The only member of his group I knew personally was Hanna Schygulla with whom I had made a movie two years earlier. It was her first film role and the first film for which I myself created the costumes. She and I had got along very well together.

Later, when Rainer was planning *Effi Briest*, Hanna Schygulla said, "Why don't you use Barbara Baum — the *Kneissl* girl — for the costumes."

Suddenly I got a call from Kurt Raab in Cologne. Would I come immediately to meet with Fassbinder about *Effi Briest*. That phone call got me pretty excited. I had heard so many conflicting stories about him and his group.

I'd seen a play he had produced in Munich, *Anarchy in Bavaria*. Of his films, I only knew *Love is Colder than Death*. I was no longer a complete neophyte in film. I had done several productions with Peter Lilienthal, Johannes Schaaf, Syberberg, Peter Beauvais, Peter Fleischmann, and Reinhard Hauff. Now I was getting lots of good advice from well-meaning people — what things I should make sure of before going to work for Fassbinder! Thus warned, I entered the lion's den in Cologne where he had just shot *Eight Hours Don't Make a Day*.

*What did you expect?*

I thought Rainer just wanted to meet me so he could decide whether I was the right person for the job. I'll never forget that day! In his apartment, several friends and co-workers were milling around. He sat in the center, issuing orders, some peremptory, some ironic. He also laughed a lot. Then, he opened the script and pounced on me. He wanted to know — scene by scene, from beginning to end — what costumes Effi Briest and all the others were going to wear. I hadn't actually thought about it in such detail. I had to improvise with lightning speed; I explained why certain witty things should be included; I tried not to lose the thread of what we were talking about. After about three hours the discussion was finished. So was I! Thank God, I'd taken copious notes. I told him that I wanted to make Hanna Schygulla's costumes myself, as well as her hats. I added that I needed 20,000 Mark right away, to buy fabric and pay the students who were going to do the sewing. He was quite impressed. Before he let me go he made a few suggestions. For instance, he wanted Effi Briest on the swing to look like Marlene Dietrich in *The Scarlet Empress*. In one scene the "young Katharina" sits in a swing. She is wearing a delicate, girlish white tulle dress. She looks like a fluffy cloud. Although the Dietrich film is set in an entirely different period, Fassbinder wanted that same aura, to show Effi Briest as a well-protected young girl.

When I left Cologne my knees were shaking. I threw myself into the preparations, organized the costume design, and did everything we had discussed. Rainer never came to a fitting. Once in a while, Kurt Raab showed up, but he never interfered. Then came the shoot in Denmark. I arrived with many crates full of costumes whose contents I had not even checked. I felt extremely insecure.

When he saw the actors in costume for the first time, he absolutely beamed. He had a brilliant memory. He remembered everything. Before each scene he asked me will there be this or that costume now? That's not to say that he ever came out and declared that the costumes were good, but I could feel that they inspired him and that he liked them very much.

*Rainer once explained his preference for working with you, "At first, during* Effi Briest, *I hated Mrs. Baum, because she watched the costumes so relentlessly. For instance, she'd plant herself in front of the camera and say, 'We can't start shooting. Effi hasn't got her brooch on yet!' But later her conscientiousness, her insistence, her penetrating perfectionism were the very qualities I came to appreciate and love."*

Remember, *Effi Briest* was Rainer's first historical film. He had never spent so much money on costumes.

*What came next, after* Effi Briest*?*

In 1973 Rainer did a play for television based on Ibsen's *A Doll's House*, the film was later titled *Nora Helmer*. All the costumes were designed by me and executed by the Theaterkunst Company. There were absolutely no problems. After *Nora*, Rainer called me quite often to ask whether I felt like making the costumes for an upcoming project. But he had the unfortunate habit of asking me too late, after I'd already started on some other production. That was the reason I had to decline *Despair*. Not long afterwards he came up to me at a film festival in Berlin, madder than a wet hen! "I hated you every day we were shooting *Despair* because you hadn't done the costumes! From now on, please ask me what my plans are before you accept an engagement anywhere else." He then turned on his heel and disappeared As soon as I recovered from that attack, I realized it was a declaration of love. I called after him, "It's a promise!" I never did have to ask him, though, because soon after that encounter he offered me *The Marriage of Maria Braun* and *Alexanderplatz*. During *Alexanderplatz* I already knew that *Lili Marleen* would be next. After *Lili Marleeen*, there was to be *Kokain* (based on a book by Pitigrlli). Unfortunately that project fell through. As you know, we made *Lola* instead. Right after *Veronika Voss*, early in 1982, came *Querelle*.

*Those are all very different films*

Every film was a fresh challenge. Never again would Rainer discuss the script with me in as much detail as he had for *Effi Briest*. A brief descirption of how he visualized the film, a few important climaxes, and the names of a few films he considered important for our work; we went to see those together. That was how he inspired us all. It was a fantastic time. For instance, he told us that *Lola* should be like an "early American color film." That was the key. He ordered me, in staccato terms, to go ahead and decide about the costumes, the dramaturgy, the actors, and the roles. He did not look at a single costume before the shooting started. He trusted me to do it right. I created the external appearance of the characters, then he took over and, with his actors, made a terrific film.

*But still, he always had very definite ideas. Can you describe those?*

He did not want pure naturalism or realism. That would have been wrong for his films. He often said, "We are making a certain film about a certain period — but from our point of view." Everything had to be transposed and somewhat heightened to make its meaning clear. That was actually the most important thing for me: Rainer gave me the courage and the drive to do things I might not have dared otherwise. Rainer always stood behind my work and defended me against the producers when there were problems.

*What about* Lili Marleen?

We had our first talk in Berlin with Rolf Zehetbauer, who was doing the sets. I brought along a lot of photos and documents I had found in picture archives and libraries. Material about Lale Andersen, about "wish concerts," about music at the front, about certain high Nazi officials who played a part in the script, about uniforms, and so on. I described the results of my research, to clear up as many points as possible in the shortest possible time. Rolf Zehetbauer, who had not had any time to study the theme in such detail, kept saying "That's really very interesting" during my little speech. Rainer was greatly amused. And besides, it reassured him that we were on solid ground and could proceed to heighten the theme "from our point of view."

For the costume of Lili Marleen in the final scene he gave me very specific instructions. He wanted her dress "to hold her together like a suit of armor," without which she would not be able to go on stage. That gave me the inspiration for the silver lamé dress with the silver turban. The fabric looked like metal, the entire costume like armor.

*Your costumes were a great success.*

And yet every new film would plunge me into doubt. Had I really done the right thing? As the first day of shooting approached, I became more and more anxious. There would come that crucial moment when Rainer would see the actors before the camera for the first time. If he beamed, I was so relieved! Of course I always made sure to ask very specific, probing questions when a new project got under way. If there were several possible ways to present a character, I suggested various alternatives. With lightning speed he decided in which direction we should go, and he stuck to that decision all through the shooting.

*But he interjected spontaneuous ideas, too, didn't he?*

Of course, sometimes he would have a specific idea on the spur of the moment while shooting, and I would not be able to execute it right away. But that was a kind of game for him: to see whether and how you'd deal with it. If you had complained "that wasn't in the plan" he most definitely would have made a scene! For instance, about an hour before a scene with Mario Adorf in *Lola* he casually mentioned, "You know, of course, that he is wearing a lounging-jacket." Of course I didn't! I had planned something entirely different. Perhaps he hoped I would panic. But I didn't give him that satisfaction. During the next hour taxi after taxi arrived at the Bavaria lot, each bringing a jacket. It was hilarious. A beautiful black velvet kimono with large golden peacocks was on Mario with only 40 seconds to spare.

*Lola* brought another surprise. Three or four days before the deadline, Rainer dropped another of his famous remarks: "You know, of course, that Lola is getting married in white and the ladies of the cathouse have to show up in church, dressed accordingly?" It was really almost impossible. We managed a fitting one whole day before shooting started. We sewed the dress during the night. It was a dream, an absolute haute-couture model right out of a fifties fashion magazine. At the same time my assistant, Egon Strasser, flew to London with two empty suitcases, and organized some wonderful cocktail dresses for the whores. He took them through customs as his personal wardrobe. But these extravagant challenges remained the exception. For me and my co-workers, that kind of game had its charm—and it definitely gave wings to our creativity.

*Which film was your biggest challenge?*

*Berlin Alexanderplatz.* Rainer wanted the basic tone to be gray: "We are shooting a black-and-white film, even if it is in color."

About the women around Franz Biberkopf he said, "They're all prostitutes, but only because they are poor, to get a little extra money." They were really respectable housewives. Under no circumstances must I betray them through their costumes. He let me deal with the visual creation of the characters. That wasn't easy, because of the idiosyncratic casting. The first time I saw Annemarie Dürnger it was during a fitting and I said to myself, "I'll never get this right." In the script it said, "Cilly, who almost looks like a movie star, is wearing a rabbit fur coat; a poverty-stricken Jean Harlow of the *Alexanderplatz* — a cellar child." I knew Ms. Düringer only from her films. Suddenly I was facing a dark-haired, very resolute, intelligent lady in sports clothes and horn-rimmed dark glasses. She was about fifty at the time. I didn't know what to do. She herself was doubtful that she was right for the part. She absolutely wanted to talk with Rainer about it. But he refused to see her. I had grave doubts whether the costumes I had designed would really transform Ms. Düringer into Cilly. Then she began to pose in front of the mirror, to move as Cilly. It was fantastic: she slipped out of suburbia and into the role. On her first shooting day I sneaked into the studio to observe Rainer's reaction to Ms. Dürnger. Rainer radiated joy. He thought she was stupendous. When he discovered me, he said with a boyish twinkle, "That one was the toughest, right?" I was extremely proud and happy.

*No matter your own casting opinions, you were there to understand and support and enhance the director's ideas.*

Rainer had a sixth sense for casting. His judgment of an actor's quality was foolproof. Of course, he often did quite unusual things. He cast actors from the time of "Grandpa's Movies" and galvanized them to perform in outstanding ways that had to be taken seriously.

My fantasies for costume design were set in motion by his brief, precise instructions: we understood each other very well without many words. I think it would have bored him to know the costumes in advance. They inspired him during shooting and he always used them very effectively. A costume designer can't ask for more.

People quite often asked me, "Isn't it terrible to work with Fassbinder?" And I always said, "Did you know him? Did you work with him? Where do you get your ideas about him?" His energy, his productivity, his crazy imagination, his incredible memory, his alertness that cut through pretentions like a laser, his knowledge of human nature, and his laughter were absolutely unique.

*Did you ever meet anyone like him again?*

Not in that ideal state. I don't know anyone who made so many films in such rapid succession. That sense of continuity was extraordinary. Besides, he worked with a steady group of co-workers — camera, editors, actors, production people, and so on — who knew each other well and appreciated and liked each other.

Rainer had the entire film in his head with absolute clarity. There was a precise daily schedule and a storyboard, everyone knew what had to be done. We all tried to do our job quickly and well. There were few retakes and we never saw rushes, only edited scenes. That was great, you saw everything in context.

Rainer did a lot to make us feel good. He enjoyed it! He wanted us to enjoy it too. He arranged evenings at the movies and all sorts of recreational activities: bowling, football, or Octoberfest and many wonderful coffee breaks at the studio, usually at his expense.

One Friday uring *Querelle*, just before closing time, Rainer proposed a slight change in our evening plans. He wanted to continue and shoot all the scenes that were scheduled for the following Monday and Tuesday; in other words, finish the film. We all agreed. By midnight we had done it. An incredible sense of cooperation pervaded the studio. We worked like maniacs, everyone giving his personal best, and everything functioned beautifully. Afterwards there were great fireworks on the CCC studio grounds and lots of champagne. Rainer was in a very mellow mood. I had never seen him like that. He went and thanked every one of of us individually. When he came to me, he gave me a long, emotional hug, like never before; he kissed me and thanked me for my "super-terrific" work. When he left I was in tears, overwhelmed by such closeness.

*Was that your farewell?*

No. Actually, our farewell was even more beautiful, about a month after *Querelle*, in Berlin. It began with plans for the immediate future. Regina Ziegler and Rainer must have raised new funds in Cannes, for future projects. When she called me to ask me to come and see Rainer she said, "I've got a lot of news, but I'm not allowed to tell. Rainer wants to tell you everything himself." We met in the Paris Bar. It was the last time I saw him. He was in a very good mood and radiated confidence as he talked about his upcoming projects. First he wanted to make *Rosa Luxemburg*, then a Hollywood re-make of *Possessed*, and then George Bataille's *Le bleu du ciel [Blue Skies]*. He beamed, like a little boy. He wanted me to do those films with him, and then, suddenly, he asked me, "How long have you and I been working together?" I realized that since *Effi Briest* in 1972, ten years had gone by. So we celebrated our tenth anniversary. It was a wonderful evening of wit and cheer. Rainer was happy as a child about his new projects and I was happy because he was going to make all those beautiful films with me.

# VOLKER SPENGLER

M̲r. Spengler was born in Bremen in 1939 and went to sea at the age of fourteen. From 1959 until 1961 he attended drama school in Salzburg and at the Reinhardt-Seminar in Vienna. He got his first acting job from Luigi Malipiero. In 1967 he joined the Berlin Schiller Theater where, amongst other things, he acted in four productions by Fritz Kortner. He also appeared in Munich, Cologne, and Frankfurt, returning to Berlin under directors such as Einar Schleef, Klaus Emmerich, and Peter Palitzsch. He also wrote a play, Dear William. In 1985 he produced Fassbinder's The Bitter Tears of Petra von Kant with an all-male cast. Between 1975 and 1981 he acted in nine Fassbinder films. The interview took place in Frankfurt.

## UNCOMPROMISING VIEW OF SOCIETY

*How did you first meet Rainer Werner Fassbinder?*

Well, I met his work on Christmas Eve, 1968. I happened to be in Berlin at the Schiller Theater. Bob Dorsey and I didn't know where to go that night, so we decided to go over to the Forum Theater and see *Iphigenie 68*. It was terrific.

Years later, Rainer appeared at the TAT [Theater am Turm] in Frankfurt and watched my performance of a play by Gerhart Roth. He liked it enough to ask if I would I stay on at the TAT to work with him.

*Many people who worked with Rainer in the theater have told me that he had very little patience for it, that the theater didn't really interest him.*

That's bull! He even attended dress rehearsals of other directors' plays and made suggestions. I remember *Leonce and Lena* very well. He didn't like certain things I did with the part of Valerio. I said to myself: he once played Valerio himself and now he probably wants me to do a kind of re- make. At first I didn't want to listen to his critique. But after I calmed down I said I'd be open to any specific suggestions he might have. He ran through eight points. They were extremely insightful. I went ahead and played the part accordingly. On opening night, Rainer stood in the balcony and every time I came out, he shouted "Bravo!"

*He was equally intense about film.*

Here's one example: on *Chinese Roulette* he locked us all up in a castle. The nearest bar was twenty kilometers away; there were only two cars and the wine cellar was full. He had built a kind of ghetto in which we lived and worked on the film with total intensity.

*To what extent were Rainer's anti-establishment views at the heart of his productivity?*

"Grampa's Movie [the cinema of the fifties] is dead" — that's what opposition to the establishment meant in the early days of the "New German Film." By the time Rainer started to direct, it had become self-evident that he no longer required that kind of opposition to motivate him. If, instead of "opposition" you want to say "defiance" or "aggression," he manufactured those within himself. And out of that attitude he formed his own opposition, his own defiance, and his own aggression.

Today, everything is leveled off. There is no opposition. Everything's the same sauce, with any left-leaning bourgeois considering himself an ultra-radical. In order to be creative, in any field, you have to produce this aggression, this defiance, and this opposition. Rainer was a master at this. His opposition, his rage and hatred, his really uncompromising view of society is nowhere expressed more clearly, more directly, more accurately, or more sensuously than in his film *Satan's Brew*.

*Wasn't it very similar with* Third Generation? *We all wanted to be movers and shakers. What a thrilling time it was! All of us acted and all of us worked; there were no stars.*

Sure. We made the film because we wanted to respond to what happened [terrorist attacks, etc.] in '77. Rainer as cinéast was embroiled in an ongoing argument with society.

*Would you call yourself a Fassbinder actor today?*

It's just a label. I can't deal with labels. When I am working on something with Mr. Palitzsch, that doesn't make me a Palitzsch-actor. I am an actor who has a contract with Palitzsch. I wasn't a Kortner-actor when I worked with him. I've always been against that group mentality. When I hear the word "group," I hear "grrrowl!" I only join one kind of group, the kind where individuals come together to work on a project, to achieve a common goal In the theater, that usually happens on opening night and in film on the last day of shooting. That's all the "group" I need.

*Some people claim that Rainer could not exist without a group. He always showed up with his entourage.*

But that is quite meaningless. Whoever was around went out to eat together; they got themselves invited, that's all. Rainer never tried to coerce an actor. Whatever Rainer wanted to get out of you he could — quite peacefully — make emerge from inside you.

# ELISABETH TRISSENAAR

M*s. Trissenaar was born in Vienna, where she graduated from the Max Reinhardt Seminar. Until she met Fassbinder in 1974 during a production of Peter Handke's* They are Dying Out, *she had mainly worked with her husband, the director Hans Neuenfels. She played all the great female characters of the German-language repertoire, including Miss Julie, Lulu, Nora, Medea, Iphigenie, and Elektra. Her career in film began with the role of Hanni Bolwieser in Fassbinder's* Bolwieser. *She also has worked with directors Andrzej Wajda, Krzystof Zanussi, Agnieszka Holland, and Doris Dörrie. She acted in many Fassbinder films, from* The Marriage of Maria Braun *to* Berlin Alexanderplatz. *Elisabeth Trissenaar lives in Berlin, where this interview took place.*

## AIR SIGNS, INTANGIBLE

*When and where did you meet Rainer?*

At the Frankfurt Schauspiel, in 1974. It was the only municipal theater in West Germany where collective management was the rule. In other words, everything that went on at that theater had a distinctly leftist slant. Rainer was somewhat to the left, but the idea of having to work under such conditions must have struck him as ridiculous. He had other things on his mind than political infighting. In his films, he aimed at more subtle stuff, like stripping the solid citizens of their little pretentions. I don't actually remember which film he was making when we met.

*That was* Fox and his Friends?

Right. Before taking over the Theater am Turm [TAT], he did Peter Handke's *They Are Dying Out* at the Schauspiel Frankfurt. Two very different directors, Palitzsch and Neuenfels, had led the theater decisively but in wildly divergent ways. Before Rainer could start, there ensued endless discussions about whether or not he should direct the play. That whole bureaucratic process cranked up every time a new director was introduced. The discussions, and the voting that followed—whether a certain play should be produced and a certain director asked to direct it—it made you feel you were in a lion's cage. We were young and many of the discussions turned vehement. I am sure we voted on whether Fassbinder should direct in our theater. But I can't remember the actual voting, even though it had such an important effect on my life. I was probably playing hookey that day. Between the big parts I played and those meetings every afternoon, I never had enough time for my child.

Well, it was decided that Fassbinder should direct the Handke play. Of course, he had already made a lot of films—some wonderful ones—and people had begun to talk about him. But he was not yet at the very top. Groups had formed around the two polarized directors, Palitzsch and Neuenfels. There were very few "double agents"; almost no actor worked with both directors for any length of time. It was silly, but that's the way it was. Rainer ran into that situation when he started casting. But he simply went ahead, paying no attention to any of that collective-decision business. And so I landed the part of Paula Tax. This produced suppressed howls, because I was already playing Nora, Hedda Gabler, Cressida, and one other lead. So it was by no means "my turn." But my having played all those parts in Neuenfels' high-visibility productions was probably the reason Rainer picked me. I was overjoyed, of course.

Rehearsals were very intense, very imaginative. But many rehearsals simply didn't take place. Of course, he had to go to the Cannes film festival; then he had to be somewhere else, to discuss a new project. Rainer loved the theater, he was one of the few film directors who often went to the theater to look for actors he could use in his movies. But his patience ran out rather quickly at rehearsals. When he was shooting a film, he lived for that extreme concentration that culminates in a single, brilliant moment. It bored him to look up at a stage and watch an awkward, unfinished process. It all went too slowly for him. He was always moving faster in his head. But, still, he was a theater director, too. He had the stage within his grasp. When he wanted to!

*How did you get along with the actors from Rainer's group?*

They were sort of brusque with me — they made it clear that if it had been up to their "collective decision" they would never have admitted me into the Fassbinder ensemble. I fell smack into every psycho-trap set out for me. Here we were, rehearsing at the Historical Museum. It wasn't a good rehearsal. We were unimaginative and boring. And so Rainer became boring, too. My fellow actors couldn't think of anything more creative to do than to needle me. Except for Irm Hermann and Kurt Raab, everyone had it in for me. Suddenly Rainer got up and said, "Excuse me, one moment, I'll be right back." I did not burst into tears, which I often did back then, but I was terribly down. The Historical Museum is on Römer Square; there are stalls where you can buy hot dogs, drinks. Rainer came back very quickly, carrying a whole lot of little bottles of cognac and vodka. He walked up to me and looked at me with those unforgettable eyes — an infinitely warm, understanding gaze that sank deep, deep into my being. He placed all those little bottles in front of me and said, "Sissy, these are for you"; then he abruptly turned to the others in a domineering pose I never again saw him assume — not even when everything went wrong during a shoot. "To you people, I just want to say this, because you're all gunning for Trissenaar: you are gunning for her because she is working so much with Neuenfels. But right now she is working with me — and I want to tell you: all great actresses have their directors, and so Trissenaar had Neuenfels. And now she has me. And Dietrich had Sternberg." He was furious when he said it, but his eyes told me that he loved me; and nothing would take that love away. *Basta*.

*A beautiful story.*

Not even his little well-directed bursts of sarcasm were able to damage that love. Every intelligent person turns sarcastic now and then. During *Maria Braun* for some reason there was a break that seemed endless to me: I was furious and wanted to go home for my son's birthday. I had turned away and he roared, "Why don't you throw your kid in the garbage!" Even that single knock-down drag-out fight could not really diminish that love. I understood and accepted him — in the abstract. I would not presume to say that I understood him completely. He and Hans [Neuenfels] had the same birthday, so he, too, belonged to the Butterfly Clan of the Native American horoscope. Air Signs; intangible. Beautiful to watch. Essential for me — a Fire Sign. Incidentally, Rainer was rather hip on Chinese astrology. Once he discovered where you belonged in the Chinese horoscope — we talked about that sort of thing in the evenings, sitting around after a day's shooting — he used that knowledge as an inexhaustible source of sharp little digs and jabs.

Bolwieser *was the first film you made with Rainer?*

I said yes before I had even read the book. Then, when I read it, I was overjoyed.

*What exactly was special about Rainer from an actor's point of view?*

He was a perfect casting director. He knew exactly which actor he needed for which role and that went a long way towards the actual work. You can see it very clearly in *Berlin Alexanderplatz.*

A director needs a lot more than a knowledge of human nature. He meets an actor who is probably tense and whose head is humming with a single mantra: "I want the part, I want the part." He has to find inside this actor the human being whose own special qualities and passions will make the character come to life most fully. Rainer had that ability. He could see very deeply into people. He was certainly a genius, extremely intelligent with a high-speed brain. After two or three rehearsals he knew the text by heart while you, the actor, were still stumbling and stuttering. Rainer, with friendly sarcasm, would prompt you from behind the camera.

He always took the shortest route to get the work done — beware the actor who couldn't keep up with his tempo! You might say that his brilliant casting saved him a lot of extra work. And he was unforgettably good at observing. That's essential for a director. He is, after all, the movie's first audience. If he is cheated out of a certain thought, a certain emotion, then the audience later on will also feel cheated, or will subconsciously detect something amiss. They will no doubt attribute this absence to the failings of the actor. The director can save you by watching very closely. I had unconditional trust in Rainer.

He squatted — in contortions! — behind the camera, crawled along with it, his knees to his chin when he had to cross the rails. He watched and watched during rehearsals, always as close as possible to the camera's point of view.

Shooting also means waiting. Sometimes it takes hours to set the lights; the actors sit around, smoking, bored, drinking coffee, starting to sag. Not Rainer. He sat in an unused corner of the set and worked out the connection for the next scene. Painted little pictures — the camera angles. His own concentration made the actors feel that one had to "stay with it," concentration was maintained, sometimes intensified.

*Did you learn anything else, working with Rainer?*

He taught me how to rehearse as long as it took without exhausting myself psychologically and emotionally. And then, when the scene was set, and every move and step had been practiced so that you kept landing on the right marks with perfect precision, then the real work began, all of us concentrating as if there'd be only a single take.

There was a great sense of community. Yet Rainer made it very clear: the film was his project, and his alone. One had to accept that. Once, on *Bolwieser*, I spoke out of turn. Looking at the rushes, I loudly and unequivocally told Rainer which of my takes I preferred. He cut me off: "If you can't watch the rushes quietly, you shouldn't have come. If you weren't always at your best during takes, that's your fault. Technical mistakes may occur. But you are not supposed to make mistakes. That's why I hired you."

*How did you manage to keep up with his tempo?*

He was always racing against whatever time was left on the clock. Sometimes I thought he had deliberately picked such a dangerous way of life, exhausted his resources, tried to squeeze every last thought from his brain, as if instinct had told him that his time was limited. But then again, there were those attempts at keeping fit. During *Alexanderplatz* he went on a diet, rode a bicycle. Coming back to the set after being away a short time, you suddenly found yourself looking at a fledgling ascetic. Those attempts were so intense that I often thought he would somehow manage to calm down the pendulum that swung between his body and his measureless spirit.

His system was to overtax and overstimulate himself, and it was catching—he dared you to match it. *In a Year with 13 Moons* was the most chaotic, but also the most interesting, film work I ever did. He was behind the camera in that film too. He had thought up an extremely complicated camera angle in which all the characters in the film should come together, emerging from different doors and corners. Even an experienced cinematographer would have had trouble with that.

*That's the final scene.*

It wasn't such a big acting problem for me. I just had to stand there with my arms around Eva Mattes, who played my daughter. Eva was supposed to cry. She had started to concentrate on crying early in the morning, during makeup, and she cried in take after take until it got to be afternoon and then early evening. And she just couldn't any more. During hours and hours of endless wrong camera moves she had become used to her sorrow, and had turned to stone. Her face was ruined, dissolved, as if a tank had driven over it. It looks wonderful on film.

*Did you feel Rainer's support outside of your work for him?*

Oh, sure. While we were shooting *Bolwieser* I was playing Medea in Frankfurt at the same time. We performed on planks that had been placed across the first eight rows of seats in the audience. There were passages where I had to jump around barefoot on those boards — rant, scream, weep — and then go sit in the auditorium. One time I'm about to leap to the stairs when I notice all the space is taken. Never mind, I think, I'll be able to find a spot — I'll simply squeeze between two members of the audience. As I sat there in my flimsy costume, something smooth and cool touched my arm. A leather jacket. I felt so much affection and warmth at my side. It was Rainer. He had not been able to get a regular seat in the auditorium and so we sat for a little while, huddled together. I played Medea and he watched me. That sense of closeness made many things possible.

# KARLHEINZ BÖHM

W*hen he played the "Emperor of Austria" to Romy Schneider's "Sissy," the Austrian Mr. Böhm became the epitome of Imperial Highness for German audiences of the 1950s. His subsequent work with the British director Michael Powell erased the stigma of those earlier films. In 1959 he played the lead in* Peeping Tom, *a disturbing film for its time, which didn't gain the recognition it deserved until twenty years later. After having made more than fifty films, Böhm began working with Fassbinder. First came* Martha *in 1973. Then* Fontane Effi Briest, Fox and his Friends, Mother Küsters goes to Heaven, *and two stage plays:* Hedda Gabler *at the Free Volksbühne in Berlin and* Uncle Vanya *at the TAT in Frankfurt. He created a sensation when he decided to end his acting career in favor of an enterprise he started and initially financed himself, and which he now directs: "People for People"—a project of developmental aid to Ethiopia. The interview took place in Baldham, near Munich.*

## WORKING ON AN ASSEMBLY LINE
## IS HARDER

*Rainer's life was also his work. But he himself tried, during his last years, to keep those two elements separate from each other.*

I can differentiate between those two areas very well. But I don't think there is anything wrong with comparing his sex life—what I knew of it, and I knew it from the outside only, not being homosexual myself—with his professional life. What I mean is: what he pretended to be is not what he really was.

*What do you mean by "pretended"?*

I met several women, and I'm sure you are one of them, who said that he was the most wonderful lover they had ever met; they raved, literally, despite the fact that he — pretending to be homosexual or bisexual — had affairs with men. Rainer had a very fractured relationship with his father; in *Martha* I practically depicted his father, and, because of that film, Rainer and I talked a great deal about the man — as a psychoanalyst, then, I would understand his homosexual excesses. You can't call them anything else, they frequently were actual excesses. It's true that Rainer was very good at acting a gay person, and behaving like a gay person; he acted gay roles with tremendous elegance. But I have observed him from a rather different side.

*What do you suppose made him create such an image of himself?*

Rainer adopted the image of a homosexual as a kind of protest against his father, but also to express his opposition to a society where homosexuals were not being accepted. That was the point of *Fox and his Friends*. He identified with things he didn't really approve of. Rainer was an incredibly disciplined, unbelievably hard-working person. He was one of the few artists with whom I worked — Vincente Minelli among them — who were of true genius caliber, according to Goethe's dictum that genius is 90 percent hard work and 10 percent talent.

*How did you first get in touch with Rainer?*

I was in the midst of a public identity crisis. I was trying to extricate myself from the fifties and develop autonomy as an actor. I needed money, so I did dubbing for Bavaria [Film Studio]. (Of all my acting stints, I hated that one the most.) And one day I came upon Rainer, Schygulla, Kurt Raab, and Chatel, all sitting in the canteen. I walked up to him and said, "Mr. Fassbinder, my name is Böhm. I've seen *Katzelmacher* and *The Coffeehouse* and I was enormously impressed. They were really the most exciting things I've seen in the last ten years. Furthermore, I would like to work with you some time." He looked up for a moment, looked at me with narrowed eyes, and all that came from his mouth was, "Hahhh!" — nothing else. I was furious and said to myself: that arrogant son of a bitch, that no-good, stupid, high-class, counterculture swine. I never want to have anything to do with him again.

Two weeks later, my agent called — listen, do you know Fassbinder?! So I say, "Do I know Fassbinder? Don't mention that name to me, I want to have nothing to do with that guy." "That's very strange," says she. "I've got a script here for you that he wants you to do with him." To make a long story short, I read the screenplay for the film *Martha* and twelve hours later I called him and told him yes. We started shooting immediately, in Konstanz. From the very start we developed a harmonious relationship. But it was very peculiar: during the entire film he dressed like his father.

*How do you know?*

I met his father once. A doctor from Cologne, if I remember correctly. It was a very short visit. He dressed very conservatively. During the shooting Rainer once said to me that he would dress like his father: neckties, shirts, suits. Here I was desperately trying to outgrow my own necktie period!

*Tell me about* Chinese Roulette.

It was an infernal game where people tell others exactly what they think of them; all kinds of pent-up animosities were unleashed and absolutely awful things came out into the open. I can maintain a certain objectivity in private life, but I become the underdog at work. He dominated people in such a fabulous way that one didn't even notice it. He was an absolute authority figure for me.

*You felt intimidated by him?*

"Intimidated" is not the word I'd use. I would say he guided me in a way no other director ever had. Most of them just say you go over there and then you do such and such. Rainer was not like that. He did it in a much more subtle way. He made people — and I don't mean this in a positive sense, if you'll forgive me — dependent on him. I don't know whether you want to admit to this, but all the people I knew who worked with him were somehow dependent on him, each in his own way.

*I learned a lot through him. When we met I was still very young, shy, and trying to find myself. He sensed that here was a human being who wanted to learn — among other things — how to handle sadness and sensitivity.*

Rainer as a film man was incredibly patient and he knew exactly what he wanted. When he was behind the camera and gave his directions, everything functioned perfectly. In the theater, unfortunately, he did not have that much patience. Staging a play is such a different process. But when he directed a play he also had very definite ideas. I'll never forget once, in *Uncle Vanya* or *Hedda Gabler* (I had yearned to act in those two plays and he had immediately agreed to it), he showed me a certain pose on the stage and said, "Now you go over there and then you stand there with your feet apart, like a regular macho." Those were film ideas that would have been brilliant on the screen but on the stage a part has to develop from inside the actor. And that takes endless patience. And, as you know better than I, Rainer had almost no patience.

*He had a great deal of patience with people.*

But genius that he was on the stage with those plays, he really had no patience. The *Coffeehouse* at the Witwe Bolte had made an enormous impression on me. In *Uncle Vanya* he went so far as to have a veranda built like a peep show. The first act took place inside it and it was all glassed in against the audience. On opening night the people screamed, "Louder! Louder!" Nobody could hear anything. The entire stage was glassed in so that the actors seemed to be inside a large fish tank. The next evening, thanks to an onslaught of criticism, everything was changed, the glass was cut away. That shows you a typical miscalculation: it was a brilliant film idea.

The four films we made together were among the most wonderful experiences I can remember. He had a brilliant way of utilizing an actor's capabilities. He not only saw me as the upper-class gentleman or the good-looking lover. He also saw — because he really listened to me — what had hurt me, what aspects of my character had been left undeveloped. And he recognized that, and made use of it. In that respect he was more sensitive than any other director I ever worked with.

We were in the subway station beneath Marienplatz, shooting night scenes for *Fox and his Friends*. It must have been three or four in the morning, and I am not a night person. I hate night scenes. I was leaning against a post and yawning so hard I almost tore myself apart. Suddenly Rainer comes up, grins at me and says, "Tired, aren't ya?" So I say, "Yes, I'm very tired." I was grumpy and irritable. He looked at me in a certain way and said, "Working on an assembly line is harder." That statement has stayed with me all my life. I have quoted it many times, for instance in Ethiopia where I often have to work really hard, and people come up to me and say, "Take a break, you must be tired." In such a situation I always remember: working on an assembly line is much harder.

In Frankfurt, late in 1974. Rainer had finished the script for *Mother*

*Küsters goes to Heaven.* I read it, went to see him in his director's office at the TAT and said, "I've read the script for *Mother Küsters.*" He said, "Well?" I said, "Well, I think it's good. But there's one thing I don't understand. I know you are against the right, and you are against the left, you are against the extremists, against high and against low, you are against political parties, you are against religion — what exactly are you *for*?" He started to think and after a while he said, "You know, I keep noticing all the places where something stinks. Whether that is right or left, high or low, doesn't mean shit to me. And I shoot in all directions, wherever I notice that something stinks." Believe it or not, that statement marked the beginning of my political-sociological development. I began to see the world around me more clearly — from an increasingly critical perspective. And not from any party perspective, including the Green Party, with which I felt a great deal of sympathy. Wherever I looked I began to notice: something isn't right here, and something isn't right there. And from that point I began to organize my life in a way that led to "People for People."

*You say that Rainer was the catalyst for it?*

Fassbinder was the prime mover, not only artistically but politically. All the work I did with him pointed in this new direction. Step by step we went through these new phases together. But that one remark started me thinking until I suddenly said to myself: I can identify with that. There is such an unbelievable amount of injustice in the so-called "Third World" that I'm going to do something about it.

*There are many people who hated Rainer for somehow moving them.*

The few times we were alone together, we always talked about our fathers and the problems we had with them. Did I tell you that I once invited him to meet my father? The two of them played table-tennis together.

*Did Rainer win, at least?*

They only shot a few balls back and forth. My father was close to eighty. Afterwards my father laughed and said, "You told me that he is such a revolutionary; he is a really well-brought-up young man, he is very nice." Only his clothes did not appeal to my father; he thought Rainer's shoes were really awful and he asked whether he didn't have any money for a decent pair of shoes.

The only thing I regret is that we had too little time, or took too little time, to build up a relationship separate from the group. I remember, once I invited Rainer alone, but he brought along two other people.

*Did Rainer strike you as chaotic?*

No, but the group around him was. And he used that group in the most fantastic way. Some of them were very weak people. The strong ones occasionally got into a fight with him. Schygulla, for instance, who was a great personality even then. It was unavoidable that the personalities he worked with sometimes got into hot water with him.

*One had to fight with Rainer, and the more you fought him the more he respected you. But he was not interested in fighting as such: he wanted arguments to clear the air. He couldn't stand wishy-washy situations or attitudes.*

I accept that with some self-criticism: one of my greatest weaknesses is that I can't fight. When I get in an argument, I usually think of a good, strong answer a couple of days later. In direct confrontation I am very weak, which also makes me a weak partner. I'm sure it must have bothered Rainer that either I reacted not at all or much too late, and usually by that time he had forgotten the original argument.

# GÜNTER LAMPRECHT

M*r. Lamprecht was born in 1930, in Berlin. Because of the war, he spent only four and a half years in school, was then apprenticed to a roofer, later found temporary work in a button factory, then in a firm that produced orthopedic gear. In 1953 he began to study acting under Else Bongers and at the Max Reinhardt School in Berlin. His career as an actor began at the Berlin Schiller Theater and continued in Bochum, Wiesbaden, Heidelberg, Essen, Cologne, and Hamburg. He also worked in radio and has appeared in ninety television productions to date; he has acted in movies since 1975. His portrayal of Franz Biberkopf in* Berlin Alexanderplatz *has been acclaimed, especially by American critics, as one of the greatest achievements in German film.*

## AN UNSPOKEN FRIENDSHIP

*Where and when did you first meet Rainer?*

We met in Zadek's Bochum Theater during a production of *Bibi* by Heinrich Mann. Rainer turned up with his entire company. I was a member of the Bochum ensemble, and was being conscripted for the rehearsals of *Bibi*—meaning that the managing director ordered me to play the part. Rainer's own ensemble was too small. I went to the rehearsals and every morning I observed an embittered Hanna Schygulla or a bored Gottfried John, or whoever else was there.

*"Embittered" how?*

She was always totally introverted; sort of floating miles away. The

whole company was a regular traveling circus. Everyone was a bit nutty
— some in lovable ways, some not so lovable.

We were supposed to have stage rehearsals and I had prepared myself pretty well. Rainer stood in the door of the rehearsal room and observed the whole scenario. I expect directions from a director. But there
weren't any. The book, a fragment, was very thin and I had no idea what
to do with my part. I did really weird things: leapt in the air, forwards,
backwards. I thought maybe I could provoke direction from him. Rainer
just stood there the whole time and watched us. I only wanted one thing,
to get out of there. It was really stupid, no communication at all, not
even a friendly "good morning," nothing. This went on for five, six uneasy days, and then I was called in by Zadek and he said, "Günter, you
are out of the Fassbinder production." And I said, "Fine! But why?" And
Zadek said, "He says he is physically afraid of you. He can't do anything
with you. You're out." "Thank God," said I, "that I don't have to stay
with this shit."

A few hours later — they were still rehearsing — as I walked down
the hall to the canteen, I ran into none other than Rainer Werner
Fassbinder, who now throws his arms around me, hugs and kisses me
and says, "We're making a fantastic film, you and I." I thought, "Now
I've really landed in the loony bin. A minute ago I got thrown out and
here he comes and says we're making a film." Then he says, "I have a
terrific part for you in *World on a Wire*, let's forget about *Bibi*." "That's
fine, Rainer," I say. "I am glad to be out of *Bibi*. That's no play for me.
We'll shoot something as soon as Zadek gives us a vacation." And he
said: "I've already discussed all that with him, it's o.k." So three days
later I received a contract from the WDR for *World on a Wire*. From that
moment on, when I stood in front of the camera and Rainer stood behind it, I felt an incredibly strong empathy with him. It was an unspo-
ken friendship. I was drawn to him.

Then came *Eight Hours Don't Make a Day*. He wrote in a part for me.
In 1977 I did *Maria Braun* in Coburg. I must have impressed him. I went
to see him in his trailer. He was sitting in a corner. He asked me how I felt
about Biberkopf. I said, "Excuse me Rainer, I'm sorry — but: Biberkopf?
What's that?" "You don't know Biberkopf?" And I say, "Oh, yeah, he's got
something to do with Berlin, something in literature. But right off the
cuff, I don't know who he is." So Rainer explains, "He is the main character in the novel *Berlin Alexanderplatz* by Alfred Döblin." "Oh, my God —
Döblin. Yeah, I once started reading him and after thirty pages I stopped;
I didn't understand him." "Yes, that's who you're going to play in my

film," says he. And then I again, "I can't imagine how that novel is supposed to become a film." "That's not your problem," says he. "The scripts are almost ready, I'll send them to you one of these days." I asked, "Are you offering me the part?" "Yes, you'll play that part," he says. So I say, "Man, I look forward to this, but am I curious to see those scripts. I simply can't imagine how that book can be made into a film."

A few weeks later, the scripts arrived in the mail, all fourteen volumes; it was a huge package. I took off for Grönitz on the Baltic, got into bed in a hotel room, high above the ocean, and read those books in three days. I was fascinated. It was crazy, the way he had transformed that novel into a screenplay. I wanted to start acting the part right then and there. That was how I got into *Berlin Alexanderplatz*.

Well, I'm vain enough to say that I can't imagine anyone more ideally suited for that part than myself. And Peter Döblin said the same thing to me during the press preview; he kept paying me compliments: if only his father were still alive and so on. Do you remember the dubbing? When Rainer announced loudly, "Günter Lamprecht is not a Fassbinder actor." I don't know what that was about. That remark simply hung there, in space. And then we made the famous agreement; I said, "Rainer, I hope we had a good marriage. And I hope we've made a good child together: Franz Biberkopf. And now I've got to stop working with you for a while. I need a rest. Let's give ourselves an intermission of, say, two years. I've picked up sinusitis and an ulcer, I simply have to take a cure." But no sooner was I back from my cure than the offers started all over again. First *Lili Marleen*, then *Lola*, and then *Veronika Voss*. I declined them all based on the fact that our two years weren't up yet. I just wasn't ready.

*Would you see him at all socially?.*

He was in *Kamikaze* in Berlin at the same time I was doing *Love is no Argument*, so we sometimes ate dinner at the same restaurant and would be sitting at the same table. I can still see Rainer in his corner. He'd say, "Good evening, fat Miss Bibbi," or "Bon Appetit, Franziska." Once he came out with his offer for *Querelle*, very, very cautiously. I said, "Rainer, I really don't know." And he: "Oh well, you're much too normal for that movie anyhow. Forget it."

One night, after the shooting for *Querelle* was complete, I walked into the Paris Bar and saw Rainer. He looked terrible. I was overcome by pity for him, a strong, deep sense of sympathy. But I had to fly to Zurich the next morning, so I had to leave the bar early. I got up, said goodbye, walked past his table and waved to him. Suddenly Rainer gets up and looks at me. I turn back and now comes a scene that could have been shot by Fassbinder: two men walk towards each other and kiss each other passionately. Then I turned, walked out of the Paris Bar and looked back once more, through the window. He was still standing there. That was the last time I saw him.

*When you first read the novel* Berlin Alexanderplatz, *you weren't turned on by it. But you were crazy about the scripts.*

I come from a lower-class family. We had very little money. I was a regular latchkey child. As a small boy I worked as a luggage carrier at the railroad station for fifty pennies. My formal schooling never went beyond grade school. And I never got to read any books. At sixteen, when I suddenly started reading real books, I didn't really understand Döblin. He was way beyond me. Much later, thanks to drama school, I started to catch on. I studied literature and caught up with a vengeance. I was a late bloomer. Then, when Rainer offered me the part of Biberkopf, I bought the novel and read it properly. Then, of course, I understood. My mother never read anything, you see, and she didn't go to the movies either. Later, when television came into her life, she watched a lot. My being an actor meant nothing to my parents until I appeared in two episodes of a TV series and several films directed by Wolfgang Petersen. That established my reputation as an actor and made my parents proud of me, even if they had no idea what it was all about. They liked to see their Günter on the screen and in the newspapers. My mother thought I was great in every part I played.

In the early seventies they moved from Berlin to somewhere near Hannover. They had a neighbor there with whom my mother didn't get along at all. She and my mother were both eighty, but my mother was still quite active, did her own marketing, walking with a cane. Some time after the third episode of *Berlin Alexanderplatz* my mother walks out of the house to go shopping and the neighbor comes out of the house next door and says to her, "Tell me, Mrs. Lamprecht, is that your son I see on the screen every night?" My mother, proudly: "Yes!" Then the other woman: "Then why don't you tell your son that he is a pig." So, and now comes the good part: without a word, my mother lifts up her cane and bangs the other woman on the noggin. But the other one had a cane, too, and so boing! boing! boing! the two octogenarian ladies knock each other senseless with their canes. Just try and imagine the scene! When they were totally exhausted, some passersby pulled them apart. And all because of *Alexanderplatz.*

*Because of the so-called "dirty sex" scenes.*

My father had wanted me to become a prizefighter, you know. I fought in twenty-two amateur bouts in Berlin. I was going to be a professional. My father had this image in his head of me in Madison Square Garden — world champion! He was always hanging around the ring watching me train. He really worked on my boxing career, here in Berlin. Then one day, I went and quit. I said to myself, they are making a reservation for you at the Britzer Clinic to have your nasal bone removed. That's what they used to do to you before a big fight, so you wouldn't be injured and have to give up. Of course, there's always a lot of money at stake. Because of my nasal bone, which I did not want to have surgically removed, I said, "This is it, I won't get into my shorts; I'm quitting." The promoter had invested a lot of money in me. For my father, the world fell in. Then, in 1982 I was in New York when *Alexanderplatz* opened there and I had those fantastic reviews ...

*... so you did get to Madison Square Garden after all!*

Yes. I got the publicity man, John Davis, to take me to Madison Square Garden. I looked the joint over and sent a postcard to my father — he was still alive then. I wrote, "Now I'm here and I'm a world champion. They love me here in America. Success doesn't only work for prizefighters; it works for actors, too." He died soon afterwards.

*Sounds as if you had quite a reputation in New York.*

I had appointments every day. I had to keep giving interviews — in my lousy English. (Meanwhile, of course, my English has improved.) Then a new bookstore opened up. They had published a new edition of Döblin's book. I was supposed to sign copies of the book and they drove me there in a Rolls Royce. Only in New York can you see a bookstore two stories high and nothing but copies of *Berlin Alexanderplatz* in the window. The most flipped-out people from all over New York were there. And, what was really fantastic: along the entire second floor they had fourteen monitors, each with an episode from *Alexanderplatz.* You could walk from one to the other. Really a terrific idea.

# BRIGITTE MIRA

$M$*s. Mira's career as an actress and singer began in 1930. She starred in countless films in the forties and fifties, and in the sixties began to appear on television as well. She met Fassbinder in 1972 at the Bochum Municipal Theater where she played under Peter Zadek's management. Films such as* Ali: Fear Eats the Soul, Mother Küsters goes to Heaven, *and* Chinese Roulette *established her presence in the New German Cinema. The interview took place during the Fassbinder Exhibition in Berlin in 1992. She lives in Berlin.*

## A GENTLEMAN THROUGH AND THROUGH

*One of your most beautiful roles was in* Ali: Fear Eats the Soul — *a woman who falls in love with a foreigner, a foreigner who is much younger than she is. That film was made in 1973.*

It's uncanny, as if Rainer had seen into the future, how precarious the situation regarding foreigners would become.

*Do you believe that movies that deal with such socio-political subjects can have an influence on society?*

Well, when you're an actress and you're given a beautiful part to play, you enjoy that so much that you probably don't give much thought to what the film is saying. You create a human being on stage but meanings are the director's job, you can't burden yourself with them. I don't think we will ever find a greater director than Rainer, he really knew how to say everything the world has to say...For an actor, the main thing is to play his part well, isn't it? And Rainer took care of everything else, that was so great, you didn't have to rack your brains about it.

*How did you meet Rainer and how did he treat you, a star from a different generation?*

He was a gentleman through and through, he was incredibly kind, only his methods were sometimes a little strange to me. It was hard for me because the troupe around him, his permanent crew, they all belonged to him. There I was, a complete stranger. I said to myself, "Dear God . . . it's like a wall." Later on, though, it disappeared. Everyone was very nice to me but it was quite different from what I had been used to. I said to Rainer, "Why don't you encourage me a little bit, you might have said that was well done, something like that, but you didn't say anything at all." "But when I don't say anything," he replied, "it is always well done." That was Rainer.

*Did you feel he was difficult?*

We worked together a lot and we enjoyed it. I don't understand how anyone can say he was moody or anything like that . I didn't experience any of that. I really got to know him and I remember him well. He liked to laugh a lot, like a child, like a little boy, didn't he? Very few people know that and very few talk about it.

*There are so many different opinions of Rainer as a director; what is yours?*

He had such a delicate sense of what an actor can and cannot do . . . But basically Rainer let me do things my way and that, of course, is the most wonderful thing that can happen to you. He made me feel so secure, so calm . . . he was a perfectionist, and he also — as the saying goes — did his homework. His notebooks, his director's notes, they were full of little figures and lines and that sort of thing; he knew everything down to the characters' hand movements.

*After your early difficulties, how did you get along with the community around Fassbinder?*

In 1974–75, TAT had become a real theater cooperative. And I must say — I've always had a big mouth — a cooperative with actors is impossible. And why? Because there is no profession more full of ego, every individual so vain that it makes you want to puke — if you pardon my French. And everyone is busy trying to get a leading part. That's just the way it is.

*There is a wonderful saying: All actors are vain, drunk, stupid, and besides, each one is better than the other.*

Absolutely correct — except *I'm* never drunk.

*How does an actor feel when a film like* Ali: Fear eats the Soul *runs utterly counter to the popular taste? How does it feel to play a part that is bound to meet with rejection?*

That brings us back to the terrible vanity of actors. We are basically very primitive. The actor just wants to know, "How do I come across?" The film's message is something he sees from a different angle. He sees a good part, first and foremost. To be perfectly honest, I thought the part was terrific. Besides, the subject speaks to me, I am always befriending foreigners...

*What was the audience reaction at the time?*

I remember *Mother Küsters goes to Heaven*: that practically caused a riot, people whistled and booed, not because the film was bad but because the subject was so controversial. I know nothing about politics and I don't feel entitled to make any judgments. Rainer always said, "You certainly know your job." That was high praise coming from him.

*When you worked with Rainer, were you aware of his qualities?*

You know, I am an old hand at theater and I have worked in many films with a lot of different directors and I must say, he was a revelation for me. He was the one who could get the very utmost out of you but not, as some people say, by manipulation. No, it was simply because he wanted it. By means of a gesture he could give you the feeling that you were good, and that made you good. A strong hand is important in the film business. It won't work any other way.

# BARBARA SUKOWA

*In the seventies and eighties Ms. Sukowa starred in major theaters in Hamburg, Salzburg, Munich, and Paris with directors such as Luc Bondy, Jürgen Flimm, Peter Zadek, and Giorgio Strehler. While acting in* The Women *she met Fassbinder, and she went on to play Mieze in* Berlin Alexanderplatz *and the lead in* Lola. *She discovered her talent as a singer while* Lola *was being filmed. Since then she has made a name for herself with numerous concerts in Berlin, Paris, New York, St. Petersburg, etc. — especially with her interpretation of Schönberg's "Gurre-Lieder." She has worked with directors Margarethe von Trotta, Michael Cimino, Lars van Trier, Volker Schlöndorff, and David Cronenberg. Ms. Sukowa has three children and lives in New York. The interview took place in Hamburg.*

## STRANGE DISCREPANCIES

*How did you start working with Rainer?*

The first time was in a play, *The Women*, in 1976. I had been acting mostly in the theater, with Luc Bondy, for instance, who was extremely important for my development.

It was a time when everyone tried to do things differently from the way they had been done before. Staged rehearsals, for instance, were out. The entire system of organization had been eroded during the sixties. The directors gave the actors a lot of freedom. They had no fixed concept, and they did not do staged rehearsals. They never said, now you walk from this spot to that spot. They didn't have every move worked out on a drawing board. They thought of themselves as initiators and observers during rehearsals, and they let the actors improvise.

*How did those directors treat actors?*

When I was doing my third or fourth play with Luc—I played Regina in *Ghosts*—he actually said almost nothing at all to me during rehearsals. But one extremely important remark, which he dropped in a kind of aside, was, "I have a feeling that she is somehow very clean, physically clean, too." That sort of gave me a line to follow and from then on I just improvised a lot. But when I started making films with Rainer, there were staged rehearsals once again. He said, "You stand here, you walk over there, because the camera is just making such and such a move." I had no idea what filmmaking was all about and it didn't interest me all that much. On my evenings off, I preferred to go to the theater. I was used to working in a certain way and now all of a sudden there were all these specific directions. Rainer had an exact concept of the way you were supposed to enter a room. Once, I remember, I was really puzzled when he said to me, "Why don't you just play it like Marilyn?" At the time I thought it was silly. I couldn't see why I should be like her, why should I ever be like anyone else? Later, when I saw her films I was thrilled and then I understood why Rainer had said that to me, and what I could have gotten out of it.

In one respect he was very much like Luc and the other good directors I knew: he gave you the feeling that he enjoyed what you were doing. That made you open up and relax. When I first started out I had directors who immediately pounced and criticised everything. That only makes you shut down, it doesn't get you anywhere.

*Until* Berlin Alexanderplatz *you had worked exclusively in the theater?*

And in 1978 I had a child. I didn't plan to go back to work for at least a year. On August 13, Hans was going to be a year old, and *Berlin Alexanderplatz* was to start shooting on the 12th. I felt very sad because I hadn't quite kept the promise I'd made to myself. But the week before shooting started, they called me to say that it had been postponed to the 14th. I took this as a very good omen.

*Were you looking forward to playing that part?*

I was terribly scared. When I read the scripts I saw a mixture of Elisabeth Bergner, Marilyn Monroe, and Bette Davis. I thought it would have to be something completely crazy and wonderful.

*And you didn't see yourself that way?*

No! I kept asking myself why he had picked me for that part. He said, "She is very sweet." And I: "But I am not really sweet."

He: "That's just why, because you aren't like that." And then he told me to go see *La Strada*. I was obstreperous again. But I went and I did see what he meant: the clownishness struck a chord.

*Did he make you feel secure? Or did you have doubts about yourself?*

I had never played a big part in a movie or on television before *Berlin Alexanderplatz*. Everything was completely new to me. I had to concentrate very hard to understand what was going on. That made me very tense and I tired easily. I didn't even know what they meant when they said, "Now we'll do a cross cut." I didn't have a clue.

*You know what's crazy about this? You moved with such absolute perfection, very cinematically. For instance, there were no breaks in continuity. I have seldom seen that, even with the most professional actors. How did you do that?*

I have no idea.

*Did he work more closely with you because everything was new to you?*

Everything went so fast. I remember my very first scene in *Berlin Alexanderplatz*. I was supposed to smile. But I also wanted to show the character's sense of insecurity—I would smile, all right, but at the same time I would sort of pull at my skirt with one hand. You know, the way children sometimes do when they are embarrassed. I had no idea that I was only visible down to my shoulders. That whole business of pulling at my skirt was for nothing. That's the sort of thing that kept happening to me.

*There is a long shot in which it shows. There were three different shots of that one moment.*

I once asked Rainer whether there's any difference between acting on film and on the stage. He said no, when it's good you act for the camera exactly as you would on a stage. But of course, you would have to know when you're having a huge closeup. Because then, when you move your head even slightly, it would be like a major thunderstorm. But otherwise, he said, it would be exactly the same. You don't ham up your facial expression on stage either... The fact that I know so little about film may have helped with the part: that clownish, somewhat stylized business, that playfulness stayed in. I acted in a slightly more stylized way for Rainer.

*How do you mean?*

He liked me to play with a little more emphasis. In *Lola* I was performing something definite. When I walk towards the car, when von Bohm kisses my hand, there's almost a mixture between "showing" and "being." And I noticed that Rainer enjoyed that; he laughed every time. When you work with a director whom you don't know at all, you have to find out which acting style he likes. I have a wide range of acting styles. When I saw Rainer's eyes light up, I knew I had hit on the right one. It wasn't always easy.

*Rainer never meant film to be an image of reality but an elevated presentation of ideas, of a period, of interpetation. After* Alexanderplatz, *did you realize what you had done was so good?*

He accepted me. I had no negative feedback. But very often I didn't even understand what he was doing. That scene in the woods, for instance, where Gottfried John kills me, I had expected it to turn out totally silly; I thought, what we are doing here — it's ballet! It all seemed so unnatural to me. I simply didn't know that the camera is different from the stage. I imagined the scene the way I would see it on a stage. I had no idea that when the camera moves it gives a greatly enlarged detail. I was really astonished when I saw the result.

*What was special about the way Rainer made films?*

Rainer was very good at delegating authority; he did not have to do everything himself. He never even looked at Mieze's dress, the costume for *Alexanderplatz*, before the shooting started. I arrived on the set in that dress, and the shooting began. There are directors who want to have their say down to the last bit of lace on your panties. They come on the set and want everything to be changed. Rainer trusted his people, and they had their own way of doing things. Some interesting incongruities were inevitable; some things never came together. For instance, the tablecloths and ashtrays in *Alexanderplatz*: they were all modern, from the wrong period. But that didn't interest him. Those strange discrepancies were, in my opinion, what made up his style. Take *Maria Braun*, where Schygulla and Trissenaar are stalking through the ruins in boutique clothes and high heels. You won't find any documentaries or newsreels of the time in which women run through the ruins dressed like that. Only in that film they did, and that's what I find so intriguing. If they had run among those ruins dressed as rubble-women with kerchiefs on their heads, it would not have been a Fassbinder film.

*Rainer made movies from different periods, but always with a contemporary feeling. I think that's what makes his films timeless.*

The first time I saw *Lola*, I said: "This film will be good ten years from now." And that's the way it turned out. People who did not like it the first time they saw it call me up today, after they have seen it again, to tell me that it is a really great film after all. All my friends have told me I should do a comedy. But I usually played those serious, tragic parts. Rainer saw that side of me, too.

*But you can be very funny . How about that scene in* Lola *where you are drunk and talk about the area utilization plan?*

That was even better during rehearsal. I could have used a few more takes. At the time I was not really familiar with film as a medium — and not so crazy about it either.

*If you had the choice between a terrific play and a terrific film today, which would you pick?*

Let me put it this way: If Rainer were to offer me a film today, I would do it with him.

# PETER KNÖPFLE

M*r. Knöpfle was born in Stuttgart in 1937. Having studied makeup and hair styling, he began his professional life at the Bavaria Film Studio, where he has worked on many national and international productions.* Berlin Alexanderplatz *was his last Fassbinder film; his contract with Bavaria prevented him from outside work. Today he is chief makeup artist. The interview took place in Hall 7 of the Bavaria Studio, in the same space where Franz Biberkopf's room had been set up in 1979–80.*

## TO HAVE A BIG TRUNK READY

*Did Fassbinder appreciate your work? And if so, how did he show it?*

He knew what he wanted and he wanted something original. If you realized his ideas the way he wanted, he was extremely grateful. He might just pat your shoulder at the end of the working day, to show that he appreciated what you'd done. I liked that a lot.

*Is that unusual?*

Yes, it is unusual — most directors don't do it. You shoot a film for three months, and at the end the director says, "It was great working with you; I want you on my next film." But you won't make another film together, because he's totally forgotten. After *Alexanderplatz*, Rainer asked me to work with him on each new film. Since I had this permanent job here at Bavaria, often the schedule wouldn't allow it. There were other reasons why I sometimes didn't want to.

*What reasons were those?*

I told him that I shouldn't make every film with him. An occasional change of director was important for me. He was terribly offended.

*Sad, rather, I would imagine.*

I didn't want to become a part of his clique. I didn't want to be marked into his groove. I didn't want that. I simply needed to stop once in a while. But I was always enormously pleased when he asked me.

*How would you describe the atmosphere during a shoot with Rainer?*

I've never seen anything like it. You'll hear the same from everyone at Bavaria who was there at the time.

*How was Rainer different from other directors?*

Rainer arranged everything in his head in incredible detail, but he still let others express themselves. He understood human beings very well, knew exactly how to deal with every single one of his people in his own unique way. He was simply incapable of working slowly. He said, "The actors are letting up, they're going slack." He certainly didn't say that because he wanted to go home early.

*How much independence did you have with Rainer? To what degree did you simply execute his orders?*

Makeup is not known for its independence. But with Fassbinder we were lucky. We had a lot of freedom. Even when he had a precise idea of a character, he accepted other people's views. Most directors don't even trust you to fix up the extras properly. Rainer was totally different. If he got mad, you knew the reason why. But he never got mad about your work. That builds you up, of course. When you have a director who likes your work you go to bed feeling stronger. Of course, you must not let him down either.

*How did it work with* Despair? *That was an historically and psychologically complicated film.*

Oh, Volker Spengler was very makeup-friendly. I like it when a guy says, "You know, we could do that with red hair and red eyebrows and red cheeks." We even made his eyelashes red.

*Did Rainer tell you beforehand what kind of color he envisioned for the film?*

Oh, yes! He wanted everything pale violet around Hermann, Dirk Bogarde's part, especially his factory, even the cars; the entire set was kept in those shades.

*When did he discuss the film?*

I spent an entire day with him on *Despair* at his home. He explained every single camera setup. He discussed each character with me, and you could be sure he was going to remember. He didn't just say any old thing; he stuck to it consistently during the shooting. Of course, he also had some sudden, spontaneous ideas, so you had to have a big trunk handy and be ready to dive in. A director has a right to change his mind. During *Alexanderplatz* he came to me once and said, "I need very long eyelashes right now." At a moment like that you can't offer some medium ones; you've got to be able to conjure something up. Like the crown of thorns for Gottfried John in the epilogue to *Alexanderplatz.*

*That wasn't in the script.*

Just before lunch he said, "After lunch I would like to have Gottfried look like Jesus." So I ran out into the woods and twisted a twig into a crown of thorns; we let some blood run down it and there it was. So I sent Gottfried in, and Rainer didn't say anything. When he didn't say anything, it was okay. Then, in the evening, he came by and said, "I liked it." Sometimes when something spontaneous came up, he asked me, "How long will that take?" I said, "Half an hour." And he: "Twenty minutes." Then I: "Half an hour." And he, again: "Twenty-five minutes." It really became a matter of five minutes more or less ...

*Did you get recognition for your work with Fassbinder?*

When you mention the name Fassbinder, there's always this hush. Having worked with Fassbinder has meant a great deal to me professionally, I am sure. It was enormously important for me.

# ROSEL ZECH

$M$*s. Zech was born in Berlin in 1942 and studied acting at the Max Reinhardt Seminar there. She first with Peter Zadek in 1968 and was a member of his ensemble at the Bochum Theater from 1972 to 1977. Although her first Fassbinder film was* Lola, *she gained international recognition later with* Veronika Voss. *She continued to work at major theaters with such directors as Hans Lietzau, Jérome Savary, and Hans Neuenfels. She appeared in numerous motion pictures and television productions, including* Mascha, *for which she received the German Performing Arts Prize [Darsteller-preis], and most recently in* The Doctor *by Jo Baier and Peter Steinbach. For her performance in* Long Day's Journey into Night *in Vienna she received the Kainz Medal. Among her most recent motion pictures are* Salmonberries *by Percy Adlon and* Neben der Zeit [Next to Time] *by Andreas Kleinert. The interview took place in Munich.*

## HIS INCREDIBLE AWARENESS

*What did Rainer mean to you?*

That covers a lot of ground. He was something like a big brother, my alter ego. He knew more about me than I knew myself. He exuded such strength, something so bright and vibrant that it made you come truly alive. That's what I'll always remember. He was a dynamo, a magician. I was always completely myself with him, and never afraid. Excited, yes. I might think, "Darn! Now I've said something stupid"; that sort of thing. But you could keep silent, too; you didn't always have to babble or say something clever when you were with him. He knew what was going on anyway, perhaps because he was so totally aware. I don't know what it was. He was a big riddle, but I didn't want to solve it, I only know his effect on me. I always felt completely at one with myself, that's what he did for me. He always made you be at your very best.

*Where and how did you meet?*

In 1972, in Bochum. Zadek had taken over the theater. Rainer staged two productions there, *Liliom* and *Bibi*. When Rainer left Bochum, he wanted to do *A Doll's House* with me. But I had to stay with Peter Zadek. Peter and I had only just started working together. And Rainer understood.

*Which directors were still working in Bochum at the time?*

Werner Schroeter; Pip Simmons from the Netherlands; Jérome Savary; Jürgen Flimm; Rainer, of course; Zadek; Augusto Fernandes — those were the chief directors. It really was something, to have such big guns as Rainer, Peter, Schroeter — it kept everyone alert.

*How was the relationship between Rainer and Zadek?*

There was always stuff going on; Rainer had problems with Peter and vice versa. It was often about rehearsal conditions. Peter kept the best for himself and Rainer rarely got the good rehearsal spaces, or enough time, and so on. And they played tricks on each other; for instance in *Bibi* Rainer named a dog "Zadek." Those were cat-and-mouse games. There was a Fassbinder faction, a Zadek faction, and a Schroeter faction. All those "religious sects" were in one and the same place and if one of them spoke to the other, it was an event. They were a very lively bunch.

*You were loyal to Zadek?*

I had gone to Bochum because of Zadek and I simply had to go on working with him. That cycle had to be brought to completion. It was the only reason I didn't go with Rainer. I also had an offer from Peter Stein and I told him the same thing.

*When did you meet Rainer again?*

In 1979; I was in Molière's *The Misanthrope*; Rainer was filming *Berlin Alexanderplatz* and Thomas Schühly, his production assistant, took me along to a joint where Rainer happened to be. And then it was — how shall I say — love at second sight. I felt very close to him, somehow at home. He offered me a part in *Berlin Alexanderplatz*. But I was rehearsing *The Importance of Being Earnest* with Zadek, and Zadek being as jealous as most directors — they all think it's a sacrilege when you work with another director, you just might give a good performance for somebody else! — he did not permit me to work with Rainer. I could easily have managed; I had only two scenes in *Importance*. Rainer said, "O.k., next time." And that next time was *Lola*.

I instantly felt that we had known each other a long time, that he knew all about me. I would have accepted anything from him, without question. Meeting him was important, it was such fun to work with him. It was extraordinary. It never felt like work, although we really worked a lot.

*How did* Veronika Voss *come about?*

Very simple. In Berlin, at the "Diener," the artists' hangout, he said, "Do you want to play Veronika Voss?" I said yes right away. And Rainer said, "Find a book about drugs, for some background, the rest you'll do on your own." That was it. I got the information I needed and then I shut myself off from the world.

*You and he did not talk much about your part?*

Not at all. I only knew that he filmed very fast, that one had to be prepared and always give a first-night performance. We filmed for five weeks and had very little time. But he was an experience.

*Do you remember the time when you found out that two scenes had been cut, and how you called us about it?*

That was awful. I was already crushed when I saw the rough cut and Rainer's rather angry reaction to it. Today I can understand it, of course; I know that he was just as nervous when he saw his film for the first time. And besides, the two scenes between Armin Mueller-Stahl and me were still missing. At the time I said to myself, "My God, never again will I work with Rainer." Today, I would not react that way.

*Why were you so angry?*

I felt somehow helpless after the screening and I thought we ought to do it over, make it better. I said so to Rainer and he got angry; he was right, but I was right, too. When I think about it now, he was always and in everything—even when I got so mad—a lover. He felt everything very deeply, and so did I.

*How was opening night?*

The film broke three times. It was terrible. I thought my end had come, but Rainer took it with a sense of humor.

*After that, did you still want to keep working with Rainer?*

Of course I wanted to keep working with him; it was mutual. We wanted to do a play, *Penthesilea*, and another film, *Le bleu du ciel [Blue Sky]* based on a novel by Georges Bataille.

*After Rainer's death, did you feel that your work was appreciated?*

Yes, oh yes, especially in America. When I told them I had worked with Fassbinder, people simply fell over backwards and treated me like a saint. It was also great when Percy Adlon said, "I'm going to steal a scene from *Veronika Voss*: you'll have that same halo in our film, too."

*Veronica Voss was panned in Germany. The critics called it "Mimicry of the fifties."*

That upset me, too. The worst thing was that they paid no attention at all to me. Rainer was panned into the ground, but I did not even exist. I think Mr. Krasek wrote that I was a kind of diluted washerwoman from the Ruhr.

*Are Rainer and the experience of working with him still meaningful for you today?*

Yes. I've dedicated some of my work to him. For instance Mary Tyrone in *Long Day's Journey into Night* by O'Neill, which I played in Vienna. I dedicated that part to Rainer because of the intensity with which everyone lives and experiences life in that play. I think of him often, very often. He is a part of my consciousness, it gave me courage to know that such a man existed on this earth, and that I was allowed to meet him and be together with him for a while. What I liked most about him was his incredible awareness. There are very few people who are so much at ease, and who are, in their innermost self, aware of other people, not just of themselves.

*Did you feel loved by him?*

Yes, I felt loved, accepted, and understood. We all knew how intensely Rainer lived his life. He could shoot all day, spend half the night at the October Fest and the next morning at nine he was ready to go on shooting. You might say, "Well, all right, that can't go on forever, it's just too intense." He also wrote screenplays and thought up stories. To someone who is that creative you can't say you've got to do such and such now, because this and that is good for your health. It's impossible. For him, Number One was work—at least that's how I saw it—and self-expression. For van Gogh, self-expression was also the most important thing. Health and everything else had to be Number Two. If Rainer chose such a vehement tempo for his life and work, that was his business. It's wrong to say he died so young because he had not lived right. For him it was right, it was the way he expressed himself. And he did not want it any other way.

# HORST OTTO GRIGORI WENDLANDT

B̲orn in 1922 in Criewen near Schwedt/Oder, Mr. Wendlant learned his *trade from the ground up. He began as a distribution agent for Tobis Filmkunst and, after two years as a prisoner of war in France, quickly gained a new foothold in the industry: first as business manager for Carl Froelich Film Productions, then as production director at CCC-Film. In the early sixties he joined Rialto Film where he made a name for himself as producer of movies based on the novels of Karl May and Edgar Wallace. In order to distribute the films of Charles Chaplin, he founded Tobis Filmkunstverleih in 1970. Since 1977, he has been sole owner of Rialto and Tobis, with more than ninety productions to his name. He has worked on a number of screenplays for the films he produced. His screenwriting pseudonym is H. Gregor. The interview was conducted in Berlin.*

## WE MET TOO LATE

*Weren't you offerend* Maria Braun *at some point?*

We were offered *The Marriage of Maria Braun* for distribution in 1977. I saw the film here in Berlin, we said yes, and then all hell broke loose with the Filmverlag der Autoren [The Authors' Film Publishing House] and the American distributors, United Artists. Augstein asked me to withdraw because they had a contract. So I said, "It's o.k. with me, if you already have the film then we won't take it." But when Augstein turned around and went to United Artists I was really mad. I met Rainer in Cannes on the Croisette, we looked at each other, fell into each other's arms, and I said, "I must tell you, the film is sensationally beautiful." I was the one who spoke first. He said, "I'm really glad" and he was quite embarrassed. "Well, are you taking the film?" And I: "We wanted to, but we withdrew in favor of the Filmverlag der Autoren. Let's talk about it..." And then we spent six evenings together, went out to eat together, became friends. There was such immediate warmth; I had not really expected that from him.

*What sort of mental image did you have of him ?*

Well, those pictures that used to appear in the newspapers, where he would turn up somewhere with his clique and make a lot of noise. And then a famous critic wrote that the German film would benefit by a collaboration of Fassbinder and Wendlandt. We eventually got together and started talking. He had big plans, right away. When he was here in Berlin in 1980 he called me a few times, and I told him that I had something really terrific: I offered him *Kokain [Cocaine]*. He read the book, thought it was great and wrote the screenplay. But it was at least two hours too long.

*You producers! Everything's always too long for you.*

And Rainer said, "Now we've got to go to Brazil and look at the locations." "Well, all right," I said and all of us took the Concorde to Brazil. I said, "You go out and look, I'm staying right here in our hotel." Sometime during dinner I said, "Rainer, you have to shorten the screenplay when we get home. We can't make a movie that runs four or five hours." Rolf Zehetbauer already had some sketches ready, everything looked absolutely terrific. And then he said, "Heck, you know, I have a lot of problems with shortening things, I really don't know how. You know something? Let's make *Lola* instead." And I: "For Pete's sake, we've come all the way to Brazil." He: "I think Brazil isn't really right after all. Scratch Brazil. Tell you what, I'll take off right now for Marrakesh, there are really terrific sites there." So they went to Marrakesh and I flew home. When they came back from Marrakesh, Rainer said, "You know, *Lola* would be the right project... To *shorten* a screenplay, I'd need a lot of time for that. I'll have the time after we finish *Lola*." I asked, "What have you got ready for *Lola*?" He: "I've got all of it ready, we can start shooting in eight weeks." I said, "Wonderful, so let's make *Lola*."

*You've been making films since 1968, you have worked with internationally known directors. When you compare Rainer with . . .*

Stop right there. You can't compare him to anyone. He had such an extremely sensitive intelligence and such deep feelings, more heart than I have seen in any director. Everything he did he made with his heart, not his mind. And at the same time he had the intelligence to know exactly what to do. That may explain why his images are so fantastic and his dialogue so brief and simple. He had only one aim: to finish the film as simply as possible and never to give less than his best. And he succeeded without interruption.

Whenever I had a success, it was because I had worked with my heart. We were a little bit alike in that respect. It was always important for him to have something to play with. Making movies was fulfillment for him; a child gets a rocking horse, and suddenly the child is happy. That's how it was with Rainer. When he was making a film the world around him disappeared, and he was the happiest human being you could imagine. When he could direct his people and show himself from his worst side and torment them, that's what he liked. He wanted to torment me, too, but there I'm afraid he didn't succeed. We simply never had any arguments. If he wanted something, he got it. I simply put my trust in him. That's why I held a protective hand over him during *Lili Marleen*. Luggi Waldleitner's working method was completely different. Luggi is at the studio every day; every day he looks at rushes, every day he expects to have his say in the matter. But I feel that's what you have a production chief for. As producer, I don't stand over my director from morning till night. That is not the producer's job; his job is to take charge when there are problems. And there were no problems with Rainer. Of course, he was pleased if you showed up once in a while when he just happened to be shooting an important scene.

*And if something went wrong?*

I would be the first to hear about it. It's always a matter of money, anyhow. When the film is finished, that's when I see how the money's been used. When Ingmar Bergman made *The Serpent's Egg* he worked just like Rainer. There were never any problems. At precisely seventeen hours he stood before me and said, "Finished." And about Rainer all I can say is: I would have made any film blindly, without a contract, without anything. He was someone I trusted completely. He never had any thoughts in the back of his mind of taking advantage of me. It was his film, one had to let him make it the way he wanted to.

He was such a worker — unlike many others I could name. They are ready to collapse if you ask them to make a picture every three years. Rainer was indefatigable, indefatigable!

*What did Rainer want from you?*

It really was a kind of father-son relationship. Perhaps he was look-ing for a legend in me: Wendlandt has turned out so many successful films. And success was very important to Rainer. He was not like some of those young filmmakers who made movies just to be able to show something. They didn't give a shit about success. They were sponsored, they were subsidized, they were happy. As long as they got a good re-view, they didn't give a damn whether their films sold or not. Rainer was the exact opposite; he wanted great success, to make great pictures.

*That's what they reproached him for with* Lili Marleen.

Isn't it always that way? As long as someone is making five dollars, the critics love him, since they themselves only make five dollars. When he earns 500,000 dollars they are angry at him because they are still only making five dollars.

*You once offered Rainer money to do nothing?*

Yes, indeed. I wanted him to put in a rest period, a period of con-templation. But you know yourself, no sooner was he done with *Lola* than he had to start on *Veronika Voss*. I said, "I'll give you money every month to stop making one film after the other." But he answered, "No, I can't do that, I always have to think and work and have something else up my sleeve. Who knows what'll happen?"

We met too late. We could have had an international success with *Kokain*!

# ROLF ZEHETBAUER

Born in Munich in 1929, he began working independently as a production designer for motion pictures and TV in 1952. He joined Bavaria Films in 1968 as chief architect and designer for all their important productions. He has many international films to his credit, among them Ingmar Bergman's Das Schlangenei [The Serpent's Egg], Das Boot [The Boat], The Never-Ending Story by Wolfgang Petersen, and Schlafes Bruder [Brother of Sleep] by Joseph Vilsmaier. He has received numerous prizes, including an Academy Award for Bob Fosse's Cabaret in 1972, and the German Film Prize for Robert Siodmak's Nachts wenn der Teufel kommt [At Night when the Devil Comes] in 1955 and for Fassbinder's Despair in 1978. He also received the Order of Merit First Class of the Federal Republic of Germany. His collaboration with Fassbinder began in 1977 and continued until Fassbinder's last film, Querelle. He has also made a name for himself as an architect for exhibits, including the 1992 Fassbinder Exhibition in Berlin. This interview took place in Munich.

## A QUESTION OF TRUST AND ABILITY

Despair was the first film you made together.

That first assignment seemed very strange to me. He told me what he wanted with incredible precision. Then I read the screenplay.

You didn't know the Nabokov novel?

I didn't read it until after our meeting. I developed the set and showed it to him. He'd barely had time to look at it when he declared that it was great. We built it and scheduled a viewing and discussion.

*You built a model?*

No, the complete set. I arrived for the meeting, dead on time, but he had already been and gone and left a message behind: Looks good. All systems go. Our entire collaboration was based on the fact that we saw each other very seldom, but when we did, it was with utmost concentration. Now and then he'd come on the set and have a fit because it was so hard to photograph it. But then he sort of internalized the set with all its glass, its mirror images and dissolves. What he made of it was brilliant. When he found everything he had specified, he wound up using the set from exactly the same perspective as the designer had planned. That's what fascinated me about him.

*Can you describe this more specifically?*

It was the way he worked. Sometimes we talked at great length, seven, eight hours for *Lili Marleen* for instance, and for other films half an hour would do it.

A designer has his own perspective, of course. He builds a set so that it has an optimal side and a certain spot from which it can best be photographed. The set becomes a frame. Rainer always came to the studio, looked around, and then went and stood at this ideal point. He made full use of the set. He became a raging beast if the designer messed up or misread anything. This never happened to me, which doesn't mean that I'm infallible. He simply expected the same kind of precision with which he himself prepared a screenplay.

*You won your second German Film Prize for* Despair.

That meant a lot to me. Speaking of prizes and Rainer, I've got to tell a story. I suppose I can talk about it now. I was to get the newly established Bavarian Film Prize for the production of *Lili Marleen*. But the selection committee said, "We can't expect the Prime Minister of Bavaria to present a prize for a Fassbinder film." I never told Rainer this — or Luggie Waldleitner. Thank God, the attitude towards filmmakers has changed radically since then.

In any case, Rainer and I became friends without seeing each other often. Then he came to me with other projects. Not with every film, but on a regular basis. I had become quite friendly with the men and women who worked with him. He had his own scene, that's well known. But that I, at my age, was accepted there, that he drew me into it, I thought that was just great.

*At first the sets were not central to his concern. He used existing spaces. But he enjoyed finding a film designer whose imagination harmonized with his own. It always fascinated him that you could realize his ideas so accurately, although you come from such a totally different background.*

The success of a designer's work depends very much on his sense of the director's vision. The screenplay gives some guidelines, but there is a special director's language. And to translate that language into a set design, that's what is important. It was easy with Rainer in a way because he showed only superficial interest. But on the other hand, if someone accepts a design within a quarter of an hour—as was the case with *Querelle*—you are bound to think, "Did he really look at it?" Yet when he came to the studio, he knew exactly what was what. He had originally worked out a concept with projection screens which I didn't think was all that great. We needed a set he could move around in without being tied to projection screens. But that was how we did it; our last job—unfortunately. Unfortunately—for everyone!

*You've never forgiven him for that . . .*

No, and I will say it again and again. Working with a filmmaker like him was such a terrific experience. He was so active, always full of plans. Others are elated when they finish a film. They're in no hurry to start the next one. But he always had three or four new projects in the works. He was a creative dynamo.

*When you tell your many contacts in Hollywood that you worked with Fassbinder, what does it mean to them?*

They show great respect in Hollywood. In Germany, however, I often encountered a perfectly miserable attitude. Horrible! People sniffed and asked, "How do you stand it?" And I used to say, "Listen, you could all learn from him, from his precision, his creativity." If one day he didn't feel like working, he made it up the next day. I don't think he ever overran his shooting schedule.

*For some of us who belonged to the group, that pattern was a matter of course. I only realized later what I had lost.*

It has left a gaping hole in my life. Of course, I made pictures afterwards, but this hole has remained. We never got around to making *Kokain [Cocaine]* by Pittigrilli, for example. That was a tragedy for me, really. Our preparations were already well under way. It was a bitter fate.

*What he demanded most of all of us was ambition and love of filmmaking.*

Love of the project. Absolutely. The way he would discuss it! I remember once we were in his kitchen, planning *Lili Marleen*. To discuss such an epic project at the kitchen table—that was a unique experience for me.

*Did he mention what the political aspect meant to him?*

Yes, of course. First of all, he expected you to have studied the book—not just read it, studied it. He noticed immediately whether you had immersed yourself in it or not.

*And while the shooting was going on —were you always there yourself?*

He didn't want to see me during shooting. To have the architect standing around on the set was totally uninteresting to him, as long as everything was right. When he shot *Lili Marleen* he did ask me to come to the Olympia Hall for the matte painting. He had no experience with that technique, so he wanted to be sure. Our work was driven by precision: brief talks, so I could give him what he wanted, give him the chance to work well with the camera.

Now, with *Alexanderplatz* we had a major problem. The milieu was uncongenial to me, so I begged off. He didn't understand and he resented my backing out. But that milieu—perhaps the whole thing was too big for me, not that I mind big projects, but this one went on forever. Besides it was destined mainly for television.

*Or so you thought!*

We all make mistakes.

*How did you come up with those brilliant sets for* Veronika Voss?

"It must look like a ship," I said to myself. The idea clicked with him. When you are on the same wavelength, there is always the danger that the tension will slacken, that you will no longer challenge each other. If he had felt something like that happening, I know it would have been the beginning of the end. He, of course, was always utterly engaged and he expected the same from the rest of us.

*He hated complacency. I often heard him say, "There goes another well-fed artiste."*

Exactly. Once he said to me, "You are the only older man I know who is as young as we are." That delighted me and of course it made me feel completely on his side.

*You say you never met anyone else like Fassbinder. With all those huge projects you worked on?*

It's true. I could give you a good story with the name of every director, but every story would be miles away from the story of Fassbinder.

*Even a genius like Ingmar Bergman?*

Bergman is a genius and enormously creative. He gave me as much free rein as Rainer did, but the amount of discussion he needed to come to that point — that took weeks, months. Of course I learned a lot from him. He, like Rainer, did not come to my studio, he did not want to see what I was working on. But to reach the point where you could start to build, that took months with Bergman. While the film was being shot, there was a meeting every evening about details needed for the next morning. Working with Bergman and working with Rainer — there's no comparison. There are directors who can read sketches. There are directors who can read layouts. And there are directors who can read models. And if you show a floor plan to a director who can only read models, then he has no idea what it's all about. Rainer could read everything because he had the necessary imagination. I ask every director, "How would you like it? Do you want a model, floor plan, or sketch?" Rainer would say, "If we understand each other you don't have to show me anything." It's a question of trust and ability. And so I showed him very little. And because I didn't need to show him much, there is unfortunately almost nothing left of what I did. I have no sketch of *Lili Marleen*, I have nothing. For *Querelle* we built a model, he could read it, he looked at it and said, "Yes, fine, that's the way I want it." We also had the wonderful color sketches by Frieder Thaler. And then, of course, Rainer made his own storyboards. Nowadays directors have them made by others. Rainer's story-boards were such tiny little postage stamp pictures. He was not one of those directors who go around looking for motifs on the set and end up picking the worst corner. He was completely prepared; that's one reason he always worked so fast. That had its effect on everyone, including the actors.

*What mattered to him most was precision, speed, and concentration before the camera.*

There are directors who rehearse the actors to death. They do twenty-five takes and at the end they pick the second take anyway. I've seen it many times. And there are directors who break an actor's arms during the shoot, telling him exactly how he is supposed to stand. It's good to have seen all those different methods. And that is why I can say with a perfectly good conscience: Rainer was more. For me he remains a pearl among directors.

# XAVER SCHWARZENBERGER

B*orn in Vienna in 1946, Mr. Schwarzenberger has been a cinematographer since 1970. His camera magic is inextricably connected with Fassbinder's later films, from* Berlin Alexanderplatz *(1979–80) to* Querelle *(1982). Among the pictures he worked on with other directors are* Kamikaze 1989 *with Wolf Gremm,* The Ace of Aces *by Gérard Oury, and* Night *by Hans Jürgen Syberberg. So far, he is listed as director as well as director of photography in fifteen films, including* The Silent Ocean, *the two* Otto *films, and* The Night of Nights. *The interview took place in Munich.*

## THAT COMPELS A REACTION

*You said that you remember your first encounter with Rainer with dismay.*

It was my first trip to Berlin. I arrived punctually at the apartment in Niebuhrstraße where you two lived and worked during the *Third Generation*. It was about eleven in the morning and after a lot of knocking and ringing, Harry Baer opened the door. I didn't know him. He was wrapped in a white sheet and his face was all swollen. When I told him who I was and that I wanted to see Fassbinder, he immediately closed the door on me. He was totally confused, looked at me as if I were a ghost, and probably couldn't believe anyone wanted to see Rainer at that hour. Then he came back and said he would try to wake Rainer but he wasn't very optimistic about it. He went away, returned once more and said I should come back in about three hours. It seemed a bad omen for a working relationship that would have to last almost a year.

*That was supposed to be your introductory meeting on* Berlin Alexanderplatz?

I seriously considered heading straight for the airport. But three hours later I went back. Harry Baer again opened the door. He was no longer wearing a sheet and Rainer sat at his desk, dressed from top to toe in black leather and wearing thick sunglasses. He sat there being frighteningly benign. He was actually nice and polite. We used the formal address to each other, just like two businessmen. But very soon he asked which cinematographers I liked, which directors I admired, and so on. We discovered affinities. Sternberg's name came up very quickly on our list of directors and Gianni de Venanzo's among cinematographers, two figures in motion picture history whom we both revered.

*But you were definitely going to direct the photography for* Alexanderplatz?

No. Neither of us knew if he would be able to stand the other for more than an hour or a day, not to mention a whole year.

*You had never worked on such a long project before.*

True. And besides, I had done hardly anything in Germany.

*Did the novel* Berlin Alexanderplatz *mean anything to you?*

Not a thing. I flew back home and the next day Minx called to say that Mr. Fassbinder had agreed and if I agreed, it was a done deal.

*How was your working relationship?*

At the start of *Alexanderplatz* we didn't see much of each other. During the first two or three weeks we shot very fast. Rainer and I were heading for a showdown about who would break first. It was clear that it would be me, I had to work so much harder physically, but he was determined to see how long he could force me to work at that speed.

*He would bring you his sketches, not the day before, but just as you started shooting. You must have had your own ideas of how to shoot your scenes.*

The motif was always clear, but you had to react pretty fast, since nobody knew what the continuity would be like. I was given everything just before shooting started and it had to be done precisely his way. He had drawn his little stick figures with great care and always in the right direction. Then I had to get cracking. I am a very fast worker anyway, but I wanted to be especially swift.

*Well, he was famous for fast work.*

But I, too, was known as a fast worker. So we kept egging each other on. It was terribly hard on the others. It was hard on me, too, because I kept getting into stressful situations. The lighting engineers couldn't keep up, and so on. We started around nine; he came at ten, and by four we were finished. We never worked overtime. On a normal film, you keep shooting for as long as twelve to thirteen hours. We did not even spend half that much time. Later on, this gave us a chance to play football together. But at first it was complicated. After all, we didn't really know each other. And after two or three weeks, I said to myself, "I give up, I can't do this." He was also keeping his distance; we hardly talked, there was almost no contact. I was pretty devastated.

*But remember how everyone was panting to see the cut? We kept doing it that way up until* Querelle.

The results were wonderful, but I couldn't take the tempo any more. It was as if he were trying to set an Olympic speed record. And it upset me to be kept at a distance.

We had been working a lot faster than necessary. He always wanted to know where people's limits were, how much they could take, how sensitive they were, where he could stick the needle in if he had to. I don't hold it against him, but at first I thought, "I can't do that"; I lost heart. Not so much because of the speed but because of the distance at which he kept me. He was a good psychologist when he wanted to be, so he noticed right away that I'd had it. We never talked about it, but he immediately slowed down to a more human pace, and he became more accessible. Then began that period of collaboration which meant so much to me. It was the most fruitful, agreeable, and enjoyable time for me and my camera. I never experienced anything like it with any other director.

*There is that scene in the eighth sequel where Mieze comes to Biberkopf's place, with a very slow camera move, where she sits on his lap and he calls her Mieze when she actually wants to be called Sonia. And then there is a cut with narration. It's a really terrific camera move. At the time I thought, "That's too long, we'll just cut it a bit earlier." And then, which was so typical of Rainer, I loved that in him, he said, "How can you cut away Xaver's camera move!" He probably had thought it up himself, anyway. I found that unique in him, this total loyalty, this solidarity with anyone he worked with for any length of time.*

Especially with lighting, in my case. He decided all the camera moves.

But when it came to lighting he only intervened if something was not extreme enough for him, which rarely happened.

*Did you have extensive pre-production conferences?*

We never really discussed anything in detail beforehand, never. In *Lola*, for instance, we met just before shooting started. Now, in that film it was a matter of extreme color. He said we should look at three films: *The Barefoot Contessa*, *Johnny Guitar*, and *Written on the Wind*. We did, and that was it. That was how *Lola* was made. Not a word was said about any particular color. When he liked what he saw he never said anything. But if he hadn't liked it, we certainly would have heard from him.

*Did you ever feel oppressed by him?*

Never. Normally I work on continuity with the director because many directors don't know how. That was not the case with him. Let's put it another way: I could concentrate on the lighting, and the dolly work was quite a tough job, because there were such complicated situations. I could give myself to it, which was downright pleasant.

*Did you ever meet anyone else, before or after, who could be so precise without preparation?*

Never — nobody else even comes close. That was one of the reasons I often say, "Well, all right, I'll do it myself." What's the use of arguing with amateurs?

*The five films you made with Rainer gave you enough courage to make your own films?*

When I planned my first project, he was still alive. We had actually talked about it. I'd even asked him to act in it. That was soon after *Querelle*. But we had reached a point with *Querelle* where our two paths might have parted. We might not have wanted to work together quite so exclusively.

*You had problems with* Querelle?

I never understood that film. And I never even read the book; I was simply not interested. I had never felt like that, not before and not since, certainly not with Rainer's other films. It was so alien to me. It was a story that passed me by, that didn't interest me at all. It was exciting to make the film, but I didn't know what the film was all about. Not that that bothered me. In those twenty-two days of shooting I didn't have much time to figure things out.

*Why only twenty-two days?*

He got his kicks from being fast. I can relate to that: he wanted to get finished. He was not a very patient man. We had that in common: impatience and wanting to finish up, to be done with the thing, to put it away and go on to the next. I can understand that very well. I think it was the main reason why he drove us so hard.

*Is there anything you learned about cinematography by working with him?*

What has stayed with me is the rhythm of a story, the importance of closeups, for example. And the possibility of shot-reaction-shot at the right moment. He always knew the rhythm he wanted to maintain during shooting. Rainer always had a definite, well-defined, and carefully worked-out concept. I had not come across anything like it before, and was not capable of it myself, and afterwards I never encountered it again.

*Were you hurt by the criticism of* Alexanderplatz, *that the film was too dark?*

I myself thought that it was too dark. Rainer and I had talked about it.

*What did he say?*

Somehow, I think he got a kick out of it. But there is a hitch. I wouldn't have minded the darkness if much hadn't been lost through that shitty 16-mm material and because of that stocking.

*The stocking over the lens?*

Yes, we decided on it after a while. And because we did not shoot chronologically, some parts are lighter and some are darker — that bothers me.

*But the fact that* Alexanderplatz *is a masterpiece and has since become recognized as such . . .*

Still, I noticed a lot more than others did, including the weaknesses.

*Couldn't one say that it is right the way it is? There is, in fact, only a single scene that's too dark, the Zanowitsch-scene in the first episode.*

O.k., but you can't ignore that one scene.

*Five minutes in fifteen hours!*

Well, those five minutes could have been better. I can't say it's terrific, I can't say it's the way it should be, because it just isn't so. It wasn't planned that way. And it was my mistake.

*What made Rainer special as a filmmaker?*

When you worked with Rainer, when you had been part of a film he had made — and it was always clear that he was the one who made the film — you felt that you had been part of something really important. Whether it was really so didn't matter; you just felt that way. He conveyed that in every moment. He was a man with great charisma. When you have charisma, you produce something that compels a reaction; you motivate people to work beyond their abilities. For me, Rainer was the last German film maker of importance. Until this day!

# ARMIN MÜLLER-STAHL

*M*r. *Müller-Stahl was born in West Germany, grew up in East Germany, and now lives in Los Angeles and Hamburg. He has had three "careers": in the DDR and in Eastern Europe he played sons (in films which included* Nackt unter Wölfen [Naked among Wolves] *and* Geschlossene Gesellschaft [Closed Society] *by Frank Beyer/Klaus Poche); in West Germany and Western Europe he played fathers (as in* Lola, Bitter Harvest *by Agnieszka Holland, and* Oberst Redl [Colonel Redl] *by István Szabó); and recently, in America, he played grandfathers (as in* Avalon *by Barry Levinson and* Music Box *by Costa-Gavras). He acted in many locally and internationally successful films, and for twenty-five years he also appeared in numerous plays. The interview took place during the Fassbinder-Exhibition of 1992 in the Filmkunsthaus Babylon in Berlin.*

## ANYONE CAN DO REALITY

*What comes to mind when you think of Fassbinder today?*

Fassbinder was someone for whom no boundaries existed, not between the real and the absurd, nor between safety and risk; neither between man and woman nor between life and death. Even his death was perfectly staged. One day he just took off into the beyond, disappeared without any histrionics. After staging so many films, he staged his own exit; it was perfect. He had said: I am somewhat like Mozart. I have completed my work, forty-four films, I am thirty-seven years old, I could produce repetitions, no doubt, improve some of the things I've done, but somehow I have arrived at a full-stop.

*Do you remember your first encounter with him?*

I had just come out of East Germany. Fassbinder offered me a part in *Lola*. At the time I was acting with some famous actors in a TV film called *Collin*. Fassbinder wanted to know what my price would be, what I would consider a decent fee. And I said, "I've just come over to the West, but I'll try to find out from some of the people I work with; Jürgens and Blech, they should know how much to ask." But I never got a straight answer. I soon realized I wouldn't be able to tell Fassbinder what I'd consider o.k. for my first fee in the West. So I said to Schühly, who was doing the contracts, "Make me a decent offer, in three days I'll know how much the others are making. I will accept your offer, in any case." "All right," he said "I'm offering..." "Just a moment," I said, "please understand that I mean it; I am a pro, I'll know within three days what the others are making." Three days later I knew that Sukowa made a third more than I and Adorf made twice as much. And that made me furious; that sort of thing galls you when you're a pro, especially when you've just come from the East. I had three choices: not to be angry; to be angry; to be very angry. I arrived at the second choice: I was angry. I called my wife and said, "Send me my two violins. I have a plan; I want to make my anger productive, I want to play all my colleagues to the wall — with my violin, with everything."

But what if Fassbinder wouldn't go along? We hadn't started shooting yet and it would only work if he went along. And Fassbinder sensed it all — he had, by the way, the most amazing antennae — he heard everything, knew everything that was going on. He understood the kind of team we were; he played the team as if it were an instrument, perfectly. He sensed that I not satisfied, that I was upset by his method of negotiating. He supported my anger against him. I was allowed to do anything I wanted in that film. So I played the violin; I played a big violin and a small one; the scene with the small one was cut, unfortunately — I always say that with a touch of acrimony — but in the meantime everything had become a game.

One day I came up with the idea of stirring my tea with a burning cigarette. There is no director in the whole world who wouldn't at least have made a skeptical face. Fassbinder absolutely beamed and said that it was just as if he had planned it himself.

*When you think of Fassbinder, can you distinguish between the director and the man?*

Not really; for me he was always the director. I only knew the man through observation. I don't think we exchanged more than four sentences in private.

*How did you feel about becoming a Fassbinder actor?*

I never planned to become a Fassbinder actor. Having escaped the clutches of the DDR, I had no intention of being caught again — not by a director, not by a series, and not by a country. You see, the DDR was so final for me. Working with Fassbinder was enormously enjoyable, but I still needed to take flight across some further boundaries. After *Lola* I was ready to change my ideas about life again because work had been so enjoyable, so much fun.

Fassbinder never shot any scene more than once. He was in a tremendous hurry. One has to understand that he was literally rushing through his life. Afterwards, I said to myself that maybe I'm going to be a Fassbinder actor after all. He is far and away, with the possible exception of Barry Levinson, the best director I have worked with to date. No actor was ever given so much freedom, and Fassbinder as a person was stimulus enough to make everyone give his best.

He was not a talker, he couldn't say much about actors' parts. There is this lovely story about Jeanne Moreau, who wanted to discuss her part. He said that's a good idea, let me think about it. And he walked away and half an hour later he came back and said, "I've got it: just be great!" That was it. The first time I met him we stood facing each other in total silence. He was almost shy, almost timid. We didn't say anything. We sort of looked at each other and then Adorf came along and said, "Shall we talk about the parts?" And Fassbinder said, "Good idea." Then he took a long pause and said, "Just like on a stage, that would be fine." We really acted like stage actors, you can see that in *Lola*. So, we played at top level, often deep into the red zone. And then there was Fassbinder's love of risk-taking. He needed to take risks in order to be able to work the way he did.

*How do you explain all those not exactly friendly clichés that kept making the rounds about Fassbinder?*

Yeah, that's something else again. "Ruffian," "monster" — animosity pure and simple. And unartistic, too, if you don't mind my saying so; you don't persecute a man because of his political themes. Chabrol has them, all directors have them one way or another, writers have them, of course: they have to stand for something. The point, I think, and this annoys me terribly, the point is that we Germans don't really have our own film. We are a non-artistic nation. We are a nation that doesn't need film. And one reason we don't need it is that we don't want to delve into our history. We simply let things hang, and that makes me so angry, because the press has gone along with those clichés, especially in Fassbinder's case.

*Were there any discussions between you and Fassbinder about* Lola — *any political discussions?*

Nothing of the sort. Not to say that he wasn't very open. One day I said to him that there is something missing from the ending, perhaps Böhm should be asked, "Are you happy?" He would be hanging in the air, a desperate figure, a failure. Fassbinder said, "Mmm, I don't think that's necessary," and never mentioned it again. Until one of the last days of shooting he came to me and said, "Today we shoot your contribution." I said, "What do you mean, 'my contribution?'" He had Lola's daughter lie down where Lola had lain, in the hay, and she asks him, "Are you happy?" And I find that so brilliant, so simple. Fassbinder was fascinated by everything that had to do with betrayal, with the way people deceive each other. But he was also fascinated by the absurdity of the story; it was not just reality. All of us must come to terms with reality, anyone can do reality, it is all over the newpapers, in the news, but what makes some people special is that they are able to show things in their absurdity.

*How was a Fassbinder rehearsal different from others?*

Some directors never stop talking and giving explicit instructions, "Now you go over there, look out the window, speak the line; but remember to stress the third word somewhat, though not *too* much, just a little. Now look around the corner and say good morning and now, you go over there into full-length and, by the way, I want your back to express the quiet kind of dignity you get from your father..." There is so much information that it clogs your head. You have absolutely no freedom left, you sort of lurch from one instruction to the next. Nowadays no director dares to do that to me anymore but I had to fight for that freedom.

Fassbinder will take his place alongside the great Germans. I haven't the slightest doubt that he will stand next to Kafka, next to Thomas

Mann. While the cameras rolled, he only had to be there and everyone gave the best that was in him or her. Very often you don't really need instructions. It is a matter of a sixth sense, one's own sixth sense. The problem is that nobody can do justice to Fassbinder, the person. Everyone has his own idea about him, everyone is impressed by his films. What he has created, what he has left for us in his short life, will continue to make people think.

*What especially impressed you about working with Fassbinder?*

His spontaneity, the way he accepted risk, freedom, his imagination, his artistic sensibility — and that included his pleasure in tormenting people! He was expert at tormenting people. He relished it. It is all part of the picture of the best director I've ever worked with.

# MARIO ADORF

*orn in Zurich in 1930, of a German-Italian family, Mr. Adorf studied theater arts and languages in Germany. His breakthrough as an actor came in Brecht's* Mr. Puntila and His Servant Matti *with the Munich Kammerspiele Ensemble. His first film was* 08/15 *in 1954. But his first big success came in 1957 in* Nachts, wenn der Teufel kommt *[At Night when the Devil Comes], directed by Robert Siodmak. During the sixties he worked mainly in Italy; in the seventies he again played in German films with younger directors such as Edgar Reitz, Volker Schlöndorff, and Reinhard Hauff. In 1978 he acted in Billy Wilder's* Fedora. *The interview took place in Potsdam during the 1992 Fassbinder exhibition.*

## THAT WAS IT

*Was working with Fassbinder enjoyable or stressful?*

Some say it was insanely stressful to work with Fassbinder. He had a way of treating even his best friends quite badly now and then. It gave you a kind of uneasy feeling: for heaven's sakes, how is this ever going to work? Well, I knew Fassbinder. I was supposed to play the director in *Beware of a Holy Whore*, but Lou Castel got the part. I had a contract, including the advance, but I returned it because I couldn't take the part, and that's when we got to know each other. Fassbinder sat with me on the terrace of my place in Rome. We couldn't talk at all; he just sat there not saying a thing. I am not the easiest person either when I notice that things aren't going well, so we probably sat there two or three hours in silence; we didn't talk at all.

When we started working together on *Lola*, I asked myself, "How can this continue?" And, sure enough, true to form, he hardly talked to me. I remember meeting Hanna Schygulla and saying, "Werner isn't talking to me." And she said, "You should be glad; because when he talks to you it can be dangerous: you suddenly become a member of the group and that gets tricky."

Certain actors just remained outsiders. I was one of them. The work went very well, he never said a harsh word to me, never. I remember, once, when I asked one of his former teammates, "Why on earth doesn't he talk to me?" the teammate said, "He's afraid of you." I simply couldn't understand it. It was really strange. I would have liked more contact.

*What was Fassbinder's typical way of directing?*

Here's an example: we had just shot a scene and he said, "Fine, that's it." And I said, "You want to leave it like that?" He, "Yes, why?" And I, "Well, I blew a line, I wasn't at my best, can't we do a little . . . " And he said, "You want it slightly more perfect but I couldn't care less about your perfection." That was a very significant and typical Fassbinder remark. He wasn't interested in perfection.

*He never looked at rushes, he always printed the first or second take.*

Well, there are other directors who do that, but they get everything so perfect in rehearsal. For instance, when I think of Billy Wilder — he always wanted the first take perfect, he never wanted to do a second take, that's the way he was. But Fassbinder, he didn't care, even if it wasn't so perfect, sometimes he didn't even rehearse. We rehearsed secretly with Barbara Sukowa. So, some of our scenes had . . .

*We were aware of it.*

Well, of course, nothing can be kept secret in a studio, even though we locked ourselves in the dressing room. It was a little strange, but we had come from the theater where you rehearse for weeks. And all of a sudden we were supposed to improvise. That big scene where Barabara sits on my shoulder — we didn't rehearse that at all. That business where we dance around, what we did there was not in the least rehearsed.

⌒

# CHRIS SIEVERNICH

M*r. Sievernich owned a jazz club in Berlin. In 1972 he began producing films for TV. Since 1975, he has lived and worked in New York. With Wim Wenders, he produced* Nick's Movie — Lightning Over Water; The State of Things; Chambre 666. N'importe quand; Paris, Texas; *and* Tokyo-Ga. *Among his other productions are* Stranger than Paradise *by Jim Jarmusch,* The Dead *by John Huston, and* The Innocents *by John Schlesinger. He is an advisory member of the Sundance Institute and a member of the Academy of Motion Picture Arts and Sciences. While he has not produced any Fassbinder films himself, his extensive international experience enables him to give an expert analysis of the "New German film" in Fassbinder's time, and of the influence Fassbinder films exerted on the development of movie making, especially in America. The interview took place in his New York production office.*

## A TRAILBLAZER

*You came to filmmaking by a detour?*

I was doing something else when a friend of mine, a Berlin filmmaker, got his first commission from the SFB [Free Berlin Broadcasting] to make a TV film. They told him he could make his film if he found a producer. So he came to me and said, "You know about handling money and dealing with people, managing and so on. Why don't you try it?" That was how I got started.

*To produce usually means dealing with money and keeping away from the so-called creative end.*

Keeping away from the creative end was out of the question for me. I had always been especially interested in the question of how this is going to work, how it can be organized so that creative and business people co-ordinate their efforts and produce a work of art, something to be proud of.

*You once said that filmmakers always want to decide and execute everything themselves. Yet I know that Rainer would have loved a responsible producer with whom he could have shared the work. But he had a hard time finding such a person. In actual fact, such a productive collaboration was possible only with the larger bureaucracies such as the WDR [West German Broadcasting] and Bavaria. The films he wanted to make himself he had to produce with his own firm: he had to engage his own production manager.*

After the war, the only producers and directors in Germany were those who had made films during the war. Only a few of the filmmakers whom the Nazis had driven into exile came back. Those who had produced films during the war had worked closely with the Nazis. Many had produced propaganda films.

Germany was busy rebuilding itself. It was not a propitious time for new producers to develop. Lightweight movies were being made purely for entertainment. And that, as you may recall, led to the "Oberhausen Manifesto," a filmmakers' revolt. We must make our own decisions, they said, make the films we want to make. We can't go along with the program laid down by the senior producers. It doesn't interest us, it bores us, it's cheap entertainment. We must have better access to the resources, to money, and so on. Then, against the background of the French "Nouvelle Vague" and some ideas that came from Italy, the so-called German Author's Film began to develop. And because there was no infrastructure, there were no producers, and the young filmmakers were forced to do everything themselves. What had started out as a liberation from production constraints led back to a new kind of constraint. Which is why the Author's Film developed very definite structures. The Author's Film was largely responsible for the structure of the subsidy system — how subsidies were granted, what was being subsidized, and under what conditions.

*Didn't the people who participated in the Manifesto become members of the film boards?*

They weren't board members, but they nevertheless had great influence on how the boards were run and who, in fact, was appointed to the boards. A new generation of television people had arisen. They were the same age as the young filmmakers. Enterprising, adventurous, experimental, they had "Grampa's Movies" up to there. Those movies were a dead issue for them. These new people gave an important impetus to the industry. But the problem was that there was almost no money forthcoming from private sources to finance those films. These films had to be financed partly by state subsidies and partly by the television industry. A mixed kind of financing. There was the "Filmverlag der Autoren" [Film Authors' Publishing House]. It paid some small distribution fees for films. There were hardly any producers around, so the filmmakers were forced to do everything themselves. And they had to keep on doing everything themselves. They got financing based exclusively on their names. They did not get the money because some crazy, bright, alert producers stood behind them. Strictly because of their names, and through their zeal and energy.

*That's Rainer's story.*

And with Wim, and Schlöndorff, and also with Herzog, Schamoni, and Kluge. Then there was also Johannes Schaaf and Edgar Reitz. That was the group that mainly worked in that manner and forged ahead. Its effect can still be felt today. The directors were the producers, script writers, and sometimes actors in their own films; it became harder and harder for them to share their work with others. And they had less and less confidence in the ability of others to do the work.

The principle of the division of labor is very important in film. In the long run, no one person can do it all. The result was that the "New German Film" became middle-aged; there were very few people who had grown up with it. And relatively few new talents in the area of directing had emerged from the school of those formerly young German directors.

*One man who made it is Bernd Eichinger. He very deliberately took the road of the producer. He wanted to be a producer from the very start.*

True, he did not want to direct, he wanted to produce. And he endeavored from the very start to get a clear commercial line into his work.

*Rainer found out after his first ten films that his idea of community decisions would not work.*

Yet the whole Author's Film movement was a powerhouse. It gave off an incredible amount of energy, much of which emanated from Rainer. He really was a breathless whirlwind...

*Did his energy annoy the others?*

The leading German filmmakers were very much in competition against each other. But Rainer was never competing with anyone. He was always a few steps ahead of them. There was that beautiful story in Cannes in '82 when we were making *Chambre 666*. Directors from all over the world were asked how they saw the future of film. It was amazing how little they came up with. Then Rainer came in and said to Wim, "I thought you were done with film school..." — a wonderful remark. Then he grinned in that way he had. With eight words he had exposed the inner disunity of that entire assembly. But then he sat down and proceeded to say some beautiful things about the future of film.

*Let's hear about the way the films of these new German directors came to America.*

Schlöndorff was the first to get real recognition with his Oscar for *The Tin Drum*. The film did very well in the U.S.A. It was the first substantial distribution deal a German filmmaker had ever made in America. Roger Corman bought the film for half a million dollars. And then came *Maria Braun*. That, too, was a big success in the U.S.A.

*I have seen people in the street, here in New York, look at Rainer as if he were a saint. They treated him as if he had just come from some distant planet. That amused him, of course. Rainer had been represented at the New York Film Festival as early as 1971, with* The Niklashausen Journey. *And from then on, he had a film there every year, all distributed by Talbot's New Yorker Films.*

Right. The New York Film Festival was the main sponsor of that German wave. The German film had a really outstanding reputation here, mainly through the Film Festival and the Film Society of Lincoln Center, where the Festival took place.

*Was that comparable to the so-called old German film?*

Of course, comparisons were being made. But the public did not see the historical connection. The films were new and adventurous, insolent and bold. After all, Americans are always much more receptive to new things, new films, new ways of seeing, than are audiences in other countries. Anything new is always received with a certain amount of enthusiasm here.

*Hollywood was very important for Rainer. He was, by the way, the first person Coppola got in touch with in Cannes in 1978. But Rainer was afraid that Hollywood would force him to reproduce his genius hundreds of times, possibly with stories that were not his own.*

I am sure he would have made it here in America, too. Talent is treated more respectfully here than anywhere in Europe except France. That sort of cultural bridge-building would have been fascinating, especially with Rainer. Filmmakers here also do well financially. When someone is successful, he makes a lot of money. It's been that way since the beginning of the movie industry. Talent is financially fostered; you also enjoy a kind of private appreciation: flowers, champagne, congratulations, that sort of thing. That hardly ever happens in Germany.

*What about the critics in America?*

I find them rather generous. American critics do not take achievement or failure so personally. They write their reviews more objectively; they concentrate on what has actually been accomplished.

*To what extent does government subsidy influence film today?*

It isn't good for any government to be involved in the film business to the extent it is in Germany. The subsidies are, after all, government instruments, political instruments. But can you produce a film in Germany without state and television involvement? No, sadly, you cannot.

*When I talk about Fassbinder in New York, there is always that sense of immediate admiration. I wonder, though, whether that feeling extends beyond a Fassbinder cult to the general public?*

No, it is a very definite thing. Fassbinder has become a trademark. At most universities, Fassbinder is part of the curriculum for film students. In film clubs and through university film departments, Rainer's films are being shown again and again. They are an integral part of the curriculum. In 1982, *Berlin Alexanderplatz* came to New York. It was the first time that a fifteen-and-a-half-hour film was shown in a commercial movie house. All performances were sold out in advance. Tickets could be bought only on the black market. Thousands of moviegoers lived their lives around that film for two entire weeks. It was an incomparable cultural event. Fassbinder was the trailblazer of the "New German Film" in the U.S.A. The work of many other directors was measured by his films.

# EGMONT FASSBINDER

B*orn in 1945, Mr. Fassbinder went to elementary school in Cologne, to high school in Heidelberg, and studied at the university of Berlin. Since his coming out in the late sixties, he considers himself a gay activist. In 1978 he started the gay publishing house Pink Triangle.*

## INTERESTING WOMEN

*Rainer had always warned me to keep away from the Fassbinders. It was a kind of first commandment. Why did he do that? Can you understand that?*

Beats me. Rainer didn't even know most of us. And his relationship to his father did not strike me as very intense.

*Your father is his father's twin, right?*

Yes. They were born in 1918, on August 25th. Whenever Rainer and I saw each other, we talked about family matters of which he really knew very little. That's why I am amazed that he had such definite views of the Fassbinder clan. The family was very religious, very Catholic. Lots of teachers and priests, through many generations.

*Did you, yourself, grow up Catholic?*

Yes, at my aunt Gisela's in Cologne. She was an actress, married to the composer, Hermann Schroeder.

*How did you end up living with her?*

Family problems. The economy after World War II. The apartment shortage. Gisela had no children.

*You are the cousin with whom Rainer spent the first half year of his life sharing . . .*

. . . a cradle, yes. I am about three months younger than Rainer. We were living in the country then, in Kippenheim on the Lahr. I was born there. My mother had taken over a country doctor's practice from a physician who was "at the front." Living in the country was a good thing at that time, a doctor could get paid with butter or a goose. No one went hungry in the country.

*Interesting: right after Rainer's birth, his father decides he's got to go to the country.*

That was typical Fassbinder decision-making, without asking anyone else's opinion. To be honest, I don't know all that many Fassbinders. What I remember of my grandfather, Franz Fassbinder, is mainly illness and old age. I see a very hard-hearted man when I think of him, but my mother says he was charming and open. He was a philologist specializing in German, first as a teacher, later as director of a high school. He had written a dissertation on the poet Eichendorff and gotten his doctorate. I don't think he had planned to become a professor. Financial problems probably guided his decision. If he hadn't had five children, he would have stayed in France, I suppose. He'd been lecturing in Clermont-Ferrand. He'd been very happy there and he spoke French like a Frenchman.

*That was the brother of Aunt Klara, the famous Klara Fassbinder?*

She wasn't his only sibling. There were a lot of children. My great-grandfather, Peter Fassbinder, had a very high academic position in Trier. He had many children. The oldest was Joseph, then came my grandfather Franz, Aunt Nina, Aunt Klara, Aunt Mary, and Aunt Margot. I knew them all, except for Joseph, who died before I was born. Klara and Mary were professors; Mary had studied economics. Nina was chief administrator of studies. After she retired from that job, she took up Russian.

*The women in that family went in for higher education as a matter of course?*

No, I don't think so, but they were allowed to decide: either marriage or higher education. Aunt Margot got married, had a stable full of children, and as a sort of extra occupation she wrote children's books and gave radio broadcasts for young people. She was the only one who had a real body, all the others were stick-figures. Mary was tall and thin; Klara was short and thin.

*And Klara was the one who became really famous . . .*

Yeah . . . my grandfather made a big point of being a university professor whereas his two sisters had their degrees from technical colleges.

*Klara was a pacifist.*

She was deeply involved in politics; a co-founder of the German Union for Peace. At one time that organization was considered a front for the illegal German Communist party. Besides she was very Catholic; she felt unclean if she hadn't been to church on Sunday, even while travelling — Catholics are permitted to skip Sunday Mass when they're on a trip.

Anyway, she was drafted during the war, and she set up an army library. It must have been the "war experience" that turned her into a peace activist. She travelled around, lecturing about peace. She wanted to create a synthesis of Communism and Catholicism. The *Spiegel* called her "Friedensklärchen" [Little Klara, the Peacenik], because she supposedly said to Mr. Khrushchev, "Why are your politics so twisted?" She also worked as a translator. According to Lübke, President of the German Republic, that was only "to disguise her political activities." She also wrote a book about the Soviet Union.

*And what did she translate?*

The works of Paul Claudel. She received a prize from the Académie Française for it. Lübke was supposed to present it to her, but he refused to hand a prize to "that Communist." One of the first official acts of the next President, Gustav Heinemann, was the presentation of the "Palme Académique" to Aunt Klara.

*Lilo Eder once told me that her husband, Helmut, always made her feel that she came from a lower echelon than the upper-middle-class Fassbinders.*

You have to scratch the word "upper." The Fassbinders are educated middle-class. The essense of upper-middle-class is education backed by possessions. And the Fassbinders had nothing. They were professors, teachers, priests. Compared to a businessman like my maternal grandfather, they were poor. All that intellectual stuff did not produce much cash. The Fassbinders were all more or less involved with literature. If the Nazis had not come to power and expelled all the Fassbinders from their academic positions, my father would have become a teacher, and Helmut, too, most likely. After the war they got together and founded a publishing house, but it went broke right after the Currency Reform.

*But Rainer's father became an entrepreneur, didn't he?*

Well — that's an exaggeration. He was always somewhat chaotic in money matters; he had problems with taxes. He never did get rich. He owned a few houses but they were seized by the tax people. He had to find something to do after he could no longer work as a doctor.

*Why was that?*

Because he had helped some women — he performed abortions, which was against the law. Someone denounced him. Until 1970 or maybe even later, he was not allowed to practice medicine.

*Now about you. You are a publisher, you founded the Pink Triangle publishing house; you are into literature. That, after all, shows a certain affinity with Rainer and your ancestors.*

Rainer picked the modern medium — film. How many people still read nowadays? But I decided on publishing. It didn't make me rich. If, instead of producing the kind of books people want to read, you produce the kind of books they should be reading — good and important books that nourish the heart and the mind . . . I decided not to produce garbage.

*And the family has accepted that?*

They haven't accepted the way I live, what I do, what I don't do. But they are tolerant. By now I am old enough so it no longer bothers me.

*Did they accept your homosexuality?*

I don't believe that any heteros can do that, even if they want to. As far as they are concerned, we are either perverted or sick and to be pitied.

*Did you like Rainer's films?*

Yes, I liked his films, not all of them, of course. But when *Berlin Alexanderplatz* was on TV, I didn't miss a single installment.

*You didn't meet Rainer very often?*

Maybe ten or twelve times in all. My mother had thrown Helmut out of her house. That's why Rainer and I didn't see much of each other as children. Later, whenever we went anywhere together, Rainer introduced me as a kind of kid brother. I didn't like that. And I didn't go to his funeral. I thought that, since we had not seen much of each other during his lifetime, it would be an insincere gesture. I felt I'd be showing off to the press. After all, I can't take credit for being related to Rainer. I can mourn him better alone.

# JULIANE LORENZ

*M*s. *Lorenz was born in Mannheim. She began to work in films while still a student. In 1976 she met Fassbinder. She was assistant film editor for* Chinese Roulette *and became the editor of every subsequent Fassbinder film — beginning with* Despair — a Journey into the Light *— more than forty hours of film in all. After Fassbinder's death, she worked mainly with Werner Schroeter. A master of film montage, she received the German Film Prize [Bundesfilmpreis] for* Malina *in 1991. Together with Rolf Zehetbauer she devised the Fassbinder Exhibition 1992 in Berlin, as well as a scaled down version for the Goethe-Institute. She is currently director of the Fassbinder Foundation. The interview was conducted by Wallace C. Watson in Berlin.*

## OPEN TOWARDS YOU

*Did Fassbinder talk much about his past?*

I remember a scene in *Berlin Alexanderplatz* where Mieze asks Reinhold about Franz's past. She says, "He doesn't tell me things." Rainer didn't speak very much about his past. Only about a few, very private things. He did not gossip. Most of what is known about his private life comes from books about him, not from him directly — unless you count what his films reveal about his person.

*The published interviews are very informative.*

Rainer was always very precise and clear in what he said in interviews and articles. That is why I chose his own words for the descriptive text throughout the Berlin exhibition.

*What are your future plans for the Fassbinder Foundation?*

When Lilo Eder set up the Foundation, I encouraged and supported her. I never expected to take it over. What I am now doing will, I hope, extend beyond a limited time and place. I hope it will also inspire future filmmakers. I think the 1992 Fassbinder Exhibit in Berlin was something new — a big exhibition about a film director and his oeuvre. Another of the Foundation's tasks is the conservation of negatives. As a cinéast, I know what happens when negatives are left lying in the can too long. You have to take care of them, make duplicates, so when you print new positive copies you do not have to use the original negatives. We also want to look after the movie rights of several TV films that were never shown on the big screen. For instance *Martha**, *Fear of Fear*, and *World on a Wire*, which, by the way, I consider the most fantastic science fiction film in motion picture history. Rainer made that two-part film when he was about twenty-seven. There are films like *Whity* which never came out. Another part of our activity is the archiving of all of Rainer's works — originals belonging to me and documents that belong to the Foundation.

*The Foundation will be a full-time job for you, then?*

I hope not. There are a lot of other things I want to do. It took me several years after Rainer's death to find a way through my grief. Now I have at last gained enough distance to be able to turn to other projects.

*In addition to editing, did you help Rainer with business matters?*

He liked to have his business looked after by the person who cared for him and with whom he had a relationship. That's why I did it.

*Do you agree that the period around 1976 was a time of crisis for Fassbinder?*

Yes, and a time of change. His play [*Garbage, the City and Death*] had been dropped and there were charges of anti-semitism. He could not make *Soll und Haben* [*Debit and Credit*, a novel by Gustav Freytag], nor *Die Erde ist unbewohnbar wie der Mond* [*Earth is uninhabitable, like the Moon*], a film based on a novel by Gerhard Zwerenz. The German tabloids really tore him to pieces. It was awful.

* After being shown at the 1994 Biennale in Venice, *Martha* did get into the movie houses.

*Did he talk with you about it?*

No, but I saw him every day and I could feel it. I saw how seriously he took his responsibility as an intellectual and political artist. And I recognized his pain at being misunderstood. And then there was his private problem with Armin, his lover, who was a very warm person but by no means an intellectual partner.

*Was there a pattern with Armin and Salem?*

I didn't know Salem personally, but Rainer told me about him. The most important aspect of his relationship with Salem was Salem's ability to learn new things easily. Salem came from a small village in Morocco, and he had taught himself French and, later, German. Rainer said Salem was a miracle. You must know that Salem was ten years older than Rainer; he had a wife and two children back home. He was very attractive, as you can see in *Ali: Fear Eats the Soul* and in the other early films. Maybe he was also a kind of father to Rainer. I think he saw a "real" man in him. Rainer did not care where a person came from, his social background, whether he was gay or straight, black or white, rich or poor.

*You were doing film editing before you started working on Fassbinder's films. Had you seen his films before you went to work for him?*

I had studied political science and worked in a film laboratory for half a year. Before I met Rainer, I had edited two documentaries. I wanted to make films, but I also wanted to be a writer. I greatly admired the work of Visconti. When I was fifteen, I saw *Ali: Fear Eats the Soul* on TV, and was extraordinarily impressed. That was all.

*Can you say what he liked about your editing?*

I don't know. Maybe that I was quick to understand what he wanted. There was rarely a problem of communication between us. He trusted me, and I tried to keep him and the others from being aware of how young I was. At the time of *Despair* I was just twenty-one!

*Was there some specific editing technique of yours that he liked? Did he deliberately select you to replace Reginald Beck, who had preceded you as film editor?*

Editing, of course, is not primarily a matter of technique. It is an artistic process which demands a great deal of empathy. Naturally, technique matters—in editing as in directing and cinematography. But a true editor must first of all understand the film; the film as a whole, its motivation, its soul. The editor must be able to bring out what is inherent in the material. He's like a sculptor or a diamond cutter who gives the substance the form hidden inside it. An editor usually starts with a lot of inchoate material created by the story, the actors, the director. The editor gives it its final form. Needless to say, I was not yet that kind of creative editor in Rainer's time. He didn't need a creative editor. He himself formed his films very precisely during the shooting stage. But I think it was my fate to become Fassbinder's editor and that process gave me the strength to become the editor I am today. First I mainly worked with sound as assistant editor on *Chinese Roulette*, and then as co-editor on *Bolwieser*.

*Despair* was the first film Rainer and I edited together. During that famous night, when we cut the film, I learned the difference between an editor and a machine. An editor becomes an extension of the director's sensibility. Yet, the editor must be his own master who gives the "gift" of his skill to the entire work. Next to the director, Rainer said, the editor is most important, and must take that responsibility. And the director must allow the editor the freedom to see the film in his own way.

*Do you know why Xaver Schwarzenberger replaced Michael Ballhaus as Fassbinder's cinematographer starting with* Berlin Alexanderplatz?

1976–77 was a time of separations, including the separation from Ballhaus. Michael is a wonderful cinematographer, no question. Rainer once said about him, "I don't want him to keep forcing me to hurt him. We must go our separate ways." Rainer and Michael had worked together for a long time. Perhaps they had tried everything that could be tried during that time. I do remember that Ballhaus was not very happy during the shooting of *Maria Braun*.

*What about Kurt Raab's departure from the production team?*

Well, that's another, very special case. First let me say that I only met Kurt three times. During the shooting of *Bolwieser*, and then after he and Rainer separated. Kurt was a very talented actor. But his role as "art director" simply can't be compared with that of Rolf Zehetbauer. Kurt never created spaces. He just arranged them. Starting with *Despair*, Rainer greatly changed his attitude concerning set design. It became increasingly important to him in his later films.

*So he outgrew Raab professionally? What about the personal difficulties between them?*

I can't tell you much about that, because Raab was just leaving when I arrived in 1976. Kurt was very weak, very self-destructive. He drank a lot and he felt abandoned by Rainer. To me he seemed like a wife who thinks her husband is playing around, and who keeps complaining you don't love me. I don't believe that Rainer really needed all those people from his early days of the antiteater. I disagree with those who claim he needed people in order to be creative. He would have made his films in any case. But he had a special talent for forcing others to live up to their creative potential. He felt responsible for them. He turned those people into actors, production managers, and so on. Nobody starts out as a star or an actor, an editor, whatever. You need somebody who believes in you, and that really means love. It is incredible how much love Rainer had for people who were not even all that talented to begin with, or who treated him badly.

All right, listen: the real reason why Rainer had to separate himself from Kurt Raab was that Raab had hired someone to kill Rainer. Yes, it is true. And Rainer told me that and said, "Now that's enough. He's losing his marbles, I have to let him go."

Another big problem at the time was that everyone wanted to be loved more than any of the others. As we all know that is a very dificult demand to satisfy. And because Rainer was so attentive and so open, you could easily become accustomed to it. When he then gave his attention to someone else, you felt abandoned.

*Did he love you?*

Oh, yes. He loved me. I didn't recognize it at first, because I never wanted to be loved. But he really loved me, and when I realized this I gave him love, in my way. I didn't show it to the people around him. I was afraid we might lose some of our strength if anyone else got too involved in our relationship. I wanted to be with him, because I revered his work and I wanted our love to be treated as a secret.

*Katz writes that you may or may not have been Fassbinder's second wife, and that after you were married in Fort Lauderdale late in 1979, you tore up the marriage license after he went to bed with a man on your wedding night. Is that the way it happened?*

No. Let me explain again how Rainer and I met and what kind of relationship we had. Rainer was the first man in my life who took me seriously. He noticed every little thing I said; I realized that when he started quoting me. Then I thought, "How strange! He is so famous, he could have so many more experienced people around, but I'm the one he listens to." On the other hand, I was very precocious. Yes, and at times a bit arrogant; I thought I knew all about life, as young people do. I had strong opinions and he often laughed at me. That was the beginning.

Then came Rainer's separation from Armin. I thought that Rainer preferred men. Then Armin died. Rainer was very much alone: everyone concentrated on what he was doing professionally, hoping to get work through him and so on. We spent more and more time together after work. I focused on him, completely; I was interested in his feelings, his life. I also felt very sad about his loneliness. Sometimes Rainer talked about dismal personal relationships, especially in marriage. He spoke very frankly about all that. So when he asked me to marry him — that was in Tangier, in June 1979, our first trip alone, before shooting began on *Berlin Alexanderplatz* — I was confused. What he asked of me was so contrary to everything he had said about personal relations. And for me, too, marriage didn't have the most blissful connotation. Rainer sometimes talked about his horrible time with Ingrid [Caven]. He said she exploited their marriage. And when they met during the time that Rainer and I were together — which didn't happen often, only on official occasions when Ingrid was singing in Germany — I noticed that those old scars were still sensitive.

I was astonished when Rainer asked me to marry him again in Fort Lauderdale after everything he had said about the exploitative side of his earlier marriage. Then he gave me reasons why we should marry. Today I know that I was just a stupid little girl with a romantic vision of love, untouched by official papers. I did not know the real meaning of marriage then. Once, after Rainer's death, Lilo said something wonderful to me. She knew that Rainer had wanted to marry me. She said, "Juliane, perhaps there was something he wanted you to learn together." But to get back to Fort Lauderdale: I did not shrug off his wish. I looked in the Yellow Pages and located a Justice of the Peace to whom I said, "We want to get married." I was told that we needed a blood test. Then Rainer said, "I won't have a blood test. Not ever!" This made the situation somehow more bearable for me, somehow humorous. And I said, "Let's get married anyway, just for fun." So we went to the Justice of the Peace who said, "Okay, if you want to have your ceremony, I'll marry you now. But you will have to do it over again, in a place where no blood test is required, in Germany or wherever." After this mock "ceremony" we went back to our hotel and had fun. Everything was fine until Rainer said to me that he could not believe I didn't really want to be married. He repeated his notion that all women want to be married for the sake of money. That made me mad.

When we got back to Germany, Rainer must have told the others about our "unofficial" marriage. I was asked if it was true. I was afraid of becoming crushed by all the publicity, and so I frustrated Rainer's wishes in that respect. Anyhow, we lived together, I didn't see any need for a marriage license, and our life went on as before. Today I know what it would have meant to Rainer. He wanted order, structure; perhaps he was afraid something would happen to him. In March 1982 Rainer again asked me to marry him. By then I realized that it was really important to him. We set the date for December 31, and a few days later Rainer said that he wanted Rosel Zech and Thomas Schühly — the co-producer of *Veronika Voss* — to get married on the same day. He wanted to make a big event of it.

*Did it disturb you that he loved men, too?*

Not at all. I understand the different elements that make up a human being. We all have both inclinations within ourselves. We are both genders simultaneously. Society teaches us to show only one side. And so we think it is "normal" for a man and a woman to live together. It fits more easily into the official image of a "family." But there are other possible lifestyles. They are "normal," too.

You must understand my situation when Rainer and I met. I was very young and open to every aspect of life. Rainer was living with a man at the time, Armin Meier. They lived together for just two years when problems developed. Then Armin died and I entered Rainer's life. After shooting *In a Year with Thirteen Moons*, he said to me, "Let's live together." A different kind of relationship had begun for him. In the last four years of his life he did not have a close relationship with a man.

*Katz presents this as wishful thinking by you and Mrs. Eder.*

I am not trying to make Rainer more "normal" than he really was. There was a time when he lived as a gay man, and there was a time when he lived as a bi-sexual person. I think he preferred to sleep with men. With a woman . . . it was work for him, and he was also afraid of it. He needed a woman who could accept his way of thinking. I was happy about the way we lived. He was always very open about being attracted to someone else, which I think showed more respect for me than if he had tried to hide it. I was always sure of his love. He treated me as a woman and as his wife. There were three times when he took a lover for a few days. I don't think there is anything more to be said about it.

# NOTES ON FASSBINDER'S LIFE AND FILMS

Between 1966 and 1982, Rainer Werner Fassbinder made forty-four films including two shorts; his first film, now lost, brings the number to forty-five. He produced or co-produced twenty-six of his films himself, first under the name of "antiteater-X-Film," later under the firm name of "Tango-Film Rainer Werner Fassbinder." He acted in nineteen of his own films and in twenty-one films by other directors. He wrote fourteen plays, created new versions of six classical plays, and directed or co-directed twenty-five stage plays. He wrote and directed radio plays and wrote song lyrics. In addition, he wrote thirty-three screenplays, including an eight-part family series (of which only five parts were produced), two two-part TV films, and a fourteen-part motion picture. He collaborated with other writers on thirteen screenplays.

## CHRONOLOGY

1945–48     Born May 31, 1945 in Bad Wörishofen, a resort town near Munich.

        Soon after his birth, his parents, Dr. Helmut Fassbinder and Liselotte Pempeit Fassbinder, move to Munich. Dr. F. opens a private practice adjoining their living quarters, Sendlingerstraße 5. He decides to send the child to Kippenheim bei Lahr (in the Black Forest region) to live with an uncle and country-doctor aunt. In spring 1946, the boy returns to Munich where, in the meantime, several relatives have moved in with his parents. Later, the entire group relocates to Stielerstr. 7. Again, the doctor's office is part of the family living quarters.

1950     Mother is hospitalized with tuberculosis.

1951     Parents divorce. The father moves to Cologne, mother and son to a small ground-floor apartment in Munich. She begins to earn her living as a translator.

1951–55   A few months in a public grade school, then three years at the Rudolf Steiner School. The boy begins to write stories and poems, puts on short plays with his classmates and records them on tape. He makes clandestine visits to a movie house on Goetheplatz near his home. While his mother is in the hospital, relatives, friends, and neighbors look after the boy.

1955–61   Gymnasium (Grammar School); first at Munich's Theresiengymnasium, then (1956–58) at boarding school in Augsburg (St. Anna Gymnasium). Mother undergoes lung surgery followed by 2 years at a sanatorium. F. attends a second boarding school: the Realgymnasium, Augsburg.

1961–63   Lives with his father in Cologne while attending night school. The teenager has to earn his living in his father's real estate business. Writes short plays, poems, short stories.

1963     F. returns to Munich where he lives until his death, when not traveling (France, North Africa, the United States) or working in other cities (Bremen, Berlin, Bochum, Cologne, Frankfurt).

1963–66   A short stint in the archives of the Süddeutsche Zeitung and private acting lessons from director Max Krauss, followed by two years at the Fridl Leonhard drama school (March 1, 1964–May 31, 1966). There he meets Hanna Schygulla and Irm Hermann. He makes his first 8-mm films and takes on small jobs as actor, assistant director, and sound-man. Fails the State Examination for Actors. Writes (among other things) the play *Just one Slice of Bread: dialogue for an Auschwitz film*. The play shares third prize in a drama competition at the Junge Akademie in Munich. To gain entry into the new film school in Berlin, F. submits a film version of his play titled *Parallels*. He also enters several 8-mm. films including

*This Night* (now lost). After a week of entrance exams in Berlin, he fails to gain admission to the school. Encounter with Daniel Schmid. *The City Tramp* — a short 16-mm film.

1967    *The Little Chaos*, short film, 35-mm. Several brief periods of stage and screen acting. First contact with members of the Action Theater (including Ursula Strätz and Peer Raben) in Munich. Second unsuccessful attempt to enter Film High School in Berlin. F. joins the Action-Theatre; begins to direct.

1968    F. revises and directs a play by Marieluise Fleißer, *For instance Ingolstadt*. Writes and co-directs the play *Katzelmacher*. After the Action-Theatre closes, F. and several former members, including Peer Raben, establish the "antiteater" which performs in various Munich locations. F. writes four adaptations of other plays; he stages and co-stages (with Peer Raben for the most part) five plays. Writes and co-stages *The American Soldier*. In April, the West German students' movement reaches its first climax.

1969    Writes three plays, including *Preparadise Sorry Now* and *Anarchy in Bavaria*, and two adaptations. Stages two himself, co-stages two others. Begins producing films under the firm name "antiteater-X-Film."

   Four films: *Love is colder than Death*, *Katzelmacher*, *Gods of the Plague*, and *Why did Mr. R. run Amok?* (co-directed with Michael Fengler). F. acts in seven films, including *Baal*, directed by Volker Schlöndorff, and three of his own films. The Theater am Goetheplatz in Bremen, under Kurt Hübner, presents a "Fassbinder-Showdown." The antiteater-Ensemble is invited. All Fassbinder plays are performed. Start of relationship with Günther Kaufman, which lasts one year.

1970    Seven films: *Rio das Mortes*, *The Coffee House*, *.Whitey*, *The Niklashausen Journey*, *The American Soldier*, *Beware of a Holy Whore*, *Recruits in Ingolstadt*; F. writes two radio plays: *Preparadise Sorry Now* (from his stage play) and *All in White*. He marries the actress and singer Ingrid Caven.

1971    Writes two plays: *Blood on the Cat's Neck* and *The Bitter Tears of Petra von Kant*; writes and stages the radio play *Iphigenie in Tauris by Johann Wolfgang Goethe*. Collapse of the "antiteater."

   The films of Douglas Sirk are shown in a retrospective at

the ABC Kino in Munich. F. establishes "Tango-Film Rainer Werner Fassbinder." The company's first film is *The Merchant of Four Seasons*. F. becomes involved with El Hedi ben Salem M'Barek Mohamed Mustafa; writes and stages the play *Bremen Freedom* for Margit Carstensen.

Death of Wolff Eder. F's mother, Liselotte Eder, begins to oversee the hitherto chaotic financial affairs of "antiteater" and "antiteater-X-Film."

At the annual New York Film Festival at Lincoln Center, the Fassbinder film *Niklashausen Journey* is shown. Dan Talbot in New York takes on a number of Fassbinder films for future distribution. Among those films: *The Marriage of Maria Braun*.

1972    Four films: *The Bitter Tears of Petra von Kant, Jailbait, Eight Hours don't make a Day, Bremen Freedom*. F. stages a play, *Liliom*, at the Bochum Schauspielhaus (Manager: Peter Zadek). First shooting phase of *Fontane Effi Briest*. F. writes and directs the radio play *No one is evil, no one is good*. Divorce from Ingrid Caven.

1973    Four films: *World on a Wire, Nora Helmer, Martha, Ali: Fear Eats the Soul*. F. stages *Bibi* in Bochum and *Hedda Gabler* at the Freie Volksbühne in West Berlin (Kurt Hübner, manager.) End of relationship with El Hedi ben Salem M'Barek Mohamed Mustafa.

1974    F. plays the lead in his film *Fox and his Friends [Faustrecht der Freiheit]*, stages a show, *Like a Bird on a Wire*, with Brigitte Mira, and a Peter Handke play, *They are Dying Out*, at the Frankfurt Schauspielhaus. Becomes co-director of Frankfurt's Theater am Turm (TAT); stages *Germinal* and *Uncle Vanya*. Writes a screenplay based on a novel by Gerhard Zwerenz, *The Earth is Uninhabitable like the Moon*. Writes his last play, *Garbage, the City and Death*. First Fassbinder Retrospective at the Cinémathèque Française. Relationship with Armin Meier.

1975    TAT engagement ends prematurely.

Three films: *Mother Küsters Goes to Heaven*; F. writes — with Daniel Schmid — a screenplay for the film *Shadow of Angels* from his play *Garbage, the City and Death*, in which he plays one of the leads; and *I Only Want You to Love Me*. First part of shooting *Satan's Brew*. Fassbinder Retrospective at the New York Film Festival.

1976    Three films: *Satan's Brew* (second shooting period), *Chinese Roulette, Bolwieser* (two-part film). Separation from Kurt Raab.

1977    Four films: *Bolwieser*, edited for motion picture presentation; *Women in New York*; *Despair — a Journey into the Light*; recording of screenplays for *Berlin Alexanderplatz* (completed in three months). The search for terrorists in Germany culminates in hostage crisis and Mogadishu skyjacking. Episode for *Germany in Autumn*. Together with Douglas Sirk and film students of the Munich Film School, F. shoots the 30-minute film *Bourbon Street Blues* in which he acts the part of a writer.

1978    Two films: *The Marriage of Maria Braun, In a Year with Thirteen Moons*. Armin Meier dies, presumably of an overdose of pills. F. begins life with film editor Juliane Lorenz.

1979–80    Three films: *The Third Generation, Berlin Alexanderplatz* (13 parts and an epilogue), *Lili Marleen* (1980). F. dictates the screenplay for *Hurra, We're Still Alive* onto tape.

1981    Three films: *Lola, Theatre in a Trance, Veronika Voss*, for which he receives (at last!) the Golden Bear medal at the Berlin Film Festival. Writes a screenplay commissioned by Horst Wendlandt, *Kokain*, after a novel by Pitigrilli.

1982    His last film, *Querelle*, and an appearance in the documentary film *Chambre 666. N'importe quand* by Wim Wenders. Exposé and preparations for the film *I am Happiness on Earth [Ich bin das Glück dieser Erde]*. Production notes for *Rosa L.*

Rainer Werner Fassbinder died on June 10, 1982 at approximately 4 A.M. in his apartment in Munich, Clemensstraße 76.

# Index of Names

# Index of Titles